CONVERSATION

MW00830692

AMSTERDAM STUDIES IN THE THEORY AND HISTORY OF LINGUISTIC SCIENCE

General Editor

E.F.K. KOERNER

Zentrum für Allgemeine Sprachwissenschaft, Typologie
und Universalienforschung, Berlin
efk.koerner@rz.hu-berlin.de

Series IV – CURRENT ISSUES IN LINGUISTIC THEORY

Advisory Editorial Board

Raimo Anttila (Los Angeles); Lyle Campbell (Christchurch, N.Z.)
Sheila Embleton (Toronto); John E. Joseph (Edinburgh)
Manfred Krifka (Austin, Tex.); Hans-Heinrich Lieb (Berlin)
E. Wyn Roberts (Vancouver, B.C.); Hans-Jürgen Sasse (Köln)

Volume 203

Neal R. Norrick

Conversational Narrative. Storytelling in everyday talk

CONVERSATIONAL NARRATIVE

STORYTELLING IN EVERYDAY TALK

NEAL R. NORRICK

Saarland University

JOHN BENJAMINS PUBLISHING COMPANY
AMSTERDAM/PHILADELPHIA

™ The paper used in this publication meets the minimum requirements of American National Standard for Information Sciences – Permanence of Paper for Printed Library Materials, ANSI z39.48-1984.

Library of Congress Cataloging-in-Publication Data

Norrick, Neal R.
  Conversational narrative : storytelling in everyday talk / Neal R. Norrick.
  p.   cm. (Current Issues in Linguistic Theory, ISSN 0304-0763 ; v. 203)
  Includes bibliographical references and index.
    1. Discourse analysis, Narrative. 2. Conversation analysis. I. Title. II. Series.
P302.7.N67   2000
302.3'46'014--dc21   00-040333
ISBN 978 90 272 3710 1 (EUR) / 978 1 55619 981 3 (US)   (Hb ; alk. paper)
ISBN 978 90 272 4829 9   (Pb ; alk. paper)
ISBN 978 90 272 9955 0   (Eb)

© 2000 – John Benjamins B.V.
Paperback 2010.
No part of this book may be reproduced in any form, by print, photoprint, microfilm, or any other means, without written permission from the publisher.

John Benjamins Publishing Co. · P.O. Box 36224 · 1020 ME Amsterdam · The Netherlands
John Benjamins North America · P.O. Box 27519 · Philadelphia PA 19118-0519 · USA

For Swen, even without pictures

Table of Contents

Preface

This book aims to advance narrative theory in two ways. First, it includes types of storytelling not previously treated in the literature. Second, it integrates perspectives on narrative usually kept separate. By analyzing a more diverse collection of data, and by comparing different narrative types from a range of perspectives, I seek new insights into the forms and functions of storytelling. By treating storytelling in a broad array of contexts, this monograph also contributes to conversation analysis. I initially envisioned a book consisting of approximately half transcribed narratives and half sample analyses. The analytical component has grown in proportion to the data, but my original orientation toward exemplification and away from theorizing will still be evident in parts of the book.

My research began with the collection of conversational data. This phase of the project took place at Northern Illinois University, where I worked and taught from 1985 till 1997. During that time I had the pleasure of mentoring some excellent, highly motivated graduate and undergraduate students. Several of them shared their recordings and their transcriptions with me. I would like to express my gratitude to members of this Northern Illinois group: Mary Jandek, Amy Julian, Jason Turner, Shelley Synovic, Ed Leidl, Todd Laufenberg, A. J. Grant, Steve Marsden, Sandra Anderson, Lynne Pantano, Katharine Parr, Than Than Win, and, especially, Kelli Lyon. Virginia Robinson served as an undergraduate research assistant to me in the spring of 1997, and she produced first drafts of many of the transcriptions consulted and used. Bill Baker of Northern Illinois University worked along with me in the early stages of developing the treatment of Beckett's "Endgame" in chapter six. I would like to express my gratitude to Katharina Barbe and Don Hardy for reading and commenting on earlier versions of portions of this book as well.

The second phase of the research took place at Saarland University in Saarbrücken, Germany. In my present position as chair of English Linguistics, I have continued to collect oral narratives and to transcribe stories from my store of tapes. I would like to express my ongoing gratitude to the staff here in Saarbrücken. Cornelia Gerhardt, Claudia Bubel, Alice Spitz, Nicole Valentin,

Jens Harder, Oliver Naudorf and Sylvia Monzon have all been involved in various phases of the project, transcribing stories from tapes, compiling bibliography, producing and proofreading several drafts of the manuscript.

In the spring of 1996, I presented the basics of my approach to co-narration in a paper delivered at the annual meeting of the American Association for Applied Linguistics in Chicago. I first aired my ideas on the Nurse's story from Shakespeare's "Romeo & Juliet" in a panel I organized at the International Association of Literary Semantics conference in Freiburg, Germany, in September 1997. I discussed aspects of the jokes analyzed in chapter six in a panel on humor and cognition organized by Victor Raskin at the annual conference of the International Society for Humor Studies in Oakland, California, in June-July 1999. I owe a special debt of gratitude to Wally Chafe for extensive comments on my work-in-progress. Input from anonymous reviewers has led to numerous improvements in the final version as well. Remaining weaknesses are, alas, due to my own shortcomings.

Saarbrücken, February 2000

Transciption Conventions

Each line of transcription contains a single intonation unit.

She's out.	Period shows falling tone in the preceding element.
Oh yeah?	Question mark shows rising tone in the preceding element.
well, okay	Comma indicates a continuing intonation, drawling out the preceding element.
Damn	Italics show heavy stress.
bu- but	A single dash indicates a cutoff with a glottal stop.
says "Oh"	Double quotes mark speech set off by a shift in the speaker's voice.
[and so-]	Square brackets on successive lines mark
[Why] her?	beginning and end of overlapping talk.
and=	Equals signs on successive lines shows latching
=then	between turns.
(2.0)	Numbers in parentheses indicate timed pauses.
{sigh}	Curly braces enclose editorial comments and untranscribable elements.

These conventions are presented in detail in chapter one.

CHAPTER 1

Approaching Storytelling in Conversation

Stories only exist in stories
(whereas life goes by without the need to turn into stories)
Wim Wenders "The state of things"

Introduction

This study describes the forms and functions of storytelling in everyday conversation. It aims at a fuller picture of conversational storytelling than has hitherto been available, both through analysis of a wider range of data than previous research, and through an integrated approach to both the internal structure and the contextual particulars of stories in everyday talk. Conversational storytelling assumes special importance in narrative studies, just as narrative passages thrive in conversation, and this investigation of conversational storytelling seeks to contribute both to narrative research and to conversation analysis.

Under appropriate conversational conditions, participants engage in storytelling for a range of purposes. Generally, one conversationalist becomes the storyteller, while the others become listeners. The teller introduces the story so as to secure listener interest, gain control of the floor and ensure understanding. Then the teller must shape remembered materials into a verbal performance designed for the current context. This may include interruptions and comments from listeners; indeed, recipients may seek to redirect the story line, to reformulate its point or even to become full-fledged co-tellers of the story. In any case, story recipients can apparently understand and evaluate the story they hear rapidly enough to respond appropriately to it, perhaps with matching stories of their own. A description of these processes is a fundamental goal of any complete account of language in use.

The tradition in narrative theory pioneered by Labov & Waletzky (1967) provides a method of analyzing the internal structure of stories, but it requires extension to describe the conversational emergence of stories, since it is based on interview-style stories. Labov & Waletzky treat oral narrative as a decontextualized phenomenon rather than as a conversational strategy for accomplishing some interactional end. Their data consist only of stories elicited in interviews from a single teller with a particular question, either about an important fight or a close encounter with death. Storytelling by a single individual naturally differs from the polyphonic storytelling typical of conversation. Especially the lack of listener response during and at the end of the narratives, and the lack of hesitations, hitches and so on results in what one might consider "an academically hybridized form" (Schegloff 1997: 104). We must distinguish not only interview-style narration from conversational storytelling, but also spontaneously told stories from those solicited explicitly, and those related in response to some general request from those related in response to other stories. We should also differentiate stories told for their own sake from those told for a specific purpose such as explaining a position or illustrating a conversational point, as well as separating the story proper from the storytelling performance. Research on conversational storytelling should concentrate on the interactional achievement of a story between teller(s) and listener(s), observing the differences between first-time tellings, retellings and often-told stories as well. Finally, we must make an effort to include in our purview stories on a range of topics and with different functions: personal anecdotes told for humor or solidarity, put-down stories told for self-aggrandizement, family stories told to ratify membership and so on.

Observing these principles leads to a better understanding of the interrelated roles of verbalization and remembering in conversational storytelling. I hope to show that we can profit from treating tellings and retellings as purposeful contextualizations of something remembered. Certainly memory must play a role in storytelling, and its interaction with telling strategies in concrete contexts represents an important research topic. My data persuade me of this all the more when I find verbatim repetition of descriptions and dialogue in two versions of what is ostensibly the same story told by a single speaker on separate occasions. Hence, I study real conversational stories, indeed a wide array of types, including inchoate and marginal examples, noting why they are told and how they are negotiated in the concrete context, while I look for common ground between stories and versions of stories as well as recurrent verbalization patterns.

Labov & Waletzky take a remembered sequence of events as the pre-existing substructure of personal narrative. But stories from genuine conversation show tellers recreating their memories of past events to fit the present context. Far from simply recapitulating past experience, storytellers often seem to relive, re-evaluate and reconstruct remembered experience. Furthermore, the sequential organization in the stories we tell and hear does not necessarily entail that tellers remember events as a set of ordered states and actions. After all, we routinely impose sequential order in verbalizing future events; we serialize instructions and travel directions, convinced this is the natural order; and we serialize items in lists and arguments in talk, as if they, too, were ordered in time. Storytellers may thus simply verbalize memories in sequential order to simplify interpretation for listeners accustomed to this mode. In fact, if temporal sequencing represents a principal strategy for producing stories, then tellers can concentrate on other features in remembering and performing them. And if temporal sequencing is a predictable property of stories, recipients can also orient themselves to more salient organizational features. My own conversational data exhibit storytellers organizing their performances around repetition and formulaicity as much as sequence; they also illustrate more stability in evaluation and dialogue than in the sequence of events in retold stories. The comparative salience and stability of recurrent features in stories will be of central interest in what follows.

For an understanding of teller strategies we must take seriously the micro-analysis of storytelling and its integration into turn-by-turn talk. Chafe's (1994) work on discourse and consciousness and Tannen's (1987a, 1989) research on the 'poetics of talk' demonstrate that the structures behind teller strategies and listener comprehension are accessible through meticulous analysis of real conversational data. Formulaicity, repetition and disfluencies such as false starts with abrupt cutoffs and restarts or self-corrections loom large in spoken language, by comparison with written language (see Chafe 1982, 1985; Ong 1982). These same features play a prominent role in the organization of conversational stories. They enhance coherence and contribute to involvement in Tannen's sense; and they facilitate verbalization and remembering, as described by Chafe. Since tellers and listeners must apportion limited cognitive resources to constructing and understanding stories respectively, they rely on repetition, formulaicity and disfluencies to gain planning time, focus attention, segment story sections, reinforce evaluations and so on. These features help organize the storytelling performance, ensure comprehension, guide interpretation and facilitate remembering.

Previously related stories may possess a degree of verbal stability, but the exigencies of real-time verbalization for an active conversational audience usually render the actual performance discontinuous and polyphonic. This concrete performance makes up the input listeners must rely on for their understanding of the story, yet they respond in ways that demonstrate understanding almost immediately. We can gain insight into the forms and functions of narrative through assuming this recipient's point of view, working from the storytelling performance to an underlying framework. Distilling a 'primary sequence' of narrative clauses (Labov & Waletzky 1967) or proposition types (Polanyi 1981) represents a plausible approach to analyzing narrative structure from the point of view of a recipient who must make sense of a polyphonic storytelling performance. We have no direct access to the remembered forms of storyteller consciousness except through introspection, but we can examine the spoken record captured on tape from the perspective of teller strategies as well. The contributions of the story recipients, including polyphonic co-narration, must receive careful attention in this regard. Micro-analysis of oral storytelling is necessary to describe the significance of such phenomena as hesitations, false starts and repetition, for instance, in differentiating between those stories which report experiences for the first time and those which represent retellings. A major goal of this book consists in developing an account of how a listener might reconstruct a coherent story structure from a diffuse, polyphonic conversational narrative performance.

Reception Theory is suggestive at this point, because it stresses the role of the recipient in constituting the text and the fundamentally interactive nature of meaning. According to Ingarden (1973) and Iser (1978), the text presents only a skeleton of 'schematized aspects' from which the reader must construct a consistent and cohesive aesthetic object. Then the recipient fills in the blanks at points of indeterminacy in the text in order to be able to respond appropriately. But the recipient of a conversational storytelling must work even to actualize a narrative skeleton from the often disjoint, polyphonic performance. The basic narrative structure proposed below represents an attempt to model the construction of a coherent underlying skeleton. The recipient of a conversational storytelling then goes on to fill in the blanks in the story, as in the interpretation of any text.

The teller of a story is also a listener of a special kind. Each performance of a story helps solidify its form for the teller, but it may also affect the memory of events in subtle ways. Bartlett's famous experiments on remembering showed such effects on story form over time (Bartlett 1932). Tellers may use verbalization to relive past experience. Retelling can put them back in touch with details and emotions they could not access otherwise. Questions and comments from their auditors may also influence their perception and evaluation of past events. Psychotherapy presumes that retelling personal stories can give us new insight into our self-understanding. And we all use verbalization of experience to better understand what happened and why. Therefore, we must reject Labov's definition of narrative as a method of recapitulating remembered experience, insofar as it entails that the memory of the past experience remains unchanged by the telling.

In the interview situation, the method of elicitation pre-selects specific narrative genres with clear boundaries; by contrast, conversational data presents the researcher with questions about what occasioned a particular narrative, what sort of genre it represents and where to draw the boundary between narrative and non-narrative talk. Ervin-Tripp & Küntay (1997) recently showed a systematic relation between conversational circumstances and the presence or absence of certain story features. Conversational storytellers reconstruct remembered events in words for a particular audience and for some contextual purpose. In order to understand these spontaneous stories, we must investigate the conversational contexts which occasion them and the purposes they fulfill. But the frequent appeal to stories elicited in interviews and the focus on temporal sequencing and narrative clauses in much past research has tended to narrow the data base, excluding diffuse and collaborative stories as well as unsuccessful or incomplete stories, and marginal, narrative-like exchanges. I will seek to remedy this situation by including a wide range of conversational storytelling, particularly types which have received little or no attention in the study of narrative so far. Personal and third-person anecdotes and tales of trouble, put-down stories and dream reports are analyzed and compared. Communal tellings of family stories and common experiences show participants fitting separate versions of a story together, while collaborative fantasies show participants inventing a storyline *ab ovo* rather than verbalizing events from memory. Response stories and sequences of stories receive special attention, as do borderline pseudo-narrative exchanges like accounts of recurrent past experiences and diffuse stories, which require considerable reconstruction by auditors. Consideration of flawed narrative performances, marginal stories and narrative-like passages throws into relief the interpretive processes recipients must perform. In addition, the immediate reactions of participants to these borderline narratives give us direct access to the storytelling process and the perceptions of narrative by auditors.

An investigation of everyday talk also reveals a wide array of occasions for storytelling, where research based on elicited stories postulated narrow conditions on tellability. We will see how tellers employ prefaces and abstracts in order to gain the floor for their stories and to signal what sort of response is expected. These prefaces and abstracts sometimes establish tellability through claims of either originality or topical relevance, but they sometimes simply announce a story of current interest or a familiar story, offering the possibility of co-narration. Moreover, conversationalists manipulate topical talk and stories in progress to segue into stories of their own. The net effect of analyzing a wide variety of authentic data will be a much fuller picture of conversational storytelling than has hitherto been available.

Consequently, I propose to supplement the structural description of the narrative structures underlying stories with a micro-analysis of teller strategies, to develop a rhetoric of conversational storytelling along with a description of the contexts which occasion conversational stories and the effects they have on the surrounding interaction. I will explore the functions of repetition and formulaicity in the organization of the narrative performance. Frequently retold stories, co-narration of familiar events, and spontaneous conversational retellings of the same basic story provide special windows on the recall and verbalization of experience. I will enrich the data base with a variety of narrative data in order to determine how stories emerge from non-narrative talk and how they affect interaction. The resulting description of conversational storytelling with regard to both internal structure and contextual integration will then provide the basis for an investigation of related genres like anecdotes and jokes, and literary representations of storytelling. Fludernik's (1996) 'natural narratology' similarly advocates working from conversational narrative toward an account of literary narrative.

Remembering and verbalizing in narration

One of my main research questions concerns how we remember and verbalize stories. How do memory and telling strategies interact in the process of verbalization? Do we simply rehearse a sequence of events experienced in the past and committed to memory? Or do we recall stories at least partially in verbal form? To what extent is our verbalization governed by the local context of foregoing talk and the other participants?

Labov & Waletzky (1967) seem to assume that past experiences are remembered as sequences of events. These events are verbalized as the 'primary sequence' of a story, generally introduced by an orientation and accompanied by evaluation of various kinds. Their definition of narrative in terms of sequential ordering of clauses follows from the assumption that narrative is a "method of recapitulating past experience." Smith (1981), however, argues that memories are shaped into sets of sequential events only through the process of verbalization itself. Middleton & Edwards (1990) stress the influence of the local context and social norms on how an individual verbalizes remembered events. M. Goodwin (1997a, 1997b) demonstrates that the context of reporting past events influences how characters and their actions are portrayed. Further, Chafe (1994) has demonstrated the significance of various linguistic factors besides sequence in the organization and remembering of stories. Hopper (1997) questions the ontological assumptions behind a posited underlying sequential order of discrete events in memory which are recapitulated in storytelling. Indeed, Bamberg (1994) argues that events, scenes, actors and actions are products of more global discourse activities rather than prerequisites for them. Moreover, the storytelling process acts as a catalyst to activate memory rather than simply extracting information from it and arranging it for inspection. Telling and retelling can deepen our understanding of a story, and put us back in touch with details and relationships presumed forgotten. Ferrara (1994) documents the expansion of a story from an initial telling through the two following ones. Ochs & Capps (1997) also raise serious doubts about the correctness of recall as reconstructed in narrative form.

If we cannot remember discrete events except within the narrative framework, perhaps words and phrases underlie our narrative performances. Of course, there is no shortage of evidence that we can memorize texts word for word, given sufficient time. Professional actors commit entire plays to memory. Many people can recite extended passages from favorite books and authors as well as whole poems, to say nothing of the current texts from popular songs and advertisements we memorize apparently without special effort. While reproduction of such texts sometimes seems like replaying material etched into a plastic disk, it probably depends on fitting words and phrases into structural and prosodic patterns.

More to the point for present purposes, many of us can produce a serviceable performance of a joke or anecdote after a single hearing — and this may include verbatim duplication of a punch line or piece of dialogue at the end along with some pivotal phrasing in the build-up. We can hear or read a news story and organize that into an accurate retelling as well. A retelling could, of course, borrow phrasing directly from such a source. Moreover, once we have verbalized an experience, we have better recall of at least portions of the verbalized text along with or in place of the original, pre-verbal memory of the experience. Many of the stories I have recorded and many of those investigated by other researchers are previously verbalized in this sense, though this aspect of the narrative performance has rarely been addressed. Some stories bear clear marks of previous telling: The teller may actually say she is telling "the story of so and so" or she may ask whether her auditors have already heard about the time she did such and such. We will consider these matters in greater detail in the chapters to come.

Bartlett in his monumental *Remembering* (1932) tested his subjects' ability to reproduce stories they had read after various time intervals. His data run somewhat counter to my focus here, first because his subjects read stories and reproduced them in writing, whereas I work with stories told in spontaneous conversation, and second because he chose unconventional types of stories to test how subjects schematize information for recall, whereas my tellers base their stories on their own past experience. Bartlett's subjects apparently restructured unusual plots into more familiar narrative patterns before committing them to memory. Their regularization processes were magnified through repeated retellings, so that their productions allowed Bartlett to draw conclusions about the role of schematization in memory. One major finding of importance for the present study was that the form of a story remained fairly constant once a subject got it into a particular shape after a few replications. Still, this tendency might reflect either memory alone or in combination with stable narrative strategies. In fact, it seems two different kinds of schematization must be at work: first, understanding of events according to familiar patterns, and second, organization of event descriptions into familiar narrative patterns. These two separable types of schematization are embodied in current versions of Frame Theory.

Frame theory — also variously called schema theory or script theory — has its roots in the thinking of Bateson (1953, 1972) and Goffman (1967, 1974). Fillmore (1976, 1985) championed frame theory within linguistics as an account of semantics. But it was Tannen (1978, 1979; cf. Tannen, ed. 1993) who showed how frame concepts account for expectations about story patterns themselves as well as for relations between the elements of a narrative. Quasthoff's (1980) narrative macro-structures accomplish much the same things. Frames encode prototypes for objects, sequences of events, and causal relationships, which facilitate recognition, categorization and memory of stories; in addition, they guide tellers in what sorts of stories are appropriate and what to include in them as well as suggesting to hearers what to expect and how to respond to stories.

Also of great significance for the present investigation of verbalization strategies is the notion of chunking introduced by Miller (1956) in his famous article on 'the magical number seven'. Miller shows that we can remember ever larger amounts of information by chunking them into manageable units, which then act as a single bit of information on the next higher level. We employ various strategies for chunking information of different kinds. In this book, I explore some of those strategies, namely the ones we use to organize narratives in conversation. Certainly the imposition of temporal sequence counts as one sort of chunking strategy in this sense, but there are others as well. Hence I will be investigating stories apparently told for the first time as compared with often repeated stories, separate retellings of the same story, and group co-narration of familiar stories. I will develop methods of description which foreground organizational elements, and seek to demonstrate the significance of hesitations, false starts, repetition, formulaicity and dialogue in verbalization.

Chafe (1982, 1994) has investigated conversational data, suggesting certain teller strategies for remembering and verbalization of narratives. He has demonstrated the importance of the information unit in narration versus the sentence in writing. In a recent article, Chafe (1998) analysed two spontaneously produced tellings of the same story for clues to the nature of memory and verbalization. In my published comments on his article (Norrick 1998b), I contrasted Chafe's interest in clusters of ideas in consciousness with my own focus on teller strategies evident in the verbal performance. Where he sees repetition of a phrase as evidence of a teller preoccupation, I look for its organizational function in the narrative performance. In each of Chafe's stories,[1] the teller says she was "eating a popsicle" to set the scene. Again in both, she says she was "*just* eating *my* popsicle" to indicate duration and to segue into the Complication of the story. Then her finishing the popsicle leads to disposal of the stick and the confrontation of the initial Climax. Whether the popsicle counts as a preoccupation or not, its repeated mention clearly serves identical demarcation functions in the paired stories, so that I consider it as evidence of a teller strategy.

In order to test for stability of narrative structures, I have collected versions of typically oral children's stories from a wide range of informants. In each case I asked subjects to tell "The three little pigs" and "Goldilocks" as if for a child listener. Then I compared the taped results.[2] Although the narratives varied considerably in the ordering of events and even in the presence or absence of whole sub-plots, certain features remained quite constant, for instance the houses of straw, sticks (or wood) and bricks (or stone), but most conspicuously the dialogue. All tellers who said they knew the story of "The three little pigs" included essentially verbatim the words of the (big bad) wolf: "Little pig, little pig, let me (come) in," the response of each successive pig: "Not by the hair of (or *on*) my chinny chin chin," and either the wolf's threat: "I'll huff and I'll puff and I'll blow your house down" or a parallel description of his action: "And he huffed and he puffed and he blew the (little pig's) house down" or both. This dialogue and repetition served to frame the action in each version. Clearly, word-for-word memorization and reproduction of the dialogue was a precondition on telling "The three little pigs" for the subjects in my sample. Dialogue regularly functions as a framing device and recurs unchanged from one telling to the next in many stories I have inspected.

These reflections on remembering and verbalizing in narration have consequences for my analysis of conversational storytelling. They also suggest consideration of data where memory plays different roles, for example, collaborative verbalizations of shared experience, co-narration of familiar stories and creative fantasies with no basis in memory.

Narration in the conversational context

In order to concretize the discussion at this point, I would like to consider two initial examples, one an elicited story and the other a genuine conversational narrative. A comparison of the two should bring out the complex interrelations between the teller, the recipient and the context in conversational storytelling. At the same time, this first look at data will illustrate something of my approach and themes to be developed in more detail in the chapters to follow.

The story below was elicited during the first session of a graduate seminar in English at a large midwestern American university. The students were asked to take turns telling stories until each had told two or three. The teller, whom I call Tammy, had related a dog story as her first contribution. Others had also related personal narratives, but otherwise no coherence with the context was evident.

Barn Burning
  1   I guess the only time
  2   I've ever really seen my father cry
  3   was when I was a child,
  4   and it was August
  5   and it was very hot and dry.
  6   and we had the family habit of every night
  7   uh we'd drive into town to the Dairy Queen
  8   and get a special treat.
  9   and this particular night
 10   as we were driving home,
 11   we could see the glow in the western sky
 12   and it shouldn't have been there.
 13   and the closer we got to home,
 14   the more we realized
 15   that there was an awful big fire someplace.
 16   uh, that big fire turned out to be our barn
 17   which was a humongous affair.
 18   it- it housed the kennels,
 19   it housed ah cattle
 20   and horses and a couple of sheep
 21   and all kinds of things
 22   as well as the equipment.
 23   and by the time we got there
 24   the thing was engulfed in flames.

25 um, the animals were still in it.
26 and there was one act of tremendous kindness,
27 a a stranger from off the highway,
28 who was driving by
29 happened to see the flames.
30 and he had gone in
31 and gotten the horses out
32 and gotten one dog out,
33 but we had to listen to all those other animals die.
34 and I was so interested,
35 the fire was all gone,
36 and nothing but ash and the foundation left
37 to see my dad sit out on the porch and weep.
38 ah, I think that
39 was one of the most heartrending things
40 I'd ever seen.
41 somehow, when your father cries
42 it's ten times worse tragedy
43 than when somebody else does.
44 and, I think that still sits very strongly in my mind.

I follow Chafe (1994) in presenting spoken language one intonation unit (prosodic phrase) per line, rather than trying to reorganize it into the sentences so important in written texts. This form of representation brings out other characteristics of spoken versus written language as well. It highlights the frequency of units beginning with *and*. This characteristic in turn reflects the additive character of spoken language by contrast with the subordinative character of written language (see Chafe 1982, 1985; Chafe & Danielewicz 1987; Ong 1982; Tannen 1982, 1989; Halliday 1987 among others).

Yet even in this transcription, Tammy's story does not look so different from a written narrative. Presumably, Tammy had told the story on previous occasions. The passage contains few disfluencies such as the false starts "it- it housed" and "a a stranger" in lines 18 and 27 and the filled pauses such as "um," "ah" and "uh." Otherwise, the individual intonation units match grammatical clauses for the most part. Still, phrases like "an awful big fire" in line 15 and "a humongous affair" in line 17 suggest an informal spoken performance rather than a written text.

The story is carefully organized. Tammy begins and ends with her father's weeping. She uses the present perfect to introduce the theme: "the only time I've ever really seen my father cry." Then she relates the body of the narrative in the past and past continuous, using past perfect only in the digression about a stranger's act of kindness, and returning to the present tense in her final general comments. Tammy also moves from the general setting to her family's habit of visiting the Dairy Queen, then on to the particular fateful night. She leads the audience step by step to the burning barn, before revealing the background information about its contents. Only after the digression about the stranger in lines 26–31 does Tammy come to the aftermath of the fire and her father's reaction.

Conversational storytelling performances often give a less organized impression than Tammy's initially. First of all, they grow out of the local context and segue back into it. They are designed for and co-determined by the current audience. Whether tellers are relating experiences they have previously verbalized or not, the polyphonic nature of conversation will contribute to the form of the performance. These factors emerge clearly in the passage below. This storytelling was occasioned by Patricia's burning her finger while preparing dinner for the assembled family: her husband Ralph and their two daughters Amy and Marsha. After some discussion of ice to prevent swelling, talk returns to food and drink, amidst which Patricia introduces her story about burning her finger the previous week at line 6. She forges ahead despite extraneous talk about napkins, and interruptive joking about her term "Arabian" in lines 17–20. Patricia even interrupts herself to drink (line 27), but the reactions from Marsha (lines 9, 13, 36 and 49) and Amy (line 44) count as support rather than interruptions. Since Patricia's story of the burned finger was occasioned by a freshly burned finger, the family apparently feels that it closes the matter and requires no further response. After a brief comment by Amy, eating and food again assume center stage.

Sewing Machine

1	Amy:	I want some fruit juice,
2		can I get some?
3	Marsha:	oh, I'm sorry Mom.
4		{sound of chair scraping on floor}
5	Amy:	what's the matter with this chair?
6	Patricia:	I want you to know
7		that I burned myself
8		the day of the garage sale.
9	Marsha:	m-hm.
10		{to Amy} could I have a napkin while you're up?

11	Patricia:	Nancy sold ah
12		Nancy was selling her mother's sewing machine.
13	Marsha:	m-hm.
14		{to Amy} thank you.
15	Patricia:	so what- a an Indian couple came
16		or an Arabian or whatever they were
17	Marsha:	that's scary.
18	Amy:	Arabian {laughing}.
19	Marsha:	{Laughing} Arabian.
20		they come in on little camels.
21		{General laughter}
22	Patricia:	they were asking me about the sewing machine,
23		and I am telling them that
24		it's not my sewing machine,
25		and I don't know anything about it,
26		the woman isn't here,
27		I don't know how to sew, {4.0 Pause to drink}
28		so he's talking to me
29		and I said I can just show you
30		how it opens and whatever
31		and her husband is right behind me
32		and I'm talking and talking.
33		and I thought he would help me
34		because I had a cigarette in my hand,
35		I thought he would help me y'know?
36	Marsha:	uh-huh.
37	Patricia:	and I swung around,
38		and he's gone
39		I don't know where he went.
40		talking to somebody in the garage.
41		and I don't know what I did
42		as I tried to open the top,
43		the cigarette went underneath my fingernail.
44	Amy:	{Ingressive Hissing}
45	Patricia:	in two shakes, I ha-
46		by the time I got back to the garage
47		I had a blister.
48		that's how bad I burned myself.
49	Marsha:	mm, mm, wow, gee.

50	Patricia:	I could have gladly killed that guy.
51	Amy:	ow, gee.
52	Marsha:	this is pretty good with the ham on it.
53	Ralph:	what?
54		you like it with the ham?
55	Marsha:	yeah.

The organization of Patricia's narrative comes out more clearly if we remove adventitious talk and interruptions to constitute a coherent basic narrative.

Sewing machine 2

```
 1   I want you to know
 2   that I burned myself
 3   the day of the garage sale.
 4   Nancy sold ah
 5   Nancy was selling her mother's sewing machine.
 6   an Indian couple came
 7   or an Arabian or whatever they were
 8   they were asking me about the sewing machine,
 9   and I am telling them that
10   it's not my sewing machine,
11   and I don't know anything about it,
12   the woman isn't here,
13   I don't know how to sew,
14   so he's talking to me
15   and I said I can just show you
16   how it opens and whatever
17   and her husband is right behind me
18   and I'm talking and talking.
19   and I thought he would help me
20   because I had a cigarette in my hand,
21   I thought he would help me y'know?
22   and I swung around,
23   and he's gone
24   I don't know where he went.
25   talking to somebody in the garage.
26   and I don't know what I did
27   as I tried to open the top,
28   the cigarette went underneath my fingernail.
```

29   in two shakes, I ha-
30   by the time I got back to the garage
31   I had a blister.
32   that's how bad I burned myself.
33   I could have gladly killed that guy.

Patricia begins her story in the present tense with "I want you to know," then switches to the past tense for the topic, "I burned myself the day of the garage sale." The concluding unit in line 32 similarly starts off in the present tense, "that's how bad," and repeats the central phrase "I burned myself" in the past tense. Patricia returns to the present tense to report her own verbal action in line 9. She again switches tenses to report her own speech in line 15. Everything else is in the present tense, except the two identically worded clauses "I thought he would help me," which flank the first mention of the cigarette at line 20, and the crucial events involving the cigarette and the blister (lines 27–29).

To highlight the rhythm of the story, I match parallel units and place repeated phrases in italics.

Sewing Machine 3

A   I burned myself the day of the garage sale.

B   *they were asking me* about the sewing machine,
C   *I am telling them* that it's not my sewing machine,

D   *I don't know* anything about it,
E   *I don't know* how to sew,

F   *he's talking* to me
G   *I'm talking* and talking.

H   *I thought he would help me*
      because I had a cigarette in my hand,
I   *I thought he would help me* y'know?

J   *I don't know* where he went.
K   *I don't know* what I did

L   as I tried to open the top,
      the cigarette went underneath my fingernail.
M   that's how bad I burned myself.
N   I could have gladly killed that guy.

This form demonstrates how Patricia introduces the cigarette between repetitions of "I thought he would help me" in lines H and I, and how the cigarette under the nail follows repetitions of "I don't know" in lines J–K. This latter pair also echoes two parallel clauses with the phrase "I don't know" in lines D–E. Moreover, these pairs alternate with other pairs of *verbi dicendi*: *ask* and *tell* in lines B–C, *talk* and *talk* in lines F–G. Finally, the single pair with "I thought" in lines H–I is both preceded and followed by a pair with "I don't know." These epistemic verbs provide background information along with the verbs of saying, but they do not describe the action of the story.

The narrative units which bear the action of the story appear below. They come to life in the frame provided by the paired elements, but they do not seem to provide the salient structure for telling or understanding the story.

1   an Indian couple came
2   I said I can just show you how it opens
3   I thought he would help me
4   I swung around,
5   the cigarette went underneath my fingernail
6   I had a blister.

Thus, in my attempt to understand how tellers organize their stories, I find it necessary to consider the chunking of intonation units, verb classes and tenses as well as lexical repetition. I believe this organization reveals strategies of remembering and verbalizing narratives. My investigation of spontaneous retellings, often-told stories, and group co-narration of familiar stories also follows from this interest in teller strategies. For my purposes, reduction of a story to its basic plot line represents only one particular step in narrative analysis. Distillation of a coherent sequence of clauses may reflect the kind of processing a listener must accomplish to make sense of a conversational storytelling, but not some underlying structure in the storyteller's memory, as Labov & Waletzky suggest. It seems, instead, that background information, evaluative comments and dialogue are often the most stable part of a conversational narrative performance.

Tammy's **Barn Burning** illustrates the sort of data Labov and his associates generally described, namely elicited oral stories with a single, undisturbed teller, rather than spontaneous conversational storytelling. Hence, Labov's definition of the narrative in terms of sequential clauses may be seen as a touchstone or an analytical tool, rather than as a *sine qua non* condition for any excerpt to receive our attention. In genuine conversation, stories often surge up and recede again in topical talk. They may consist of fragments produced by separate speakers among extraneous talk and random interruptions, so that it is often difficult to say just where they begin or end. Indeed, it is sometimes impossible to determine the legitimate teller, or even the main teller. Listeners must piece together narrative structures and reconstruct chronologies to make sense of the storytelling they experience. Consequently, the analyst, too, must sometimes perform various operations on conversational materials to make them add up to a narrative, though I assume that these operations mirror the sorts of cognitive processing required of hearers in the original contexts of the stories.

The corpus

The corpus for this study consists of many hours of audio-taped conversation recorded by my students and me. Selected stories from the corpus have been transcribed according to the conventions described below.[3] Permission to tape the interactions was usually secured beforehand, and our recorders were placed in view of everyone present, though some conversations were recorded surreptitiously and permission to use them was secured after the fact. Most of the excerpts come from real conversations among family members and friends, fellow students and colleagues. More often than not, we were ourselves participants in the conversations we recorded, so that I had access to background information about the settings and participants from the ones doing the recording in each case. I have subsequently assigned fictional names to all participants to preserve anonymity for everyone involved, as my students and I promised those we taped. These names differ in some cases from pseudonyms I used for these same speakers in excerpts from this data base analyzed in earlier talks and publications. All my own recordings were completed some time before I began to think about investigating conversational narrative as such, and I have included no examples of my own narrative performances.

The so-called observer's paradox states that it is impossible to observe how people behave when they are not being observed. Won't conversationalists talk differently if they know the tape recorder is running? One response to this problem is simply to recognize that all talk obeys certain constraints. We all monitor our own speech based on a whole range of contextual features, so that our awareness of being recorded adds just one more ingredient to the recipe. Another response could be to record conversation surreptitiously, and ask permission to use the recording after the fact. Many linguists view this method of data collection as unethical. Some of my own early recording was done surreptitiously before I became sensitized to the ethical ramifications of this practice. After incurring the wrath of two friends I had recorded and increasingly experiencing pangs of conscience, I decided always to ask in advance of taping. Moreover, my comparison of openly recorded versus clandestinely recorded conversation turned up only momentary taping effects. As often as not, my subjects registered surprise that the recorder was still running — proof positive that they had forgotten they were being recorded. My experience has been that conversationalists can only orient themselves to the tape recorder for a short period, and that their behavior returns to normal fairly rapidly. While we constantly react to the contextualization cues of our interlocutors, and we can adjust our speaking register to accomodate all sorts of changes in our visible audience, we seem hard put to key on hearers not directly present vis-a-vis. A tape recorder on a book shelf or a coffee table has little if any effect on a speaker directly engaged in conversation with a friend.

Still there are obvious effects of recording on many of my tapes. Tannen (1984) describes her host's recurrent comments on the recording equipment cluttering his Thanksgiving table. Such recording effects occur most frequently at the start of a cassette, reflecting the attention of conversationalists to the moving or restarting of the recorder. Occasionally, members of the present group state that they flatly refuse to talk while the machine is running. Sometimes someone converses only in whispers, at least for a time. The opposite effect is probably more common, namely the desire to perform for the recorder. Some speakers switch to a dramatically higher register or to a resonant stage voice. Others switch into a second or foreign language — whether to show off their language skills or to prevent understanding is not always clear. Of course, neither of these behaviors lasts for very long. My recordings also contain scattered examples of speakers producing a string of profanities, usually close to the microphone. Occasionally, speakers explicitly comment on their dislike for being recorded. In one passage examined below, a young man announces that he wants to go on record with a prediction; and in another passage, a speaker takes advantage of the recorder as a reason to tell a joke. In the final analysis, while I feel it is necessary to take explicit recording effects like these into account, I do not view the presence of taping equipment and conversationalists' awareness of being recorded as factors capable of skewing the data, particularly not now that we have large corpora to compare. The observer's paradox will not go away, but we have good reason to trust the data we have observed, even though our presence as observers was known.

All the recordings of conversation were made in the United States between 1985 and 1997. Most of the participants were native-born white Anglo-American English speakers, many of whom were born in and most of whom live in the upper Midwest, though a handfull hail from the East Coast. A few tellers are African Americans, Asian Americans or Hispanics living in this same area, while a few are European or Asian guests. One conversational source of several stories is an extended Italian-American family from middle New York State. I will give pertinent background information about the participants in particular exchanges as they appear, especially in cases of longer excerpts and connected passages. Despite the obvious cultural bias and the particular idiosyncrasies inherent in this or any corpus of conversation, I hope to have selected narratives resembling those my readers are used to hearing and telling. Furthermore, I trust that the illustrations of story introductions and conclusions, of reactions and response stories recall strategies most readers recognize and use themselves.

Of course, the transcribed stories are not as polished as the thoroughly practiced materials we hear on stage or in the electronic media, and they certainly lack the usual trappings we find in literary narratives. But these real-life passages have a genuine personal validity lacking in carefully authored and edited texts. Close attention to the sequencing and effects of real, organic conversational storytelling should yield an 'ah-hah effect' as the reader recognizes strategies and habits familiar from personal experience. Consequently, I will not be overly eager to generalize from the particular examples to abstract rules or hypotheses. The data speaks eloquently for itself in many cases. It provides ample evidence that narrative grows from and thrives in the concrete conversational context; it brings out the interactive nature of storytelling and the key role the audience plays; and it serves as a natural antidote to the over-rich diet of carefully selected, written, literary narrative we have come to consider the norm.

On the down side, for readers unaccustomed to it, transcribed conversational narratives initially appear rather jumbled and chaotic on the page. We are of course perfectly at home conversing and telling stories ourselves. We also feel comfortable listening to conversations and narratives, whether live, video-recorded or audio-recorded. However, everyday talk takes on a foreign aspect when transcribed. Interruptions, listener feedback, simultaneous talk and disfluencies such as false starts and self-corrections, stutters and filled pauses like "um" and "ah" all make a conversational transcript less linear and fluent than the carefully marshalled paragraphs of a short story and less orderly than the artificially discrete speeches assigned to successive characters in a play script. I have simplified the transcriptions where the minutiae of timing and overlap were irrelevant to the point being made, but often such details can be quite revealing. For instance, disfluencies routinely mark the opening sentences of stories, and the particulars of audience participation correlate in interesting ways with differences between genres such as personal anecdotes versus narratives about problems. Hence, in many instances, I opt for fairly detailed transcriptions with as much set-up and explication as seems necessary. The effort we invest in careful transcription and close attention to details of the performance and reaction to conversational narrative repays the reader many times over in the insight so gained.

Representing oral storytelling

Written texts are structured around complete sentences, while spoken language is organized around intonation units. Intonation units tend to be about five words long and to contain one new idea unit each, typically a subject and a predicate, according to Chafe (1986, 1994). In terms of prosody, intonation units are likely to begin with a brief pause and to exhibit a coherent intonation ending in a contour interpreted as clause-final. They generally contain one or more intonation peaks. Two sequential intonation units from Tammy's **Barn Burning** above are typical in all these respects, where italics mark intonation peaks.

> and *I* was so *in*terested,
> the *fire* was all *gone*,

In terms of function, intonation units typically identify some referent given in the foregoing discourse or the physical setting of the utterance and say something new about it. A second pair of intonation units from **Barn Burning** illustrates this principle. In the first unit, *we* identifies the protagonists of the story already active in the foregoing text and says something new about them, namely that they could see a glow. Then the second unit picks out *the glow* in the previous unit for attention with the pronoun *it* and predicates new information of it, namely that it should not have been there.

> we could see the glow in the western sky
> and it shouldn't have been there.

This characteristic flow from given to new information is based on intonation, and thus distinguishes talk from written language, according to Halliday (1967, 1985). Language in both mediums can be analyzed into clauses with Themes and Rhemes, but written language lacks the organization into Given and New information characteristic for spoken language with its patterns of intonation. Printing each intonation unit on a separate line and using punctuation and italic print to suggest intonation contours yields a reasonable representation of speech and information flow for most purposes.

I use regular spelling with appropriate contractions for normal-speed casual talk even when a spelling like *hafta* or *gotcha* comes closer to the actual pronunciation than *have to* or *got you* respectively. This lets me reserve such markers for especially rapid and exaggeratedly careless speech, where they signal a style switch by the speaker as part of dramatization in a narrative. The only exception I have made to this rule is the rather frequent single unit *y'know*, which must remain distinct from the two-word phrase *you know* to reflect the rhythm of talk and to avoid confusion.

A single dash directly after a letter or word signifies an abrupt cutoff with a glottal stop, typically when a speaker hears interrupting talk or wants to rephrase a sentence in progress. The units cited below contain two such cutoffs.

> my- I have a little-
> uh my parents have a little Lhasa apso.

Timed pauses of a second or more appear as an appropriate number of seconds and tenths in parentheses, as in the turn below. Pauses were timed only when they seemed particularly relevant for the rhythm or meaning of the excerpt under scrutiny, and only when they were atypical for the particular speaker or significantly longer than other silences in the same conversation.

> and I just thought that was so cute. (1.8)
> {inhales} anyway.

Periods, question marks and commas indicate intonation contours, rather than complete declarative and interrogative sentences or pauses. Thus a period shows a final falling contour, not necessarily a complete sentence, as in the passage below on Ned's initial *No* and on *well* in Frank's second turn. A comma indicates a continuing intonation, drawling out the preceding element either with a level contour or with a slight rise. This pattern appears on several words after the *well*, as Frank puts together a halting, but clearly ongoing chunk. A question mark indicates a final rise, an intonation which expects a response, though not necessarily a real question like Ned's "Have you?" Thus the rising contour on *minute* shown by the question mark conveys a lack of certainty, rather than a request for confirmation, as we see in Frank's continuation with a dependent clause.

> Frank: have you ever seen this *Simp*sons thing?
> Ned: no, have you?
> Frank: I *think* I well.
>   I, I saw it, for,
>   I guess, a minute?
>   when I first heard them yelling about it.

Sometimes a teller produces one or two utterances with rising contours in the orientation section of a narrative, as if to ensure that the listeners are attentive and able to assimilate the background information offered, as Mark does in the next passage.

Jacob: she was like screwing around
           like around Christmas time?
           and like she, I-
           I guess this was like
           when they had candles on trees?
           she lit her hair on fire.
Mark: oh wow.

Italic print highlights specially emphasized syllables, whether produced with a higher pitch, with greater volume, a longer vowel or some combination of these devices. A transcription like "that's *won*derful" indicates that the speaker emphasized the initial syllable in *wonderful* beyond normal expectations for an intonation peak in such a unit.

The representation of laughter presents special problems. The quality of the laughter can range from a nasal exhalation at the end of a word to a booming *ha ha ha*. In my past research on conversation, I tried to approximate these distinct varieties as closely as possible within the normal orthographic conventions of English, in the spirit of Jefferson (1979, 1984, 1985). However, in the chapters to come, my transcriptions will contain such comments as {giggling} and {General laughter} in hopes of suggesting what one could hear in the recordings themselves. If a speaker's turn consists entirely of laughter, I represent this simply as: {laughs}. If audible laughter precedes the words in an utterance, I place {laughing} at the beginning, and if laughter bubbles up within the utterance and continues on after the words I place {laughing} at its end. When the laughter of auditors accompanies the progress of a narrative without seeming to affect its flow, I simply insert a comment like {Audience laughter} at the point where it becomes clearly audible, so as to avoid interrupting the visual presentation of the story any more than seems appropriate. In following these conventions, I accede to the wishes of many colleagues, editors and readers, who struggled with and objected to my attempts to render laughter in the unsuitable medium of print. This change seems particularly appropriate at the present juncture, since narrative stands at the center of attention here, while humor was the focus of much of my work in the recent past. I continue to worry that characterizations like {brief laugh} and {chuckling} tend to lose sight of conversational dynamics and prosodic features such as the duration and intonation of the laughter, its overlap with speech or laughter of others. Nevertheless, I trust that the increase in readability more than makes up for the loss in accuracy of transcription.

Simultaneous speech is quite common in everyday conversation. For one thing, listeners typically intersperse attention signals like *uh-huh* and *yeah* and evaluative comments like *really?* and *wow* in ongoing talk by others. Also, a second speaker may begin to talk during a pause, only to have the first speaker continue at the same time. And genuine interruptions also occur. Especially in joint performances of narratives familiar to two or more present participants, alternate speakers often break into ongoing talk to offer corrections and comments. I use sets of square brackets on successive lines to enclose overlapping sequences of all these kinds. Thus in the first exchange below, Marsha begins her response at a potential utterance completion point, although Ralph goes on to render his question more precise, so they end up speaking simultaneously. Significantly, Marsha registers the overlap as a potential understanding problem, so that she repeats her answer "three" along with a further modification.

Ralph: so how many cars spun out there,
            [counting you.]
Marsha: [three.]
            three while we were there.

The next passage shows Addie continuing her turn after completing a sentence and reaching a natural stopping place. Brianne starts at the same time, contributing an important detail to Addie's story, which Addie explicitly acknowledges by incorporating Brianne's comment into her next turn.

Addie: she gave her a five dollar bill.
            [and-]
Brianne: [and she] promptly freaked.
Addie: and she freaked out
            because she didn't have enough change to give her.

Occasionally a second speaker times a response or comment to fall exactly at the completion point of a word or phrase in the talk of the preceding speaker, so that neither an overlap nor a transitional pause occurs. This phenomenon is commonly termed "latching," and it is represented with paired equals signs attached respectively to the end and beginning of the turns affected, as in:

Cal: that you've got a guardian angel
            and that=
Shelley: =and that you *don't?* {tsk}
            everybody has a guardian angel.

Here Shelley blends her correction so closely into Cal's phrasing that it ends up sounding as if she knew better than Cal himself what he intended.

Yet even this extension and enrichment of our standard orthography cannot provide a complete description of the actual audible performance, especially since conversational narratives often include regional or social dialect features and performed speech, various sound effects in imitation of animals, car brakes, door bells and the like, to say nothing of facial expressions, gazes, gestures and other actions in the visual domain which do not show up at all on audio tape. I will use double quotes to mark speech produced in a manner which sets it off from the regular voice of the speaker, whether it turns out to be an actual recognizable quote or, rather, a parody of a person, text or style identified somehow in the context. Thus in the passage below, Jean dramatizes her own urgent question and the unexpected response from another woman.

> and then I said
> "well nobody saw it, right?"
> she said, "*every*body saw it."

Curly braces are used to mark laughter, for comments on voice characterizations, sound effects and contextual information where appropriate, but, unavoidably, much remains for the reader to supply through empathy and imagination. A brief summary of these transcription conventions appears in the preliminary pages.

Organization

The remainder of the book is organized as follows.

Chapter 2 is dedicated to the topic of internal story structure. I propose an approach to story structure which works from details of the actual performance to a coherent basic narrative. After exemplifying my analytic techniques, I compare them with other current approaches to narrative analysis in order to clarify how they differ. Then I consider the description of relations between narrative units.

In chapter 3, I analyze the role of formulaicity and repetition in storytelling. Formulaic speech and repetitions of various kinds mark beginnings, endings, transition points and climaxes within the storytelling performance. Thus they provide special windows on narrative organization. After investigating stock formulas in storytelling, I consider the function of figurative formulas and the spontaneous creation of local formulaicity. We will see that storytellers use repetition to emphasize their evaluation and to intensify the dramatic effect of certain passages as well as to organize their narrative performances into manage-able chunks.

Chapter 4 addresses the heuristic value of investigating retelling in the analysis of conversational narrative. We shall consider story retellings and the properties of stories which are marked as retold tales familiar to at least some of the participants. I also discuss the implications of data collected through eliciting retellings and even written versions of an originally oral narrative.

In chapter 5, I turn to narrative contexts. I examine prefaces and responses to conversational narratives, with special attention to stories told in response to other stories to show understanding and to record parallel experiences. I also show how conversationalists use stories to display their alignment with other participants by indicating their attitudes and their point of view, as well as by responding with parallel stories of their own. Finally, we will observe how conversationalists signal rapport via co-telling and collaborative creation of fantasy narratives.

Chapter 6 presents a classification of conversational narrative types. Personal narratives differ thematically as to whether they aim at aggrandizement by depicting the teller in a favorable light, as opposed to depicting the teller in embarrassing circumstances, experiencing troubles or reporting dreams; and they differ structurally as to whether they aim at serious sympathy and agreement or at humor. In the latter case, I call them personal anecdotes. These personal narratives are distinguished from third-person accounts. I further differentiate collaborative retellings from collaborative fantasies, and propose two distinct new genres, namely generalized accounts of recurrent experience and diffuse stories, which emerge from ongoing talk, often without clearly marked introductions or endings or responses.

Chapter 7 extends the foregoing analyses to narrative jokes and to comic narrative passages in drama. Insofar as conversational storytelling performances often aim at humor, it is instructive to compare them with conversational performances of narrative jokes, and then to investigate comic narratives in plays. In particular, I analyze the Nurse's story of the young Juliet in Shake-speare's "Romeo & Juliet" (Act I, scene iii) and Nagg's story of the tailor in Beckett's "Endgame." I hope to demonstrate that real conversational evidence in conjunction with the analytical methods developed in this study for conversation-al storytelling can contribute to our assessment of literary texts.

Chapter 8 summarizes the major themes and conclusions of the present study, and suggests various directions for future research.

CHAPTER 2

Internal Narrative Structure

Formulated, the experience has the reality of a formulation.
Bruce F. Kawin (1972) *Telling It Again and Again*

Introduction

In this chapter, I will first define some basic terms and methods for describing the internal structure of narrative. I will consider two examples of conversational storytelling in order to illustrate the methods, and compare my analytic techniques with other current approaches to narrative analysis in order to clarify how they differ.

Some definitions

In this book, I use the terms *story*, *storytelling* and *tale* in what I take to be their usual everyday senses. *Teller* and *storyteller* will be used interchangeably and should also be taken to have their usual, non-technical meanings. In calling a story conversational, I mean that it arose in the course of natural everyday talk. Such talk characteristically involves face-to-face interaction, dynamic development of topics, frequent speaker change with no fixed order or turn length, and attention signals like *m-hm* and *uh-huh* from those currently listening. As my examples will demonstrate, everyday talk often evokes stories told to make a point, tales of shared past experience, reports of newsworthy happenings from the local media, dream tellings and so on. Even in conversation, a storytelling may be elicited by a request for a particular story, for example "the one about your old car," or a general request for a story about someone's first job. And one conversational storytelling often leads to a *response story*, fitted to the topic or type of the immediately preceding story.

I will further use the terms *listener*, *auditor*, *recipient* and *audience* more or less interchangeably in the everyday senses, though the passages analyzed will amply demonstrate that auditors are far from passive. They ask for stories, encourage and correct tellers, contribute details and dialogue. Moreover, they respond to stories with evaluations, discussion and stories of their own. If two or more participants contribute substantial details, evaluation or dialogue to a story, they may be considered *co-tellers* or *co-narrators*.

I define *narrative element* as a past tense clause describing an action or change of state; and I define *narrative* as a coherent set of two or more narrative elements. Coherence between elements is a product of the interpretive process, whereby, in responding to the minimal narrative below, we naturally equate what John drove off in with the car Judy loaded and assume that Judy's loading not only preceded but also precipitated John's driving off.

> Judy loaded the car
> and John drove off.

Reversing the order of the elements forces us to search for some different sort of coherence between them and destroys the original story.

> John drove off.
> Judy loaded the car.

A description of an event like that below which grows out of an emotion or sensory impression will not count as a narrative on the narrow definition, even though it also depicts a scene.

> I was really scared the other day,
> when John drove off
> after Judy loaded the car.

Generalized descriptions of the past with no order matching particular events similarly fail as narratives in this narrow sense.

> Judy used to load the car all the time
> and sometimes John would drive off.

Given this technical sense of *narrative*, we can speak of extracting an underlying narrative from a particular storytelling performance or compare separate tellings of the same underlying narrative. The analytical tools for distilling a narrative from a conversational storytelling are presented in the next section.

Analyzing conversational storytelling

To develop a comprehensive analysis of conversational storytelling, we must confront various questions arising from the consideration of real data. The production of a coherent analysis for genuine conversational narratives with their disfluencies, syntactically incomplete utterances, tense shifts,[1] speaker shifts, interruptions and digressions requires various ways of regularizing syntactic structures, discarding extraneous talk and filling in understood elements. Polanyi (1981, 1985) develops a proposal in this general direction. Following the research tradition pioneered by Labov & Waletzky (1967), she proposes that conversational narratives must first be reduced to clauses, then to propositions with the goal of producing what she calls an 'adequate paraphrase' from the most heavily evaluated propositions in the main story line. She coalesces teller and audience contributions into a narrative, a move which makes perfect sense from my point of view, insofar as it reflects the task facing a listener trying to piece together a coherent narrative structure from a polyphonic conversational performance.

In similar fashion, I first construct a basic narrative by amalgamating teller and audience contributions where necessary and by eliminating disfluencies, corrections, adventitious information and interruptions. The basic narrative should be both complete and coherent in that it contains no extraneous material. I assume this form reflects the sort of structure a listener must piece together in order to make sense of a narrative and to be able to respond to it appropriately either by commenting or producing a response story; it would underlie any summary or retelling as well.

Then I go back to the original storytelling and see how the teller has chunked the intonation units into narrative elements and sections. Loosely following Labov & Waletzky, I identify the abstract, main action, resolution, and coda as well as various types of orientational information (background, general frame, narrow frame) and evaluation (general versus local). This tagged narrative is useful for comparing different stories or separate tellings of the same story.

The storytelling performance may include repetitions of individual units or sections. In such cases, it is instructive to compare the basic narrative and the tagged narrative with the original storytelling performance to identify rough equivalence relations between the shared materials. Taking note of recurrent phrasal patterns and lexical repetition provides evidence of teller strategies.

Finally, a consideration of formulaic elements, dialogue, disfluencies, tense and perspective shifts as well as verb classes and the chunking of intonation units may reveal both teller strategies and the sorts of cues hearers use in making sense of a conversational storytelling performance, as we saw in the analysis of **Sewing Machine** near the end of chapter one.

Let us now consider a transcription of a story embedded in spontaneous conversation.

First Job

1	Ellen:	what was *your* first job?
2	April:	first job, um *oh*
3		that was at the Halsted Burger King
4		in Halsted Minnesota.
5	Ellen:	that near your house?
6	April:	about six miles away.
7	Ellen:	m-hm.
8	April:	and they- they built it brand new,
9		and I was one of the *first* employees.
10		and because of that
11		we ah- um we had a head honcho woman
12		from International Burger King
13		come and train everybody in.
14		because there was like thirty of us?
15	Ellen:	wow. Yeah?
16	April:	and uh we had about a week of training
17		and I remember
18		the most embarrassing moment of my *life*
19		happened then. {laughs}
20	Ellen:	{laughing} what does that *mean*? {laughing}.
21	April:	{laughing} um no this is just-
22		I can't believe I did this
23		but- um I was really nerv-
24		well it was my first *job*,
25		and I was nervous
26		and there's so much to learn.
27		I mean y'know there's so many things at Burger King
28		you have to [make and uh-]
29	Ellen:	[how old were you?]
30	April:	I was like a sophomore in high school.
31	Ellen:	okay.
32	April:	yeah, [the summer after my sophomore year.]
33	Ellen:	[you were young,] okay.

34 April: and um we were learning the drive-through
35   and just the thought of speaking on-
36   into that microphone
37   and y'know into outside-
38 Ellen: yes.
39 April: and you have to pretend to take orders
40   and, and I was so embarrassed.
41   and the *first* time I had to do it
42   I said "welcome to McDonald's
43   [may I take your order?"]
44 Ellen: [oh *no* {laughing}.]
45 April: and everybody just *laughed* at me {laughing}.
46 Ellen: {laughing} did you try and pull it off like a joke
47   like you meant to say that?
48 April: no. {laughing}
49 Ellen: no.
50   {laughing} good job.
51 April: yeah, that was my very first job.

Notice first all the disfluencies and repetitions in the transcript. False starts and pause-fillers like *ah*, *um*, and *well* cluster especially in the introductory section immediately following the apparent beginning, "I remember the most embarrassing moment of my life happened then," in lines 17–19. Disfluencies are also prominent just before the crucial elements in lines 40–42, which — we should note — are delivered without a hitch. Inspection of large numbers of conversational narratives confirms that this pattern occurs frequently. Even experienced storytellers performing narratives they have told before typically embed false starts, repetitions and corrections in introductory materials. Such disfluencies give the listeners a chance to atune themselves to the coming narrative; they encourage audience attention and participation. To the extent that April's repetitions reflect fortuitous exigencies of production rather than expressing significant evaluation or creating separable story sections, I will streamline her description of how much she had to learn and how nervous she was in reducing the story to the basic narrative below.

As is often the case in conversational storytelling, it is not obvious just where the story begins and ends. Although all the material from line 1 to line 16 counts as background information for the embarrassing incident reported, the story proper begins in line 17 with a characteristic abstract "I remember the most embarrassing moment of my *life* happened then." Statements about the most, the first, the last and so on constitute serviceable abstracts. "I remember" performs several introductory functions at once, signaling past time and personal experience, and requesting permission to expatiate upon the remembered experience. Yet in claiming the story starts in line 17, we cannot ignore the background material which precedes it; this is fairly typical for narratives which arise in and flow back into regular conversation.

Ellen instigates the story and steers its progress at several crucial junctures, forcing us to consider her contributions as part of the conversational storytelling. The provocative question, "what does that mean?" in line 20, and the exchange initiated by Ellen about April's age in lines 29–33 affects the trajectory of the storytelling performance and significantly expands the orientation. Ellen apparently considers April's behavior overwrought, and she continues her questioning until she satifies herself that April was young enough to have reacted in the manner described, saying "you were young, okay" at line 33. Stories often begin with a general frame, containing information about the place and time of the actions reported. In the present example, this frame locates the Burger King in relation to April's home, but April neglects to say how old she was, so that Ellen has cause to request this information, and it becomes part of the orientation of the story as negotiated by the two women. This provides an illustration of how we must sometimes amalgamate teller and listener contributions in order to construct a basic narrative.

Contrast the sequence Ellen initiates at line 46 by asking whether April tried to "pull it off like a joke." Although this question-answer sequence also occurs during the storytelling performance, it fails to become integrated into the narrative as such for two reasons. First, April responds negatively to Ellen's query, and second, she bridges over it by delivering a standard sort of coda: "that was my very first job," returning to the main theme of the story. This final clause completes the story appropriately and brackets out the sequence 45–48 as an interruption. Deleting other extraneous information and interruptions yields the basic narrative:

> I remember the most embarrassing moment of my *life* happened then
> and I was nervous
> and there's so much to learn.
> I was like a sophomore in high school.
> and um we were learning the drive-through
> and just the thought of speaking into that microphone
> and you have to pretend to take orders
> and I was so embarrassed.

and the *first* time I had to do it
I said "welcome to McDonald's
may I take your order?"
and everybody just *laughed* at me {laughing}.
that was my very first job.

Going back again to the original storytelling, we can separate these elements into sections to yield a tagged narrative. Beyond the skeleton of narrative clauses describing the complicating action (or main action, as I will call it), Labov & Waletzky identify other material typically found in stories. This is assigned to specific function elements surrounding the main action in more fully developed narratives, namely:

The abstract, which answers the question, "What was this about?"
The orientation, which answers the questions, "Who, what, when, where?"
The main action
The evaluation, which answers the question, "So what?"
The result or resolution, which answers the question,
"What finally happened?"
The coda, which puts off any further questions about what happened or why it mattered.

Labov & Waletzky collect all sorts of background information and framing devices into their notion of orientation, but it seems to me important to distinguish three separate types of materials under this basic heading. First, the general frame contains information about time and place. In the story above, this frame consists of the location of the Burger King and its proximity to April's home. April acts as if the setting of a hamburger place close to home presupposed a summer job during the high school years, but Ellen seems to expect explicit data about April's age in the general frame, and we saw above that the two women collaborated in determining the relevant time frame, namely "the summer after my sophomore year."

What I call background information goes beyond the setting to encompass all sorts of details, whether necessary for the point of a story or not. In **First Job**, this includes the presence of the "head honcho woman," the fact that there were thirty trainees, that they had much to learn, and that they had to make many things.

Both these sorts of information differ from the narrow frame, leading directly into the particular action of the story, here the facts that they were learning the drive-through, and that this was the first time April had to do it. Though April does not do so here, this narrow frame often includes terms which specify "this particular time," "this one night" and so on, by contrast with background information about "every time" and "all that summer," which belongs under the rubric of general frame. The outline below represents an attempt to schematize this breakdown, distinguishing background information from the general frame and the local frame. These distinctions highlight the sorts of clues a hearer might use in understanding the story, and they reveal teller strategies of recall and verbalization.

Abstract
>   I remember the most embarrassing moment of my *life* happened then.
Evaluation
>   {laughing} Um no this is just-
>   I can't believe I did this
>   but- um I was really nervous
General frame
>   well it was my first *job*,
Background
>   and there's so much to learn.
>   I mean y'know there's so many things at Burger King
>   you have to make
General frame
>   I was like a sophomore in high school.
>   the summer after my sophomore year.
Narrow frame
>   and um we were learning the drive-through
Evaluation
>   and just the thought of speaking on-
>   into that microphone
>   and y'know into outside-
Background
>   and you have to pretend to take orders and,
Evaluation
>   and I was so embarrassed.
Narrow frame
>   and the first time I had to do it
Main Action
>   I said "welcome to McDonald's
>   may I take your order?"
>   and everybody just laughed at me {laughing}.

Coda
    yeah, that was my very first job.

Now that we have a basic narrative and a tagged narrative, we should again
return to the original storytelling to look for significant patterns of repetition and
formulaic structures as evidence of teller strategies. The repetition of the phrase
"first job" itself provides a clear example, occurring initially in Ellen's question
in line 1 and April's response in line 2, but then again with stress in line 23,
echoed in the phrase "first time" in line 40, and finally in the coda, line 49. April
is even more repetitive in her insistence on the newness of the situation in the
phrases "brand new" and "one of the first employees" in lines 8–9, beyond the
references to "first job" already cited, and on the amount of learning required
("so much to learn" in line 25, "so many things to make" in lines 26–27, and
"we were learning" in line 33). All this repetition contributes to the coherence of
the narrative, and it helps insure that the listeners get the point. It also functions
as evaluation, because it embeds April's feelings of insecurity within descriptive
elements of the narrative. Further, we must distinguish the objective descriptions
of terms like *first* and *new*, which take on evaluative force only through repetition, from the local, emotive evaluation of intensifiers in "so much to learn" and
"so many things to make."

    In addition, April interlards her story with external evaluation. She explicitly
records her embarrassment in the abstract at line 17, saying "the most embarrassing moment of my life", and again in line 22 with "I can't believe I did this,"
and "I was so embarrassed" in line 40. She emphasizes her nervousness in lines
23 and 25, and again in the phrase "just the thought of speaking on- into that
microphone" in lines 35–36. All kinds of evaluation work to create interest in the
audience and to ratify the narrated events as genuine past experience, but they
also serve to signal the teller's attitudes and cue the hearer's expectations.
Evaluative elements can suspend the action to set the scene and let the suspense
build for the *faux pas*, as April demonstrates. This is typical for humorous
personal stories, though evaluation can appear anywhere in a story.

    Now let's look at a second example of conversational storytelling which
reveals interesting patterns of repetition.
In the excerpt below, Vivian is telling the story of a neighbor who mistook her
two sons for twins. One of those sons, Earl, and his wife Alice are Vivian's
conversational partners. The humor she finds in the recounted events and her
enjoyment of the memory entice Vivian into repeating salient elements of her
story during the initial telling. Vivian then repeats two pivotal utterances of her
story once again to summarize and conclude the topic, after Earl tells a related

story of his own two similar looking children. Notice that Vivian is already repeating from Alice's introductory passage, which contains three separate wordings for the same state of affairs, namely: "are they twins?"; "they're twins"; and "our kids are twins." Thus, there is definitely a formulaic feel to the phrase by the time Vivian repeats it in the second version of the story.

Twins

 1   {Alice and Vivian looking at pictures of (grand)children}
 2   Alice: people have asked us, "are they twins?"
 3   not just once.
 4   {to Earl} how often have people asked us
 5   if they're twins,
 6   if our kids are twins.
 7   Earl: well.
 8   Alice: I mean seriously.
 9   Earl: fairly often.
10   Alice: fairly often.
11   Earl: more often than I would've imagined.
12   yeah, I consider it such a stupid question.
13   for me it's=
14   Vivian: =when we moved to Pennsylvania,
15   Delbert and Earl walked to school by some neighbors, and I met that lady one day
16   when we were very new,
17   and she said,
18   "oh, you're the one with the twins."
19   and I said,
20   "oh no,
21   maybe you mean my boys
22   that are a year and a half apart."
23   "oh no, they're twins."
24   {laughing} this lady was telling me,
25   "oh no, they're twins."
26   I said, "I have sons a year and a half apart."
27   "ah, well I think they look like twins."
28   and I could've just throttled that woman=
29   Earl: =this was like the guy who said to me,
30   when I said Lilly has just turned three-
31   no, *she* said,

32		"oh, you mean four."
33	Vivian:	isn't that charming,
34	Earl:	I said,
35	Vivian:	when somebody tells the parents what-
36	Earl:	"she's my daughter.
37		she's three."
38	Vivian:	I could've just *kicked* that woman.
39		"oh, no, they're twins." {laughing}

Looking just at the story Vivian tells, abstracting away from Earl's intervening story, and eliminating all repetition, we might propose the structure below as the basic narrative.

1   when we moved to Pennsylvania, Delbert and Earl walked to school by some neighbors,

2   and I met that lady one day when we were very new,

3   and she said, "oh, you're the one with the twins."

4   and I said, "oh no, maybe you mean my boys that are a year and a half apart."

5   "oh no, they're twins." {laughing}

6   and I could've just throttled that woman

I assume this stripped down narrative reflects the sort of structure a listener could construct in order to make sense of a narrative and to be able to respond to it appropriately, either by commenting or producing a response story; it would underlie any summary or retelling as well. We can further separate these elements into sections, as shown below. The first clause gives information on the time and location of the story, which I reckon to the general frame. The next four clauses describe the main action of the story, while the final clause functions as its resolution.

General frame

1   when we moved to Pennsylvania, Delbert and Earl walked to school by some neighbors,

Main action

2   and I met that lady one day when we were very new,

3   and she said, "oh, you're the one with the twins."

4   and I said, "oh no, maybe you mean my boys that are a year and a half apart."

5   "oh no, they're twins." {laughing}

Resolution

6   and I could've just throttled that woman

This tagged narrative provides a simple form for comparing with other stories or different versions of this same story.

If we now reconsider the original storytelling by comparison with these two analytical structures, we realize how much of interest they leave out. Labeling the first five units Vivian produces without interruption as A–E, we see that the next three elements appear to paraphrase B–D in reverse order. (Alternatively, the second clause labeled as C may be heard as a separate statement attributed to the neighbor with no important consequences for the point at issue here). Labeling the resolution as F, the two final elements following Earl's story also repeat E and F nearly verbatim, though in reverse order, as shown below.

A   when we moved to Pennsylvania, Delbert and Earl walked to school by some neighbors,

B   and I met that lady one day when we were very new,

C   and she said, "oh, you're the one with the twins."

D   and I said, "oh no, maybe you mean my boys that are a year and a half apart."

E   "oh no, they're twins." {laughing}

E   this lady was telling me, "oh no, they're twins."

D   I said, "I have sons a year and a half apart."

C   "ah, well I think they look like twins."

F   and I could've just throttled that woman=

F   I could've just *kicked* that woman.

E   "oh, no, they're twins." {laughing}

The repeated elements would count as free clauses of evaluation for Labov & Waletzky, but they can be seen to reflect teller strategies as well. The repetition of elements F and E practically verbatim following Earl's response story nicely illustrates the salience of dialogue and evaluation in personal anecdotes. At the same time, it shows how Vivian gets the final word on her own story, rather than letting Earl determine its interpretation with his comment and response story.

Diffuse and polyphonic patterns of narration present additional problems in determining the basic narrative and the tagged narrative, as we shall see later on, but otherwise these initial examples illustrate fairly well the range of problems we will face in analyzing conversational storytelling.

Comparison with other approaches

In this section, I compare the analysis of narrative sketched so far with that developed by Labov and his co-workers, then with Polanyi's approach.

Labov (1972: 360–61) considers narrative as "one method of recapitulating past experience by matching a verbal sequence of clauses to the sequence of events" reported. This matches the definition of the narrative as a sequence of clauses which are sequentially ordered with respect to each other from Labov & Waletzky (1967). Defining narrative in terms of sequentiality is intuitively plausible, because a sequencing of reported events seems to underlie our ability to recognize causal connections and to summarize the action or the gist of a story (see Polanyi 1981, 1985; Stubbs 1983).

Since Labov works exclusively from elicited, interview-style stories, he has no need to reduce the storytelling performance to a basic narrative, except to recognize 'coordinate clauses', which are unordered with respect to each other, while fixed as a unit in the overall structure of the narrative. The middle pair of clauses B–C represent coordinate clauses in this sense.

A   I started drowning.
B–C   the other guys kept going; they left me
D   another guy saved me.

As stated above, Labov assigns the clauses of a story to specific function elements. An elicited narrative analyzed by Labov & Waletzky illustrates the central elements, Orientation, Complicating action, Evaluation and Resolution:

Orientation
A   yeh I was in the boy scouts at the time
B   and we was doing the 50-yard dash
C   racing
D   but we was at the pier, marked off
E   and so we was doing the 50-yard dash
F   there was about eight or ten of us, you know,
    going down, coming back

Complicating action
G   and, going down the *third* time, I caught the cramps
H   and I started yelling "help!"
I   but the fellows didn't believe me, you know
J   they thought I was just trying to catch up
    because I was going on or slowing down

K   so all of them kept going
L   they leave me
M   and so I started going down

Evaluation
N   scoutmaster was up there
O   he was watching me
P   but he didn't pay me no attention either

Resolution
Q   and for no reason at all there was another guy,
     who had just walked up that minute ...
R   he just jumped over
S   and grabbed me

With relation to this story, Labov & Waletzky discuss pairs of coordinate clauses like I–J and K–L, and the notion of 'restricted clauses' like O, which might occur anywhere after H, but not before. After identifying the narrative clauses and assigning them to function elements, they isolate the 'primary sequence':

G   I caught the cramps
H   and I started yelling
I J the fellows didn't believe me; they thought I was ...
K L all of them kept going; they leave me
M   I started going down
Q   there was another guy
R   he just jumped over
S   and grabbed me

This represents the narrative sequence with the most explicit statement of the 'a-then-b' relation. Labov & Waletzky (1967: 31) consider this "the underlying form, and derive other equivalent narratives from it." The tagged narrative structure A–S above represents one step in the integrated approach to narrative proposed here, since it has heuristic value as a model of the sort of framework a listener might construct from the conversational performance as the basis for recognizing causal connections and summarizing the events or gist of a story. By contrast, the primary sequence G–S has no particular psychological significance nor any analytical value from my point of view, since it obliterates most of the storytelling mechanisms. My simplified versions of stories, like those for **First Job** and **Twins** above, grow out of the concrete storytelling performance and could represent an actual performance themselves. An auditor could reconstruct this sort of structure on the fly to clarify a diffuse story or to make sense of a narrative as it emerges from topical conversation.

Focusing on sequentiality and adopting the primary sequence as the underlying form for the storyteller leads Labov & Waletzky to neglect several aspects of the story which are fundamental in my view. First, verbatim repetition of the phrase "we was doing the 50-yard dash" in the orientation (clauses B and E) bridges the introduction of background information in C and D: "racing, at the pier, marked off," while it reinforces the setting and ensures understanding. Second, the three-time occurrence of the phrase "going down" organizes the story both structurally and semantically. It initially contrasts with *back* in "going down, coming back" (clause F). Then it appears in the clause G in the phrase "going down the third time," which matches a formulaic description of drowning, though it here means 'on the third time down' the 50-yard stretch. Nevertheless, it immediately precedes the report that the teller "caught cramps" and "started yelling 'Help!'" Finally, in clause M, the phrase "going down" clearly expresses the meaning of 'drowning'. Before the third occurrence, we also find the apparent self-correction: "I was going on or slowing down," which certainly echoes the phrase "going down" as well. Particularly since this story describes a near drowning, the phrase "going down" must count as pivotal in its organization. Also "help!" enjoys special prominence in a story of near-drowning. Although it does not alone constitute dialogue as such, it represents the only speech reported in the story. The perspective shift and suspension of action produced by the vision of the passive scoutmaster in clauses N–P just before the resolution plays an important structural role as well. Its absence in the primary sequence looms especially large.

Labov & Waletzky do not record observations of this type for this story or any others. They discuss repetition and perspective shift as means of expressing evaluation, but do not consider their potential as structural units in verbalizing, understanding and remembering narratives. Although Labov (1972) stresses the significance of evaluation in personal experience narratives, and remarks on the power of perspective shifts (Labov 1997), he excludes them from the underlying form unless they participate in the 'a-then-b' relationship. By contrast, I look for evidence of teller strategies and for the cues a listener must attend to in trying to comprehend and evaluate an oral performance. The investigation of perspective shifts and units of evaluation simply proves more productive than a consideration of sequential ordering in the search for teller strategies. In fact, repetition, constructed dialogue, formulaicity and disfluencies are elements often central to the organization of conversational storytelling. These features can be collected under the heading of the rhetoric of storytelling. Not only do they enhance coherence and modulate involvement in the sense of Tannen (1989), they also facilitate verbalization and remembering, as described by Chafe. Since tellers and listeners can allot only limited cognitive resources to the construction and understanding of narratives, they rely on repetition, dialogue, tense shifts and formulaicity to focus attention, to reinforce evaluations and to segment stories into manageable chunks. Elements so central to production, comprehension and remembering surely belong in a complete account of narrative.

Polanyi (1981, 1985) seeks to reduce conversational narratives with the goal of producing what she calls an 'adequate paraphrase' from the most heavily evaluated propositions in the main story line. Polanyi formulates her adequate paraphrase to summarize the narrative and to serve as a tool for comparing narrative performances.

Polanyi amalgamates teller and audience contributions to a narrative to coalesce a coherent narrative structure from a polyphonic conversational perfor- mance. Then, she dissects the narrative, separating Main Story Line Event Clauses from Durative-Descriptive and Non-Storyworld Clauses, and then Main Story Line Event Propositions from Durative-Descriptive and Non-Storyworld Propositions. This compartmentalization facilitates formulation of the adequate paraphrase, but it obliterates the organizational function of words and phrases in the narrative performance.

Let us consider the central portion of Polanyi's conversational narrative "Eating on the New York Thruway." In Polanyi's transcription, intonation units are separated by three spaced dots ..., and single-word back-channels are enclosed in parentheses within the body of the story as in (Betsy: Right).

Carol: I mean ... I mean ... Did I ever tell you the story about the water ... I mean coke? I went i ... I always drink coke, right (Betsy: Right) So Betsy is thr ... walking around with this gallon of spring water and I can't understand why she's walking around with this gallon of spring water. And she keeps talk ... she keeps telling me these ... vague ... making these vague comments about the the restaurants on the New York Thruway and at least we have this spring water. And I don ... you know, I don't know what she's talking about. So we go to this restaurant ... and I order a coke ... and I ordered some sort of sandwich. Now I don't think you ordered anything.

Betsy: I didn't order anything (C: Right) I sat there making faces

Carol: Well, one thing about this restaurant was that every person in it was retarded. (laughter) That's all. I mean the people who worked there. They were, I mean ... one after the other of the weirdest looking people I've ever (laughter) either they were retarded or they were let out for the day from the mental hospital. I ...you know

Betsy: They didn't seem to be able to distinguish between washing the floor and making a hamburger. Both things were done in the same way (laughter).

Carol: So this coke appears ... I was very thirsty. ... and I went like this ... straw in ... took a sip of this coke and (laughing) I started in screaming "I've been poisoned!" (laughter) and Betsy very calmly offered me this spring water. (laughter) I mean ... I have never in my life tasted anything so bad ... (laughter)

Polanyi proposes the following adequate paraphrase for this narrative:

> Carol was "poisoned" by sipping a coke prepared by weird incompetent people who worked at the restaurant on the New York Thruway. She was saved by Betsy who had brought along (an otherwise mysterious) gallon of spring water.

What I find particularly fascinating about the story goes entirely uncommented on by Polanyi, namely Carol's self-correction in the preface and the way she constructs her story around successive mentions of "coke" and "spring water." Carol prefigures the action of the story in her preface by juxtaposing water and coke: "Did I ever tell you the story about the water? I mean the coke?" In her orientation, she says "I always drink coke, right?" then mentions the spring water three times before the Main Line Story Event commences. The main action moves from "I order a coke" to "So, this coke appears." The crux comes in the phrase "took a sip of this coke." And the resolution comes with the reintroduction of the "spring water." The preface is also of interest to me because it reveals that this is not a first-time verbalization. By asking if she has ever told her audience "the story," Carol shows that she has related this incident before. Therefore, I have found it expedient to develop an approach different from that of Polanyi, in order to clarify the role of retelling and to evaluate the functions of disfluencies and repetition in the narrative performance.

Relations between narrative units

Labov and Polanyi do not concern themselves with semantic relations between narrative clauses, apparently satisfied with the relation "and then." Other research on narratives addresses such relations at some length. Thus, Sacks (1972) gets at relations between narrative elements in part by recognizing 'membership categorization devices', which provide for assigning the mother and the baby in his own example below to the same family group.

> the baby cried.
> the mommy picked it up.

Sacks also postulates 'viewer's maxims', which provide for construing the mother's behavior as adhering to a norm that mothers should try to soothe crying babies. So-called Story Grammars in the narratology tradition (e.g. Prince 1973) or the artificial intelligence camp (e.g. Rummelhart 1975) set up semantic relations between story elements such as 'Cause' and 'Motivate', so that the mother's behavior could again be characterized as motivated by the baby's crying.

Frame concepts from such sources as Bartlett (1932), Bateson (1953), Fillmore (1976, 1985) and Tannen (1978, 1979) can also account for such relations, as described in chapter one. Moreover, frame concepts account for expectations about story forms themselves, as well as for relations between elements of a narrative. We can imagine a frame for babies and caregivers (including mothers), which would specify that babies cry and that caregivers react with attempts to sooth them, but we also recognize frames for varieties of conversational storytelling such as personal anecdotes, dream tellings, fight stories and so on. The former group of frame concepts include and supersede the relations of causing, initiating and so on which story grammars recognize between narrative elements; moreover, they motivate semantic relationships between superficially different clauses in separate versions of the same basic story, as we shall see in chapter five.

The second group of frame concepts concern storytelling itself. These frames describe macro-structures for recurrent types of stories in the sense of Quasthoff (1980). They specify appropriate topics and degrees of development, as well as appropriate prefaces and endings, so that, for instance, the two-line story of the crying baby and the mother would hardly count as tellable for an adult under normal circumstances, whereas April's personal anecdote about a verbal pratfall at her first job would. Further, with regard to April's **First Job** narrative above, Ellen's questions reveal particular expectations on her part. Her question "that near your house?" assumes that the Burger King was not too far from April's home; the question as to April's age shows that she feels the information should have been included in the general frame, and also that she may consider April's nervousness somewhat overwrought, unless she was quite young. Notice Ellen's response to April's confirmation that she had only finished tenth grade at the time: "you were young, okay." Thus, Ellen's input to the performance exhibits a concern not only with the facts of the story, but also with the appropriateness of April's behavior, and hence with the tellability of the story. Frames capture intuitions about what kinds of emotional responses we can expect, what sort of stories we should tell and about storytelling practices more generally. A consideration of the conditions and conventions governing specific storytelling types must wait till chapter six.

Conclusions

We have developed various analytical techniques to describe conversational storytelling. First, constitute a complete and coherent narrative by amalgamating teller and audience contributions where necessary and by eliminating disfluencies, corrections, adventitious information and interruptions.

Second, set aside repetitions and digressions to distill a basic narrative. This form reflects the sort of structure a listener must piece together in order to make sense of a narrative and to be able to respond to it appropriately either by commenting or producing a response story. It would underlie any summary or retelling as well.

Third, identify repetitions of elements and sections from the basic narrative in the storytelling performance. A version of the storytelling performance labeled to display such repetitions is useful for comparing different stories or separate tellings of the same story.

Fourth, describe relations between narrative units reflecting macro-structures for story types. I display these relations by tagging elements as abstract, background, general frame, narrow frame, main action, resolution, coda, and general versus local evaluation. This tagging helps us recognize tellers' strategies for recalling and verbalizing stories and listeners' cues for interpreting stories.

Fifth, note patterns of disfluencies and fluid speech, formulaic elements (including local formulaicity), parallel syntax, tense shifts, dialogue, esp. around openings, transitions, climaxes and closings, as evidence of teller strategies and listener cues in the organization of narratives.

These analytic procedures will be explicated and refined in chapter three based on an exploration of formulaicity and repetition in narrative organization; they will be applied and assessed in chapter four based on an investigation of retelling and retold stories. Then in chapter five, I show how these internal elements of narrative organization interact with external factors such as contextual preliminaries to storytelling and interpersonal relations between tellers and listeners. Finally, chapter six describes various types of stories for which conversationalists must recognize macro-structures and specific conventions.

CHAPTER 3

Formulaicity and Repetition in Storytelling

Why is my verse so barren of new pride,
So far from variation or quick change?
Why with the time do I not glance aside
To new-found methods and to compounds strange?
Why write I still all one, ever the same,
And keep invention in a noted weed,
That every word doth almost tell my name,
Showing their birth and where they did proceed?
William Shakespeare, *Sonnett LXXVI*

Introduction

Formulaicity and repetition play a special organizational role in conversational storytelling. Ong (1982), Tannen (1982, 1987, 1989), Heath (1982), Norrick (1984, 1987) and others have demonstrated the importance of formulaicity and repetition in spoken language generally. In oral storytelling, specialized formulas and repetitions of various kinds cluster around prefaces and codas, transition points and climaxes. In marking story sections, formulaic speech and repetition provide special windows on narrative organization. This chapter first investigates the occurrence of formulaic speech in conversational storytelling. In addition to exploring stock formulas in storytelling, we will consider the function of figurative formulas and the spontaneous creation of local formulaicity. Then we turn to the repetition of key words and phrases within particular stories and from one story to the next as evidence of narrative strategies and structures. Besides serving an organizational function in storytelling, repetition can also intensify the dramatic effect of reported scenes and highlight the teller's evaluation.

Formulaicity in storytelling

Formulaic speech plays an important role in the organization of conversational narrative from the perspectives of both production and comprehension. Any relatively fixed unit of two or more words which recurs in the discourses of a linguistic community counts as formulaic speech. This includes phrasal verbs like *keep on*, binomials like *free and easy* and recurrent collocations like *live it up* as well as proverbs like *The early bird catches the worm* and proverbial phrases like *putting on the ritz*. We also see formulaicity in patterns like *fan the flames* and *fan the fire*, which alternate with *fuel the flames* and *fuel the fire*. In this section, we begin by investigating the functions of formulaicity in story openings and closings. Then we examine a narrative structured around a figurative formula, and, finally, consider how formulaic phrasing can arise spontaneously in ongoing conversational narratives. Just as repetition in fixed form leads to formulaicity in the linguistic community over time, so can repetition of a multi-word unit lead to local formulaicity for the space of a single conversation or story.

Formulaic story openers

In order to enlist auditors and clearly mark the beginning of a narrative, tellers naturally draw on formulas. Conversely, listeners naturally atune their ears to formulaic markers. As we saw in the foregoing section, statements built around phrases like "the most or first such and such in my life" commonly introduce narratives in conversation. Sacks (1972) has pointed out the particular genius of gambits like "Guess what" as strategies to coerce the addressee to respond "What?" thereby setting the stage for telling a story. We saw, further, in the case of the story **First Job**, the force of the introductory statement, "I remember the most embarrassing moment of my life happened then." An echo of this introduction, "I was so embarrassed," also immediately preceded the climax of the story. In a series of connected narratives included in the appendices under **Bakery**, where two female college students are sharing stories about the place both used to work, formulaic phrases introduce each new section: first "this is the latest thing. this just happened today"; second "there was this other story too. this is a good one"; and finally "it- it was *so* funny."

Another formulaic introduction for a story familiar to at least one of the listeners is "remember the time …?" or "remember when …?" In the passage below, Louise first attempts to introduce her story at line 6 with the phrase, "well remember the time," but breaks it off and waits for Jean to finish. Then Louise tries again to introduce her story at line 16 with "remember when," and again pauses to let Jean make a concluding remark. When she continues, she also constructs her statement around a formulaic phrase, "the first time" at line 18, and follows it with a standard evaluative comment, "it was the funniest thing" at line 20. Since several of Louise's auditors do in fact "remember the time," she receives more help telling the story than she may have reckoned with, a matter we return to in the pages to come.

Poodle

1	Jean:	Annie gave me a permanent once, too.
2	Louise:	Annie did?
3	Jean:	once and only once.
4		{General laughter}
5		I would never allow her to touch my hair again.
6	Louise:	well remember the time-
7	Jean:	yoooh.
8		talk about afro
9		when afro wasn't even in style.
10		my god.
11	Annie:	well see I started [something.]
12	Jean:	[frizz ball.]
13		I was a frizz ball.
14		it wasn't even afro.
15		I was just frizz.
16	Louise:	remember [when-]
17	Jean:	[it was] terrible.
18	Louise:	Jennifer, the first time Jennifer had a perm
19		when she came home.
20		it was the funniest thing.

I return to the complete transcript of this storytelling as an example of collaborative narration in chapter six.

Formulaic story closings

Formulaic story conclusions are also common. They are much more varied than story openers, since they need only signal closing to presumably attentive listeners, rather than to gain the attention of the audience in the first place. In his lectures, Sacks (1992) several times noted the use of proverbs and clichés as story conclusions. Woody begins the following story amid general laughter from a group of five fellow graduate students. The stock phrase "and I lived to tell the story" as a coda works particularly well in this case, given the general opinion that that superglue is both a potentially dangerous adhesive and a poison as well. Woody tells the story for its humor, assuaging listeners' fears through his description of the call to the poison center, and delivering the description of his glued mouth to good dramatic effect.

Superglue

1	Woody:	my former-
2		my former significant other
3		was also one of these uh people-
4		one of these women with many projects,
5		going all the time
6		and uh, one afternoon
7		I came in for lunch
8		and she had fed the children
9		and um, told me that there were some rolls
10		over on a plate for me.
11		and in the *meantime*,
12		she was gluing some uh earrings together
13		uh with superglue.
14		and uh these were fresh,
15		hot rolls right-
16		y'know right out of the oven.
17		and y'know slap a little butter on them.
18		they're irresistible.
19		so, I did that.
20		posthaste.
21		butter on two of these rolls,
22		gobbled them up.
23		and I began to notice a strange sensation
24		on the inside of my mouth-
25		the right inside of my mouth.
26		and it felt like the mouth was actually going numb
27		*and* that things were beginning to freeze together.
28		and sure enough,
29		I had swallowed superglue.
30		um I had chewed superglue into my teeth
31		and into my mouth

32		so that my uh my cheek was was caved-
33		was glued to the upper part of [my teeth,]
34	Audience:	[{scattered laughter}]
35	Woody:	and my gums.
36		and uh when she realized what sh-she had done-
37		apparently had been working
38		with the glue on one paper plate
39		and then set that aside
40		and put the rolls on top of that,
41		she needed to call the poison center.
42		and uh even though there was this toxic warning
43		on the superglue,
44		these uh poison center people
45		said that it's not toxic at all.
46		y'know "just,"
47		uh y'know "just suck a lot of water down."
48		*but* my mouth-
49		the right side of my mouth,
50		was pretty much frozen shut
51		{spoken with clenched jaw till the word *teeth*
52		–and amid general listener laughter} like this
53		and I was talking through my teeth.
54		and we administered lots of water
55		and uh I lived to tell the story.
56	Scott:	how long did it take for it to un-stuck?
57	Woody:	uh it was about forty-five minutes of uh fl-flushing.
58		regular flushing,
59		although that may be exaggerating.
60		*but* anyways.

Woody is a skillful storyteller, and his auditors listened pretty much silently, except for the laughter noted. So it is significant that Scott immediately cuts in as soon as Woody marks his conclusion with the formulaic phrase. Clearly, story auditors wait for signs of closure, and stock formulas offer them important cues.

Again in the following excerpt, after a longish tale explaining how he decided to return to graduate school, Conrad produces a whole series of formulaic conclusions, beginning with "that was like the- the last nail that needed to be driven in to the- the board," in lines 27–29.

Return to School

1	Conrad:	{laughing} and it was- it was just a *quiet* year.
2		and then uh as time went by
3		and I was thinking about it
4		and then I had this hormone kick me,
5		and I was going to quit my job.
6		go back to school.
7		"I'm going to do it."
8		and *then*, my company decided
9		that they wanted to cut back on- on *staff*.
10		but they didn't want to lay anybody off.
11		and what they decided to do
12		was to- to offer an early retirement package.
13		and they said "What we'll offer you is-"
14		y'know they wanted to go, "We'll offer you a
15		package." and so it-
16		you could either retire early
17		or make a transition within the firm.
18		and I heard these words and I thought,
19		"oh" y'know "God is speaking [to me.]"
20	Ellen:	[yes]
21	Conrad:	y'know God is saying,
22		"Conrad *do* it."
23	Ellen:	"here it is."
24	Conrad:	yeah.
25	Ellen:	"here's the way to do it."
26	Conrad:	{laughing} yeah.
27		and that was just the-
28		that was like the- the last nail
29		that needed to be driven in to the- the board.
30	Ellen:	that's great.
31	Conrad:	and I thought "Okay."
32		and- and actually I'd been talking to
33		y'know my boss first.
34		y'know I said y'know,
35		a few weeks before I quit,
36		I said y'know,
37		"I'm thinking real seriously about changing careers
38		and going back to teaching

39		and I just found out how.
40		I want you to know that
41		because if I do that"
42		and I just- and she sat down,
43		and she thanked me for saying it.
44		and then when I actually *did* it,
45		it still kind of shocked everybody.
46		but- but I'm glad that I spoke my mind *before* that,
47		[because]
48	Ellen:	[absolutely.]
49	Conrad:	yeah.
50		because then they-
51		you know they kind of understood
52		and then they- they didn't think I was just-
53		y'know grabbing this- all this money
54	Ellen:	[right.]
55	Conrad:	[and-] and running with it.
56	Ellen:	right.
57	Conrad:	so at least they knew that my heart was in it.
58	Ellen:	that's right.
59	Conrad:	and uh and so I did that
60		and- and "Here I am."
61	Ellen:	well we're glad you're here.

Once Conrad introduces the summarizing metaphor of the last nail in the board, and Ellen responds with "that's great" in line 30, the story could easily end, but Conrad goes on to justify his accepting the early retirement plan. Again he closes with a formulaic phrase: "grabbing all this money and running with it" in lines 53–55, based on the formula "Grab (more usually take) the money and run." Ellen's repeated "right" shows that she is prepared for the narrative to end at this point. Yet Conrad proceeds to explain his concern, and once again he has recourse to a formula: "my heart was in it" at line 57. Ellen's response, "that's right," contains yet another repetition of "right," signaling her awareness that the story could end here. Then, finally, Conrad produces the formulaic finish which ends his story at line 60: "and 'here I am'." Like the formulaic phrase, "and I lived to tell the story" in the previous narrative, "here I am" brings the teller right into the present: It makes the end of the narrated event fall together with the end of the narrative event, which is particularly appropriate for a personal narrative.

Figurative formulas in narrative structure

By contrast with the foregoing examples in which tellers employed stock phrases to announce and close stories, tellers may also build their narratives around a formulaic phrase. The phrase may stand near the beginning of a story, or it may appear closer to the middle, where it can draw together the threads of the narrative to that point and provide a controlling image for what follows. Figurative phrases are particularly appropriate for this function. In the passage below, the simile, "I was just like a leaf in the wind," summarizes preceding talk and collects separate figurative possibilities into a single image, which plays itself out in the narrative. Darrel is recounting how he came to study physics, in particular how his father sought to guide him into engineering.

Leaf

1	Darrel:	he said
2		"you might want to think about engineering
3		as a major
4		because you're just pretty flexible when you get
5		out." now I don't think he was actually twisting my
6		arm,
7	Ellen:	right.
8	Darrel:	but I was-
9		I was just like a leaf in the wind at that point.
10		so I majored in engineering,
11		but all the time I was majoring in engineering
12		I- I felt like
13		I really didn't want to go out and *be* an engineer,
14		or I- I-
15		and part of it was I didn't want to
16		but part of it was
17		I- I just felt like I couldn't uh
18		be like the other engineering majors
19		and really you know get into that kind of job.
20		I had sort of a sense of inferiority
21		about some aspects of technical things even then.
22		but anyway, I pushed
23		I- I- I pushed-
24		I got into a major
25		where I got to take a lot of physics.

26		and I liked the physics stuff
27		because it was more abstract.
28	Ellen:	right.

Darrel has a doctorate in physics, and has worked as a physicist in a research facility, but he has returned to graduate school to work on a second Ph.D. in English. The leaf in the wind (line 9) offers a particularly apt image for the story Darrel tells about his undergraduate days, especially since he still has not determined his final career choice. He reports feeling that he "really didn't want to go out and be an engineer" (line 13); that he "couldn't be like the other engineering majors and really get into that kind of job" (lines 17–18); and that he had "sort of a sense of inferiority about some aspects of technical things"(lines 20–21). Darrel comes off as defensive about his scientific background in conversation with Ellen, a fellow doctoral student in English. Notice in particular the repeated stutters on the pronoun *I* in lines 12–14 and again in line 23. Perhaps the physical scientist chooses an image like the leaf in the wind in conversation with a life-long philologist precisely to underline his insecurity in the world of engineers and to ratify his membership in the confederation of English students.

Local formulaicity

Local formulaicity refers to cases where an otherwise unformulaic phrase takes on formulaic force through repetition in a particular context; compare the notion of spontaneous formulaicity in Tannen (1987b). "it was really weird" becomes a local formula in this sense in the story **Model** below. The teller Brianne uses the phrase to record her initial evaluation, immediately following her introductory statement, "we had a model." She repeats this evaluative statement verbatim in the body of the narrative, and a third time in her conclusion. When even Addie picks up the crucial word *weird* in her comment, "oh no. weird," Brianne repeats the phrase a final time in the variant: "I mean, that's weird." The parallelism is heightened in the actual telling through diphthongizing the vowel and vocalizing the *r* to break the word into two syllables, rendering it as an entity almost independent of the normal lexical unit.

Model

1	Addie:	what about life drawing.
2	Brianne:	um we kind of had-
3		we had a section on figure drawing.

4		and we had a *model*.
5	Addie:	uh-huh.
6	Brianne:	it was really *weird*.
7		we had her come,
8	Addie:	{chuckles}
9	Brianne:	it was just about two weeks ago.
10		and then we did some figure drawing {giggling}.
11	Addie:	{laughs}
12	Brianne:	yeah.
13		everyone was kind of like,
14		"oh my *God*, we can't believe it."
15		we- y'know, Midwest College, y'know,
16	Addie:	uh-huh.
17	Brianne:	"we feel like we're in *art* school now" {laughing}.
18	Addie:	{laughs, coughs}
19	Brianne:	yeah, Frank has that for a whole semester,
20		like a
21	Addie:	oh, wow.
22	Brianne:	nude models and stuff.
23	Addie:	yeah, {giggling}.
24	Brianne:	yep.
25		and it was really weird,
26		because um, then, like, just last week,
27		we went downtown one night to see a movie.
28	Addie:	uh-huh.
29	Brianne:	and we were sitting in McDonald's,
30		like downtown,
31		waiting for our movie.
32		and we saw her in the McDonald's,
33	Addie:	{laughs}
34	Brianne:	and it was like, "that's our *model*" {laughing}
35	Addie:	{laughs}
36	Brianne:	in *clothes*
37		[{laughing} uh we were like]
38	Addie:	[{laughing} oh my God.]
39	Brianne:	"oh wow."
40		[it was-]
41	Addie:	[{laughs}]
42	Brianne:	it was really weird.

43	Addie:	{laughs}
44	Brianne:	but it was her. {laughs}
45	Addie:	oh *no*.
46		weird.
47	Brianne:	I mean,
48		that's weird when you run into somebody in Chicago.
49	Addie:	m-hm, yeah.

When an evaluative phrase recurs in this manner in a story — indeed any time a salient phrase is repeated and restructured in a stretch of natural conversation — it acquires a formulaic character of its own. Such local formulaicity can help tellers organize their narratives into orderly chunks, and hence can guide listeners through them; it can signal teller attitudes and move listeners to adopt parallel perspectives.

Addie responds in appropriate fashion to the crucial phrase and its repetition. "it was really weird" in lines 6 and 25 marks the story as funny due to some surprising coincidence or incongruity, namely seeing the nude model "in clothes" at a McDonald's downtown. Addie responds to the message of humor with laughter immediately after the first occurrence of the phrase in lines 6–8, and she continues to laugh in critical places throughout the story, although much of the laughter may reveal embarrassment about nudity more than mirth. In addition, Addie registers her recognition of surprise at the reported coincidence with the standard formulas "oh my God" in line 38 and "oh no" at line 45. Addie even picks up the adjective *weird* from Brianne and applies it herself in line 46, thereby contributing to the pattern of repetition and demonstrating that she shares Brianne's assessment of the event.

Repetition in storytelling

Research on repetition in discourse has demonstrated its key role in establishing patterns and rendering structure recognizable (see Tannen 1987a, 1987b, 1989; Norrick 1987, 1993b). When we see a recurrent word or phrase in a story, we may assume that it segments the story, if we classify the separate tokens as essentially the same. By contrast, we will postulate that recurrent wording marks a progression, if we judge that the repetitions build upon one another. Either way, we begin to impose a structure: either a division into more or less equal parts or a hierarchical arrangement. Similarly, if certain words or phrases recur in specific positions from one narrative to another, we will assume that they perform parallel functions in all the environments. Indeed, repetition plays much this same role in the analysis of all levels of linguistic organization: segments, phonemes, morphemes, words, phrases, sentence types, speech acts and so on. Hence, studying repetition within individual stories and comparing patterns of repetition across stories provides a heuristic for discovering narrative structures.

Repetition within narrative: Forms and functions

Under the general rubric of *repetition* I include such phenomena as restarting and rephrasing at story beginnings and transition points, parallel structures to mirror parallel reported events, to heighten the dramatic effect of telling and to stress the teller's evaluation of the story. Repetition and parallel phrasing serve an organizational function in storytelling, and an investigation of their forms and functions offers a special window on the telling and comprehension of narrative.

Rephrasing in introductions. Restarting and rephrasing occur regularly in the opening passages of conversational narratives to revise after false starts. Story-tellers frequently cut themselves off just as they are starting, then backtrack and restart, as in the openings in the two excerpts below.

Sherry: We had a-
            my mom always had like a dish cloth
            that had holes in it?

The shift from "we had" to "my mom had" in this first example is subtle yet contextually important, since Sherry's interlocutor Lydia had been talking about her own mother.

In the next passage, Jason begins to ask a yes-no question likely to elicit a direct response, then rephrases his introduction in a form similar to the formulaic story opener, "did you ever," which more obviously announces his intention to relate a narrative.

Jason: didn't they, didn't you ever hear that they ...

In both cases the tellers end up with formulations more appropriate to the particular contexts of their stories.

Sometimes tellers spin their wheels for some time before they light upon just the right formulation for their story openings, as we saw April do at the beginning of **First Job** above.

April: and uh we had about a week of training
            and I remember
            the most embarrassing moment of my *life*
            happened then. {laughs}
Ellen: {laughing} what does that *mean*?
April: {laughing} um no this is just-
            I can't believe I did this but-
            um I was really nerv-
            well it was my first *job*,
            and I was nervous
            and there's so much to learn.

April makes three separate runs at beginning her story, before finding a formulation appropriate to the current topic: "well it was my first *job*." Some of these initial false starts, cut-offs and restarts certainly reflect the exigencies of real-time processing and the teller's desire to fit a story into the dynamic conversational context. But as C. Goodwin (1987) demonstrates for markers of forgetfulness in story openings, any feature regularly associated with a function in conversation becomes a cue to that function for auditors and a resource for speakers. Hence, false starts, cut-offs and restarts must be reckoned among the markers of story openings just like such phrases as "I remember one time" and "did you ever hear about." Indeed, as Clark (1997) convincingly demonstrates, listeners key on disfluencies to determine what speakers mean and how to segment their productions. Disfluencies show that a speaker is beginning a story, help determine what sort of story it will be, and what sort of reaction will be appropriate.

Parallel structures for key events. Parallel semantic, syntactic and phonological structures often accentuate central events in oral narratives. In a long story about receiving false fire alarm calls for a neighbor's house, Doris first produces the parallel structures "there's nothing" and "there's no" in lines 35–36. She uses parallel structures again in lines 40–46 to describe the intervening day when no call came and the second call, then again in lines 54–57 to relate the repetitive actions which followed the call on the part of her husband (whom she calls "Dad" at line 47). In the actual spoken version, Doris accentuates the semantic parallelism of *Saturday-Sunday-Monday* (lines 40–44), *cooler-rainy* (lines 41–42), and the syntactic parallelism of *with the key-with the fire company* (lines 55–57) and so on with a sing-song speech pattern.

False Alarms (Excerpt)

1	Doris:	and I said of course we're willing.
2		they {the neighbors} left at noon on a Saturday
3		for their cabin in Michigan.
4		and I nev- one o'clock I get a call.
5		"this is the Dial One Company."
6		says "are you the people with the key-
7		or one of the families with the key for the Masons?"
8		"yes"
9		"well, we've had a fire alarm."
10		and I just "my gosh" I went-
11		my answer on the phone quickly.
12		I was- it was so unexpected.
13		I said "well they just left town one hour ago."
14		well that didn't matter to the Dial One lady.
15		she said "well we've had a fire alarm,
16		and we called the fire company,
17		so *can* you go over with the key
18		and let the firemen in,
19		to check the house."
20		so he {Doris' husband} had just walked down the hall
21		to take his little afternoon nap
22		and I said "well, we can."
23		So he went
24		and he gets their key
25		and he says "well I'll go over."
26		I'll bet he was over there two and a half hours.
27		the firemen came,
28		he had to let them in.
29		they said nothing's wrong,
30		false alarm, of course.
31		*but* they didn't know what caused it.
32		so, then they went into the house.
33		I guess *they* called this Dial Company
34		and said "you'll have to come out and check
35		something. there's nothing on fire,
36		there's no danger,
37		but why did it happen?"
38		well, the stupid Dial One people

39		I don't think ever came *that* day.
40		that was Saturday.
41		Sunday it was cooler,
42		and rainy.
43		everything was fine.
44		Monday,
45		one o'clock,
46		phone rings,
47		Dad was just going down the hall for his nap.
48	Vicky:	oh no.
49	Doris:	"are you the people with the Masons' key?
50		we've had a fire alarm."
51		and I said on the phone
52		"*not* again" you know,
53		I just couldn't believe it.
54		*ov*er he went.
55		*with* the key.
56		diddled and dawdled around,
57		*with* the fire company.
58		and finally they learned and determined,
59		that these little sensors they put up in the attic,
60		they didn't have set with high enough temperatures.

The phrases "diddled and dawdled" in line 56 and "learned and determined" in line 58 illustrate several types of parallelism at once. Both are nonce binomials which conjoin synonyms, displaying alliteration, assonance and end-rhyme. Their semantic and prosodic parallelism endows them with a force like that of real proverbial phrases, as pronounced by Doris near the end of the story (see Norrick 1988 on binomials in texts). Through parallel structures, events and evaluations receive special stress even without actual lexical repetition.

Repetition for dramatic effect. Reverbalization of a single idea in different words functions to heighten the dramatic effect of the action described. As an example of this sort of repetition for dramatic effect, consider the story I call **Spade**. Notice first the repetition in the description of the action of throwing the spade in lines 33–35, "Paul w- went back with the shovel, hurled it. I mean y'know just threw it." The teller Woody also repeats his description of the spade striking its victim: "that damn shovel came right down on his *head*" in line 38 and again following audience laughter in line 40, "I mean- I mean it came down and it

*flat*tened him." Even the effect of "*flat*tened" punctuated with a hand clap still
calls for a paraphrase in line 42: "I mean he fell flat on the ground." In each
case, Woody signals his rephrasing with "I mean," as if he wanted his listeners
to re-visualize the scene along with him. Woody seems very concerned to present
the scene in some detail for dramatic effect.

Spade

1	Woody:	yeah I mean the most hilarious thing I ever saw
2		as a kid growing up
3		was in sixth or seventh grade.
4		in sixth or seventh grade
5		we lived outside of uh Philadelphia.
6		and these two brothers lived across the street.
7		Mark and Paul Tulano.
8		and they were very loud very Italian young men.
9		they were in fifth and sixth grade at the time.
10		and uh they were always fighting
11		about one thing or another.
12		well Paul, my friend,
13		uh got stuck with uh digging up the garden
14		in the back of the yard with a spade.
15		and Mark kept coming around uh to tease him.
16		to tease Paul.
17		and uh you know, Paul's working with a spade.
18		and he says
19		"if you don't leave
20		I'm going to clunk you over the head,
21		with this thing."
22		and uh {cough} and Mark's saying
23		"there's no way that you're going to be like that,
24		because you you just won't do that stuff."
25		"I will I will I will."
26		so this guy started chasing him,
27		kind of like like around the uh
28		the patch where the garden was.
29		and finally um uh uh his- the younger brother-
30		uh Mark just ran off.
31		and uh he was-
32		he had to have been twenty-five thirty yards away,

33		and Paul w- went back with the shovel,
34		hurled it.
35		I mean y'know just threw it.
36	Grant, Ginger:	{laugh}
37	Woody:	and I mean what is the likelihood of that thing-
38		that damn shovel came right down on [his *head*.]
39	Grant, Ginger:	{laugh}
40	Woody:	I mean- I mean it came down and it *flat*tened him.
41		{Woody punctuates with hand clap}
42		I mean he fell flat on the ground.
43		I mean he had a rip in the back of his head,
44	Grant:	o-oh
45	Woody:	and he thought he was dead.
46		and of course he wasn't.
47		he was just knocked-out a little bit
48		and had a nasty concussion
49		and so on and so forth.
50		but um, I mean who would have thought
51		that that shovel
52		and that boy
53		would have connected at that distance.

Even when Woody seems to have completed his storytelling, he restarts with "but um," followed again by "I mean," and repeats his assessment of the reported event as particularly dramatic. This repetition to emphasize evaluation leads us to the next section.

Repetition to highlight evaluation. Both verbatim repetition and reverbalization in different words often serve to highlight evaluations in narratives. In the story **Spade** just above, the teller Woody repeated his rhetorical query about the likelihood of the event described, asking first, "and I mean what is the likelihood of that thing-" in line 37, then again, "but um, I mean who would have *thought* that that shovel and that boy would have connected at that distance" at the end of the story. Perhaps Woody feels it necessary to underline the bizarreness of the event, because he had introduced the story as "the most hilarious thing I ever saw as a kid growing up," rather than, say, as "the strangest thing." Moreover, Woody tells the story for its humor, eliciting laughter several times in its course, yet by its completion, he is clearly emphasizing the improbability of the event described. In any case, he delivers a good example of repetition through para-

phrase to accentuate a particular evaluation. One might also recall Vivian's story
Twins from chapter two, where she repeated crucial dialogue and her evaluation after
a brief intervening response story in order to re-establish her own perspective.

Now consider another example in which repetition serves to highlight
evaluation. In the next story **Accidents**, two young men have been discussing
how dangerous rough-housing can become, when Mark recalls an accident story
his aunt told him. Mark evaluates his story with the apparent rhetorical question
"isn't that horrid," answering his own question with the partial repetition "that's
horrid," before his listener Jacob has a chance to respond. Even when Jacob does
try to respond, Mark expands his original resolution from "blinded her" to
"blinded her for life," then repeats his original rhetorical question.

Accidents
```
 1   Jacob:  we've kept everything pretty much under control
 2           [though this year.]
 3   Mark:   [that's right,]
 4           you can't wrestle around
 5           or bad things will happen.
 6   Jacob:  yeah, Roger got [his nose]
 7   Mark:   [you know what] happened to my one of my aunt's
 8           friends out in Iowa?
 9           like when- when she was younger,
10           she had a headgear from braces,
11           and these two girls were wrestling around
12           just playing around, wrestling.
13           and one girl pulled her headgear off her mouth
14           and let it snap back.
15           and it slid up her face
16           and stuck in her eyes
17           and blinded her.
18   Jacob:  wow.
19   Mark:   isn't that horrid?
20           that's horrid.
21   Jacob:  [when my-]
22   Mark:   [blinded her] for life.
23           isn't that horrid.
24           that's just- I mean just from goofing around,
25           just from screwing-
26           a little bit of screwing around.
```

27	and if- and another thing,
28	it- it- it's terrible the things that can happen.
29	that's why I don't like
30	people screwing around with swords
31	and trying to throw people in the showers
32	and stuff like that,
33	and everything like that.

When evaluative phrases recur in a story, especially at the end like those with *horrid* in the excerpt above, they can acquire a formulaic character of their own, as we saw in the discussion of local formulaicity in chapter two. Like proverbs, clichés and other stock phrases, local formulaicity contributes to the organization of narratives.

Conclusions

We have seen that formulaic speech and repetition play an important organizational role in conversational storytelling. Since formulaic speech and repetition mark prominent points in the storytelling performance, they provide keys to narrative organization. In our investigation of formulaicity in storytelling, we found not only stock formulas, but also figurative formulas and spontaneously created local formulaicity. In our investigation of repetition, we explored not only the organizational functions of rephrasing and parallel structures, but also the use of repetition to heighten dramatic effect and emphasize evaluation. All these rhetorical devices signal teller attitudes and serve as guides to listeners.

CHAPTER 4

Retelling and Retold Stories

Let us from point to point this story know
To make the even truth in pleasure flow.
William Shakespeare, "All's Well That Ends Well" V iii

Introduction

Retelling and retold stories have special heuristic value for our understanding of narrative processes. Correlating multiple performances of the same story will reveal which elements of the basic narrative remain stable and which vary with the particular narrative context, thereby providing empirical support for recognizing a range of strategies by which tellers shape memory into contextually appropriate storytelling performances. In this chapter, we will first consider in how far it is possible to retell the same story, why tellers do so and what we can learn from such retellings. Then we consider retold stories, that is stories presented by their tellers as familiar in narrative form to at least some of the auditors. Though we can isolate a sequence of narrative clauses from separate tellings of a story, we will find the largest degree of overlap in areas of evaluation, background information and dialogue.

Retelling the 'same story'

Let us first consider stories told twice by a single individual or a group of co-tellers familiar with the events related. Retold conversational stories provide a natural testing site for analyzing narrative. Distillation of a basic narrative from separate storytelling performances facilitates comparison between them and highlights their similarities and differences. This section investigates, first, immediate retelling for a newly arrived listener, and second, relating the same story for different audiences. I develop methods for analyzing retold stories in conversation and suggest several directions for future research. I propose to investigate examples of natural conversational retelling from three settings, and suggest approaches to them with an eye to describing what conversationalists do in spontaneous storytelling.

Contrary to what one would expect from its title, "Telling the same story twice," Polanyi's (1981) article cites no examples of retold stories, nor does she give any indication of having inspected relevant data; certainly an empirical treatment of the matter is desirable. Focusing on narrative events in which tellers reconstruct a story for separate audiences yields a clearer view of what tellers repeat, which makes it possible to recognize separate performances as versions of the same story. My data show that a story can remain substantially intact from one telling to the next. This suggests that tellers redesign a basic story for the audience present, rather than reconstructing a narrative from the ground up for each new audience. Though the primary sequence of narrative clauses must exhibit overlap from one telling to the next according to Labov, we shall find significant repetition in non-narrative clauses of evaluation and background information as well.

Retold stories bear interest both for the study of narration and for research on repetition in discourse. Probably all stories are potentially repeatable but not necessarily repeated, while some stories may be narrated over and over for different audiences or even repeated at separate times for a single audience. In the following, we will examine what happens when conversationalists retell a story for different constellations of listeners.

Except for Chafe's seminal article (1998) on naturally occurring retellings discussed in chapter one, past work has explicitly considered retold stories in spontaneous conversation only rarely. Suggestive research by such authors as Watson (1975), C. Goodwin (1986) and Boggs (1985) has documented the influence co-tellers can exert on the trajectory of a narrative through their differential interest and competence in the details of talk. Tannen (1978) points out the importance of differing expectations about what counts as a story and how this can lead to dissonance between co-narrators.

When scholars have treated retellings separated in time, as do Hymes (1981, 1985) and Bauman (1986), their data have been elicited stories rather than naturally occurring narratives. Sherzer (1981) provides a fascinating account of retelling in Kuna discourse, describing how a basic narrative varies through repetition and reformulation with different contexts, purposes, tellers and audiences. As retellings make a story generally familiar, "what becomes increasingly important is not the news itself, but the way of telling it" (261). This holds *mutatis mutandis* for the sort of co-narration I consider in the third section below on group reconstruction of familiar stories (see Norrick 1997 as well).

Chafe (1980, 1991) and Tannen (1980, 1984b) investigate narratives produced as retellings of a film without dialogue, while Scollon & Scollon (1984) examine children's retellings of stories the children had previously read, and Romaine (1984) looks at multiple tellings of a single event by separate children. This work has highlighted differences between cinematic, written and oral versions of a story, as well as produced insights into interpersonal and intercultural differences in the comprehension and production of narratives. Ferrara (1994) explicitly examines retellings, but her description of talk in therapy sessions necessarily identifies different structures, functions and conditions on participation rights from those we find in everyday conversation. Nevertheless, her treatment of three versions of a single story from a basic narrative to successively more elaborate structures in later therapy sessions certainly demonstrates some patterns typical of retellings generally.

Chafe (1998) compares two natural occurrences of a story told for different audiences fifteen weeks apart. From one performance to the next, the teller expands or suppresses particular scenes, and each audience shapes the trajectory of the story as well, but the two versions share an underlying plot and primary foci of interest as well as substantial overlap in individual propositions and even wording repeated more or less verbatim. Chafe describes storytelling as if it were a process of retrieving information from memory, selecting from it, and verbalizing it; but I view the production of narrative as reconstruction rather than simple recall. I tend to see tellers caught up in a dynamic context and in their own performance, tellers who tailor a basic story to fit the current thematic needs of the interaction. In telling our personal stories, we create and recreate our past in light of our present needs and concerns, instead of simply recapitulating stored experience. Thus, where Chafe speaks of teller preoccupations and "clusters of ideas" from memory, I find a stability of storytelling strategies, for instance the use of repetition and parallel structures as rhetorical devices for organizing the conversational narrative performance.

We must clearly distinguish the story from the performance or the narrative text from the narrative event, as well as separating the story from the past events narrated, following Bauman (1986) and Blum-Kulka (1993). It is through separating the story qua underlying structure from the real-time performance that we can be said to be retelling the same story, as Polanyi (1981) argues. Polanyi was concerned in a theoretical way with what counted as the same story from the perspective of Conversation Analysis à la Sacks versus Labov's view. For Sacks (1972, 1974, 1992) each narrative performance instantiates a separate story tied to its local conversational context. According to Labov & Waletzky (1967) and Labov (1972), separate tellings of a single story may indeed occur. A primary sequence of temporally ordered narrative clauses constitutes the substratum of any particular story performance, which will generally flesh it out with an abstract, an orientation, dialogue and evaluation, a result or resolution, and a coda. The same real-world events may provide the stuff for several stories, just as the same story will receive different narrative treatments from different tellers. By examining retellings, we shall see in detail what Labov and Polanyi hypothesize, namely how the individual teller varies the basic narrative to fit the particular context.

The first example to be treated illustrates retelling a short story immediately after its original when a new listener arrives and asks whom the others are talking about. The second section examines another two versions of a long story presented to separate audiences a few days apart. This comparison naturally leads into a discussion of methods for the analysis of conversational storytelling and suggests certain principles of narrative organization in contexts.

Retelling for a new hearer

In the passage below, Jean tells one story of a bag left in a turkey between line 1 and line 15, then she tells a second story on the same topic in lines 16–20 before she is interrupted. Jean repeats this second story for Annie, who arrives from the adjacent kitchen asking "who?" at line 35.

Bag in Turkey

1	Jean:	we were laughing the other uh day at work.
2		we were talking about making turkeys and stuff.
3		and um Marge Jankowski said,
4		well, one of her girlfriends
5		one time made a turkey.
6		first time.
7		and she said,
8		"oh" she was so proud of herself,
9		she made the turkey.
10		the only thing, she left the bag in.
11		she said, and then I said
12		"well nobody saw it, right?"
13		she said, "*everybody* saw it."
14		I said "oh that was *ter*rible.
15		how would anybody keep a bag in there."
16		Mary, Mary kept watching and she said,

17		"I did it.
18		nobody saw it.
19		and I didn't tell anybody."
20		she said, "first of all, I thought-"
21	Lynn:	she left the bag *in*?
22	All:	it's the giblets- the turkey has all-
23	Jean:	with the giblets in it and stuff.
24		[you know there's a bag inside, yeah?]
25	Lynn:	[I've never made a turkey.]
26		I've never made a turkey.
27	Jean:	so I said, to Mary,
28		I said, "Mary,"
29		I said, "didn't you know?
30		didn't you-"
31		she says, "I saw the thing."
32		she said, "it said Ready to Cook so I,"
33		she said, "who- nobody told me I had to *clean* it."
34		she said, "so I put it in the oven."
35	Annie:	who?
36	Jean:	this girl at work.
37	Annie:	oh.
38	Jean:	she put it in with all the guts and everything.
39		with the bag inside and everything.
40		{General laughter}
41	Jean:	she said, "but nobody knew it."
42		but, she said, "they ate it.
43		it was good."

The first narrative passage in the excerpt above begins in line 4 and ends in line 15. It relates a story heard from Marge Jankowski about a colleague who roasted a Thanksgiving turkey without removing the bag of giblets from the breast cavity. Then starting in line 16, Jean tells a second story, which her friend Mary told about making the same mistake. The narrative elements representing the main action of this brief story may be labeled as follows to facilitate comparison with the repeat telling.

Analysis of Mary's **Bag in Turkey** story lines 16–19:

A   Mary said, "I did it." (i.e. cooked turkey with bag in)
B   nobody saw it.
C   and I didn't tell anybody.

Jean attempts to continue with Mary's rationale for her behavior, but questions and explanations regarding "the bag" occupy the floor till line 26. Then Jean's perspective shifts to the discussion she had with Mary about the incident. While Jean is reporting this discussion, Annie enters the room and asks, "who?" at line 35. In response to this question, Jean produces another version of the story labeled A–C above starting in line 36. This second version expands the A-clause to deliver the crucial background information for Annie, and retains the B-clause as a rough paraphrase of its counterpart in the original. The next clause in this second version expands the story predictably to report that the guests ate the turkey, while it ignores the information that Mary did not mention the bag to them.

A   this girl at work put it in with all the guts and everything. with the bag inside and everything.
B   she said, "but nobody knew it."
C   but, she said, "they ate it. it was good."

Given our frame for turkey and Thanksgiving, we might naturally assume from the first version that the turkey was eaten and enjoyed, but Mary explicitly states in this second version that the turkey was eaten and enjoyed. Similarly, the statement that "nobody knew it" in the second version includes and supersedes the two reports that "nobody saw it" and that Mary "didn't tell anybody." In this way, frames can account for essential equivalence in separate versions of the same story. The rough equivalence of the two central clauses A and B, along with the recognizable connections between the C-clauses in the two versions would suffice for us to claim they instantiate the same story, even without the contextual evidence here that Jean clearly means to repeat her tale for the new listener. Given this natural evidence, I feel comfortable claiming that the sorts of differences we have identified between the two versions simply would not lead recipients to hear them as discrete stories in the conversational context.

Retelling in separate contexts

By way of comparison, I would now like to examine two tellings of a much longer story by a single teller to different audiences separated by an interval of several days. After presenting the two versions, I will attempt a generalized analysis of the two tellings like those proposed above. The two renditions demonstrate the whole range of permutations and paraphrases one can expect to find between separate tellings of a story by a single teller in spontaneous conversation. In the two transcriptions, I italicize the parallel units and label the lines where corresponding constituents begin in both. I start labeling with single capital letters, then switch to double lower case letters to indicate a sub-section placed differently in the two variants. The parallel elements labeled Z are also positioned differently in the two variants. I generally ignore comments and questions from listeners, except that I substitute Ken's correction of *hook and ladder* for the apparently garbled *pumpers and shovers* in line 106. Recall that I take the skeletal structure to reflect the sort of coherent framework a listener might cobble together on the basis of a polyphonic performance to clarify causal relations and provide a basis for evaluation, rather than some underlying model from which the storyteller constructs an oral performance.

Doris and Ken are the parents of Jason and Judy, both of whom are visiting home during winter break. During the initial telling, Jason and his fiancée Vicky are talking with Doris and Ken about the effects of drugs and crime on modern life. All participants are middle-class white Anglo-Americans from the western suburbs of Chicago (an excerpt from the first version of this story was analyzed in chapter three as an example of using parallel structures to highlight key events).

False Alarm$_1$

1	Doris:	they just got her VCR that they could turn over fast.
2	Jason:	sure.
3		they sell that for twenty bucks,
4		then they can get high for another day.
5	Doris:	in our-
6	Jason:	and the next evening
7		they're back in somebody else's house.
8	Doris:	our back door neighbors do a lot of traveling.
9		and they *do* plan to take at least six weeks-
10		maybe two full months to make a trip to the east
11		coast. they will leave very late this month,
12		and maybe be gone for two whole months.
13		so *they* finally just decided
14		this time before they leave
15		they're not going to worry about it
16	A	and *installed a total burglar system.*
17		it's got these sensors all over the house
18		and if anybody ever walked [through the house]
19	Jason:	[yeah.]
20	Doris:	it sets off alarms and,
21		oh it's so complicated
22		I don't know what they must have paid for it.
23		and then they have to get two neighbors

24		to agree to keep a key and to be called
25		in case of an alarm and all this stuff.
26	Vicky:	uh-hunh.
27	Doris:	so of course we were elected {laughs}.
28	B	they left for a little trip,
29		*just up to a Michigan* cabin two weeks ago-
30		the thing had been installed two or three days
31		before- they called us over one night
32		and said were we willing to keep the key
33		and be responsible.
34		and, well I've always taken her mail
35		and she's taken mine and stuff
36		if we were gone not *too* long
37		and we've done things for each other for- for years.
38		and I said of course we're willing.
39		they left at noon on a Saturday
40		for their cabin in Michigan.
41		and I nev-
42	C	*one o'clock I get a call.*
43		"this is the Dial One Company."
44	D	*says "are you the people with the key-*
45		or one of the families with the key for the Masons?"
46	E	*"yes."*
47	F	*"well, we've had a fire alarm."*
48		and I just "my gosh" I went-
49		my answer on the phone quickly.
50		I was- it was so unexpected.
51	G	*I said "well they just left town one hour ago."*
52		well that didn't matter to the Dial One lady.
53	H	*she said* "well we've had a fire alarm,
54		and we called the fire company,
55		*so can you go over with the key*
56		*and let the firemen in, to check the house."*
57	I	*So he had just walked down the hall to take his*
58		*little afternoon nap*
59		and I said "Well, we can."
60	J	*and he says "Well I'll go over."*
61	K	*I'll bet he was over there two and a half hours.*
62	L	*the firemen came,*

63		he had to let them in.
64	M	*they said nothing's wrong,*
65		false alarm, of course.
66		so, then they went into the house.
67		I guess *they* called this Dial Company
68		and said "you'll have to come out and check
69		something. there's nothing on fire,
70		there's no danger,
71		but why did it happen?"
72	Z	*well, the stupid Dial One people*
73		*I don't think ever came that day.*
74	N	*that was Saturday.*
75	O	*Sunday it was cooler,*
76		and rainy.
77	P	*everything was fine.*
78	Q	*Monday,*
79		*one o'clock,*
80		*phone rings,*
81		Dad was just going down the hall for his nap.
82	Vicky:	oh no.
83	Doris:	"are you the people with the Masons' key?
84	R	*we've had a fire alarm."*
85		and I said on the phone "*Not* again" you know,
86	S	*I just couldn't believe it.*
87	T	*over he went.*
88		with the key.
89		diddled and dawdled around,
90		with the fire company.
91		and finally they learned and determined,
92	aa	*that these little sensors they put up in the attic,*
93		*they didn't have set with high enough temperatures.*
94	Vicky:	*oh.*
95	Doris:	and so when it got hot,
96		at one o'clock in the heat of the day
97	bb	*those stupid things set the fire alarm off.*
98	Vicky:	{inhales deeply}
99	Doris:	so *they* went round and round.
100		and *he* had to stand around,
101	cc	and- and- as *Dad came home and said,*

102		*do you realize*
103		what the taxpayers paid
104		to send firemen out two days-
105		a whole bunch of firemen
106		and the pumpers and [shovers]
107	dd Ken:	[a pumper and] *a hook and ladder.*
108		[*five* pieces] of equipment.
109	Vicky:	[oh really?]
110	Doris:	for a *stu*pid mistake
111		on the part of this installing company.
112	Jason:	well [I mean,]
113	Doris:	[so]
114	Jason:	so the installing company isn't liable then?
115	Doris:	they- they made a dumb mistake
116		and they didn't put those sensors a high enough
117		degree, you see.
118	U	*so of course when the Masons came home*
119	V	and *they* just kind of jokingly *said*
120		*"everything go all right?*
121	W	*you didn't get any false alarms, did you?"*
122		you know just jokingly.
123	Jason:	{sarcastically} Ha ha.
124	Doris:	we said "did we ever."
125	X	*and we thought of course they must be told,*
126		because if they're going to leave for two months
127	Y	*we don't want to be called over there every other*
128		*day.*
129	Vicky:	yeah.
130	Doris:	so they were really mad and embarrassed
131		and apologetic and grateful.
132		and they called their company back out
133		and just gave them what for
134		and said "you check every inch of this house again
135		so that this doesn't happen to our neighbors
136		or to the fire company again."
137		well of course they've taken care of it
138		and the company was apologetic
139		and it will never happen again.
140		but isn't that just typical

| 141 | of the complex life that you live |
| 142 | because of these drug-ridden people ... |

While this initial version of **False Alarm** served as an exemplum in a four-party discussion about drugs and crime on the first evening Jason and Vicky arrived at the home of Jason's parents, Doris and Ken, the second telling arises during a conversation about helping out neighbors between just Doris and her daughter Judy a few days later.

False Alarm₂

1	Doris:	I've had lots of requests for that.
2		you know the people behind us,
3		our best friends in the neighborhood,
4		are going to take an *eight week* trip,
5		they're going to drive to the coast.
6		they know the area they're going to [drive through,]
7	Judy:	[this is-]
8	Doris:	the Masons, Masons,
9		not- not the couple uh that you helped go to Alaska.
10		the Masons went to Alaska last year too,
11		but *this* year they're going to drive to the east
12		coast and see the sights there.
13		they just *love* to travel
14		and don't seem to care how many weeks they're gone.
15		*eight weeks* to me is too much,
16		but that's how they want to do it.
17		they've got a *van*.
18		but there are lots of little burglaries
19		in the neighborhood
20		and they certainly don't want to get broken in
21	A	and *they just had a burglar system put in*
22		and we're one of the people that's holding a key
23		and knowing them.
24		so, they put it in
25		but then they always go to Michigan
26		for just *one* week to a cottage-
27		they've done it ever since we've known them
28		just about now, you know.
29		the system got put in one day,

30	B	*the next day the two of them left for Michigan.*
31		I knew they were leaving that morning.
32	C	*one o'clock the phone rang.*
33	D	*"are you the- one of the people*
34		*holding a key for the Mason house?"*
35	E	*"yes."*
36	F	*"well, there's been a fire alarm."*
37	G	*and I- and my reaction was "oh no, not already"*
38		{laughing}
39	Judy:	{joins in laughter}
40	Doris:	I knew they had just left.
41	H	*so, "can one of you go over*
42		*and unlock the house for the firemen."*
43	I	*well Dad had just gone down the hall to take his nap.*
44	J	*he said "oh, I'll go over."*
45	K	*he spent three hours over there that afternoon.*
46	L	*the firemen came,*
47		*they could never find a thing,*
48		but they- you know they had to check it out
49		carefully. then he and another neighbor-
50		an old lady
51		met out in front and chatted.
52		I- I thought he never would come home
53		and I was ready to walk over,
54		but I thought maybe it's better if I stay here,
55		what if it is a fire.
56	N	*and uh, that was Saturday.*
57	O	*Sunday was a much cooler day.*
58	P	*nothing.*
59	Q	*Monday,*
60		*one o'clock,*
61		*telephone,*
62	R	*"There's a fire alarm for the Masons."*
63	S	*I just about croaked.*
64		*we would have never guessed.*
65		"can you come over.
66		with the key."
67	T	*he went over*
68		and was gone for an hour.

69	Z	*and the system people, the burglar people*
70		*never did come and check out the system.*
71		*a*nd that really made him and the other neighbor mad.
72		ao, it's- it's a long story.
73		but anyway,
74	U	*the friends came home,*
75	V	*and they just said "Well is everything okay?"*
76		and Martha just in passing said
77	W	*"you didn't have any false alarms, did you?"*
78		you know just as you'd say.
79	X	*and I said, "Well, we do need to talk about this,*
80	Y	*because imagine being stuck here*
81		*and having this happen to us all the time.*
82		so I just said to Martha
83		we really do have to sit down and talk.
84		so then we finally sat down and had our talk.
85	aa	*there were sensors in the attic* they installed
86		were the ones that said
87		if it would get as hot as so and so degrees
88		they would go off.
89	bb	*and it was on a hot hot summer afternoon*
90		*they would fall into alarm status.*
91		but Dad said it just makes you mad,
92	cc	because *he said*
93		*it costs the taxpayers money every time a fireman,*
94	dd	*a hook and ladder*
95		and all these people come running out.
96		and it costs the taxpayers=
97	Judy:	=our- where we are, we have-
98		you can have *three* false alarms …

The chunk labeled aa-dd acts as a coherent sub-section in both narratives, though it appears at different points (compare Chafe's 1994 notion of the "subtopic"). It makes sense either as a report on what the alarm system people determined after the second false alarm in the first version or as a final explanation in the second version. By contrast, the element labeled Z has no obvious slot in either version and can move rather freely, because it expresses something which did *not* happen. Negative statements in stories set up expectations about the following action according to Sacks (1992). This holds for the initial telling, where the failure to check out the system *leads to* the second false alarm, and also for the second telling, where this negative statement *follows* the result statement in lines 67–68: "he went over and he was gone for an hour."

Although Doris sticks with the past tense throughout the second version, she switches into the present tense and back to the past tense twice in her initial telling. In her description of the first call from the alarm company at line 42, Doris says: "one o'clock I *get* a call." She then reports the caller's question with the present tense *says*, before returning to the past tense to report her own response with "I went," "I was" and "I said" in lines 48–51. This corresponds to Johnstone's (1987) finding that tellers may switch into the present tense to render the speech of persons with authority. Doris again switches from the past into the present tense in lines 59–60. She reports her own words to the alarm company on the telephone in the past tense with "I said 'well, we can'," then shifts into the present for her husband's speech: "and he says 'well I'll go over'." While the past tense still marks Doris' response to authority, the present tense signals the transition back to the home front and the familiar voice. In my data as a whole, tense shifts from the pure past to the present seem to either highlight salient events or to mark shifts in speakers or perspectives. Whatever the general tendency, the particular tense shifts at issue here occur only in the first version, where we have also noted more parallel structures. Both features contribute to making the first version a more highly involved telling performance, better geared to its larger audience, as compared with the second telling performed for a single auditor.

Despite the obvious differences between the two versions, the number and close similarity of the parallel elements identified are substantial for a narrative of this length. The virtual identity of units N–Q, accentuated by parallel intonation in the actual spoken performance, points to significant verbatim recall of whole chunks or to consistent use of specific narrative techniques at crucial points in a story from one performance to the next. Significantly, N–P are *not* true narrative elements, since they provide background for the second telephone call reported in clause Q, rather than describing sequential actions. The story itself actually varies surprisingly little from one telling to the next, considering that Doris constructs it to fit a different topic in each case and that it must address different audiences with their different interruptive questions. This suggests that some speakers recycle stories as fairly intact units, apparently sometimes with moveable sub-sections, tailoring them just as much as necessary to fit the current context.

A generalized analysis of the two tellings follows on the model of those above. As we have noted, Doris shifts verb tense in the first telling; she even leaves verbs out entirely, especially verbs reporting speech. To reflect this in the generalized analysis below, I add appropriate forms of *say* and *ask*, and employ the past tense throughout. The floating Z element appears in its position in the original version, whereas the sub-section aa-dd appears at the end, as in the second version.

Generalized Analysis: **False Alarm₁** & **False Alarm₂**

A	the Masons (back door neighbors) installed a burglar system.
B	they left for their cabin in Michigan.
C	at one o'clock the phone rang.
D	the caller asked if they had the key for the Mason house.
E	Doris said, "yes."
F	the caller said they had had a fire alarm.
G	Doris reacted with surprise.
H	the caller asked them to go over and let the firemen in.
I	Ken had just gone down the hall to take his nap.
J	he said, "I'll go over."
K	he was over there two to three hours.
L	the firemen came.
M	they found nothing wrong.
Z	the burglar alarm company did not come.
N	that was Saturday.
O	Sunday was cooler.
P	everything was fine.
Q	Monday, one o'clock, phone rang.
R	the caller said they had had a fire alarm.
S	Doris could not believe it.
T	Ken went over.
U	the Masons came home
V	they asked if everything went all right.
W	they said, "you didn't get any false alarms, did you?"
X	Doris and Ken thought the Masons must be told
Y	they worry about possible recurrence of false alarms.
aa	the sensors in the attic were set too low.
bb	summer heat set them off.
cc	Ken said it costs the taxpayers money when the fire department has to respond to false alarms.
dd	the fire department sent lots of firemen and a hook and ladder.

Comparing this generalized analysis with the individual renditions reveals the sorts of adjustments the teller must make to adapt the basic story to diverse conversational contexts. We have seen that sub-sections like aa-dd, coherent in themselves, may be positioned differently from one telling to the next; in these various positions they will fulfill different functions. Small chunks like N–Q recur almost verbatim. The overall form of the story remains surprisingly constant in the retelling, though the storytelling responds to a new topic and must navigate around different audience responses.

The amount of material recycled more or less verbatim may vary with the temporal proximity and salience of the reported events, with the closeness of the most recent previous telling, with the number of times the story has been told in the past, as Bartlett (1932) showed, and with personal narrative style, as Johnstone (1996) demonstrates. Further research under more closely controlled conditions could help separate these factors and determine their relative importance. My own data on elicited tellings and retellings separated by various intervals of time indicate that, except for stories about very recent events, familiarity through frequent retelling looms largest in accounting for shared or parallel phrasing. The data further point to the prominence of non-narrative clauses of evaluation and background information among the verbatim or similar passages, as seen in the near identity of units N–Q in Doris' two versions of **False Alarm**. Dialogue often recurs essentially verbatim from one telling to the next as well, especially when it serves as a kind of punch line in an anecdote. Hence investigation of multiple tellings of jokes and personal anecdotes might also shed light on the role of repetition in retelling. As a methodological principle, I suggest looking first for repetition and variation among different versions of a story before distilling from them a primary sequence of narrative clauses. Focusing immediately on a skeleton of narrative clauses often loses sight of significant congruencies between tellings.

Conclusions

We have seen how the consideration of retelling offers a special perspective on conversational narrative, because it highlights the distinctions between a basic story and those aspects of the narration tied immediately to the local context, thereby clarifying the process by which tellers shape memory into contextually appropriate narration. I employed several methods for analyzing and comparing of successive tellings of a single story in conversation. We examined immediate retelling performed for the sake of a new arrival to the conversation. We then compared separate versions of a 'single story' delivered by a single teller to separate audiences on different days.

The immediate retellings provide natural evidence for claiming that the two performances count as versions of a single story in the conversational context. Looking at two renditions of a story in separate contexts revealed the range of permutations and paraphrases a teller may produce to match the story with diverse topics and audience responses. Despite the contextual differences between separate versions of the stories we analyzed, the similarity of the parallel elements identified was quite substantial. Although we can extract a sequence of narrative clauses in separate tellings of a story, the closest similarities in phrasing often appear among the non-narrative elements of evaluation and background information, as well as in dialogue. The virtual identity of certain phrases from one telling to the next suggests significant nearly verbatim recall of whole chunks or a consistent use of specific narrative techniques at crucial points in a story. Frequent retelling leads some tellers to crystalize and recycle stories as fairly complete units, sometimes with moveable sub-sections, tailoring them just as much as necessary to fit the current context.

The focus here on naturally occurring retellings provides insights on the kinds of work narrators perform in embedding a single story in different contexts. It suggests several directions for future research, for instance on the place of verbatim repetition, parallel structure and close paraphrase from one telling to the next; on the relative significance of salience and proximity of the related events versus frequency of past retellings and closeness of the most recent retelling; on retelling in personal stories versus canned narrative jokes and other third person narratives.

Twice-told tales

This section treats narratives marked as and recognized as retold, that is stories familiar to at least some of the auditors as stories, not just those recalling common past experiences. Conversation occasions different kinds of stories in different ways; tellers must negotiate tellability for specific stories in a contextually appropriate manner. Sometimes when speakers mention a familiar story in the course of a conversation, they simply deliver a brief run-through of the narrative, perhaps in deference to the other participants who already know the story and who might, therefore, ignore or cut off a retelling, as Polanyi demonstrates (1981). We will examine one such brief run-through below. By contrast, mention of a familiar story may sometimes also strike interlocutors as an invitation to join in the telling of it. We will analyze a retelling with significant co-narration below as well. Finally, we will observe an example of the opposite process, namely a case where one speaker presupposes general knowledge of a story which, however, turns out not to be familiar to the others.

According to most literature on conversational narratives, a new story must be "reportable" in the sense of Labov (1972) or "tellable" in Sacks' terms (1974, 1992): A would-be narrator must be able to defend the story as relevant and newsworthy to get and hold the floor and escape censure at its conclusion, as Polanyi (1981) argues. Telling a story without a currently relevant point constitutes a loss of face for the teller, especially when received with a scathing "So what?" (Labov & Fanshel 1977) or "What's the point?" (Polanyi 1979). Thus retelling familiar stories might be assumed not to occur at all; yet familiar stories regularly appear, and co-narration of such stories occurs quite commonly, especially within groups where some of the participants were present during the events reported as well as during previous narrations.

Further, Blum-Kulka (1993) says that family stories are triggered by the presence of an outsider, but my data are full of family stories told and retold precisely among those who already know them — not in spite of their familiarity to the participants, but because of it. Moreover, retold stories are typically prefaced in ways which label them as unoriginal, and yet these signals animate participants to involvement rather than cuing them to question the relevance and tellability of the stories. Apparently the tellability of familiar stories hinges not on their content, but on the dynamics of the narrative event itself. Story content need not be relevant or newsworthy if co-narration holds the promise of high involvement, as described by Tannen (1984a, 1989). Moreover, it is precisely the familiarity of story content which influences participation rights, since it presents the opportunity for significant co-narration. We shall be looking at structural markers of retold tales as well as the group dynamics and functions of retelling. By concentrating on narrative events where the exchange of information counts for little, we should get a clearer view of the other functions narration fulfills in group behavior.

It seems often that the principal goal of storytelling in conversational interaction consists in reliving pleasant moments and enhancing rapport. Thus we frequently retell an already familiar story with little information exchange and no new point to make. This desire to recreate and re-enjoy a common experience presumably motivates my first example. All close-knit durable groups have their own stories — stories recalled and repeated spontaneously during regular interaction between group members. And though these stories may be retold primarily for amusement, they function simultaneously to remind members of a common past and shared values, so that they enhance feelings of group identity.

Co-telling a familiar story

The story Brianne introduces in the passage below can serve as a typical example of a jointly constructed, retold narrative in many ways. Brianne and Addie are very close friends together the day after Thanksgiving for the first time since they departed for separate colleges in mid-August. Both women worked at the bakery described in the story, and they are in the middle of a long discussion about their former workplace, which derives from the series of stories included in *Appendix 3* as **Bakery**. Of particular importance in the present context is the explicit characterization of the story as familiar to both participants, though only Addie experienced the reported events directly, while Brianne read about them in a letter from Addie. This information appears right in Brianne's introduction to the narrative, "it- it was *so* funny in your letter. I was cracking up *so* hard."

Change (from **Bakery**)

1	Brianne:	it- it was *so* funny in your letter.
2		I was cracking up *so* hard.
3		Manuela was like "what's so funny?"
4		I'm like, "I can't even tell you
5		because you won't even think it's funny but,"
6	Addie:	wh- which one was it?
7		when I told you about Mom and the *change*?
8	Brianne:	yeah {laughs}.
9	Addie:	she gave her a five dollar bill.
10		[and-]
11	Brianne:	[and she] promptly freaked.
12	Addie:	and she freaked out
13		because she didn't have enough change to give her.
14		Mom gave her the five,
15		"and the *change*?
16		to go *with* this?
17		[that's an awful lot of change to give *back*.]
18	Brianne:	[she didn't have enough *ones* or whatever.]
19		oh my God.
20	Addie:	oh they're terrible.
21	Brianne:	I know.
22	Addie:	oh aren't they *awful*?
23	Brianne:	of all the things she freaks out about,

24	Addie:		I know.
25	Brianne:	and she doesn't freak out about that.
26	Addie:		oh, {laughs}.
27	Brianne:	that's just the worst.

All the features I find typical of collaboratively constructed retold narratives are present here. First, there are explicit markers that the story is already known to those present. After Brianne prefaces the story with an identification of its source in a letter, Addie immediately registers her recognition of it in line 6 with: "wh- which one was it? when I told you about Mom and the *change*?" Participants also check on the accuracy and completeness of their own recollections with questions or open-ended statements like Brianne's "she didn't have enough *ones* or whatever" at line 18. Conversely, participants confirm each other's statements, as does Addie in completing Brianne's contribution, "and she promptly freaked," with her own, "and she freaked out because she didn't have enough change" in lines 12–13. This give-and-take with its successive stages of agreement heightens rapport.

Second, there is substantial co-telling. Brianne announces the story by reference to Addie's letter, and Addie confirms the identity of the story in lines 6–8. Then once Addie has begun to tell the tale, Brianne contributes the information that Thelma "freaked" in line 11, as well as the detail that she "didn't have enough ones" in line 18. At the completion of the story, the women literally take turns adding evaluative comments. Significantly, Brianne demonstrates her knowledge of the more comprehensive context for the story through her over-arching evaluation of Thelma's behavior in lines 23–25: "of all the things she freaks out about, and she doesn't freak out about that." This global evaluation leads back into the more general frame of the women's common experiences at the bakery.

For other illustrations of co-telling, compare the collaborative reproduction of a story familiar to everyone present in chapter five.

Synopsis of a familiar story

In the next excerpt we shall see first how a speaker may perform a quick synopsis of a familiar story, so as to go on record as having told it without the risk of boring other participants who already know the story. Then in the section following, we shall go on to observe how expectations that a story is familiar to other participants can backfire.

Lydia opens the storytelling in the next passage by reproducing an anecdote about Sherry's thrifty coupon use, keeping the narrative to a minimum, apparently because she presumes everyone has heard it before.

Lydia: how I know she's the coupon lady.
           I've told the cute story about Elizabeth saying
           when her mom's ready to go out to the store,
           "got the coupons Mom?"
           I thought that was the cutest thing I'd ever heard.

Now this does not count as a story at all on the narrow definition, since we cannot find two narrative elements ordered to correspond to the events reported. Nevertheless, given the analytic tools we have developed so far, we have little trouble reorganizing the synopsis here into a minimal acceptable narrative like the following.

A   Sherry got Elizabeth ready to go to the store.
B   Elizabeth asked, "got the coupons, Mom?"

In any case, co-conversationalists hearing a brief run-through like that Lydia produces can certainly choose to hear it as a version of a more complete narrative, especially if they are familiar with the basic story.

Presupposed familiar story

Lydia's story about Sherry leads into another frugal-story which Sherry tells on herself after prompting by husband Brandon. This second story is new to all but Brandon and Sherry, since it happened just "the other day." Following Sherry's story, Lydia begins what turns out to be an unsuccessful, truncated narrative, again about her frugal habits with her own children. She apparently presupposes general knowledge of this story as well, but instead of receiving signs of recognition from her listeners, she elicits a question about the reference to "rubber wallets" and Ned's statement that he does not remember. Consequently, the continuity of the storytelling sessions dissolves.[1]

Rubber Wallets
1	Frank:	we don't tear out coupons.
2	Brandon:	I think you've got to enjoy the process.
3	Frank:	we don't.
4	Brandon:	*I* don't,
5	Frank:	so,
6	Brandon:	she does.
7		she's religious about it.

8	Sherry:	what, hon. {just tuning in to this conversation}
9	Brandon:	coupons.
10	Lydia:	how I know she's the coupon lady.
11		I've told the cute story about Elizabeth saying
12		when her mom's ready to go out to the store,
13		"got the coupons Mom?"
14		I thought that was the cutest thing I'd ever heard.
15	Brandon:	did you hear the one the other day?
16		tell the one about you in the grocery store Sher.
17	Sherry:	I was- I saw this *new* yoghurt.
18		that had only fifty calories.
19		and you know they have the Yoplait
20		that's a hundred and fifty,
21		and the other is ninety,
22		and Weightwatchers has a ninety calorie one-
23		this one was *fifty* calories
24		and I just looked at it and I went- wow.
25		and Elizabeth said, "what.
26		did you see a really good price Mom?" {laughs}.
27	Lydia:	isn't that em*bar*rassing {laughing}.
28	Sherry:	{laughing} and I just started *laugh*ing and laughing.
29		and I hugged her.
30		and she was saying,
31		"well, was it?
32		was it?"
33		said "no honey," uh
34	Lydia:	maybe you'll have the joy
35		of having *your* children tell *you*
36		what I've had them say to me
37		about my uh rubber wallets?
38		and their scrounging cheap mother.
39		I've been *told* that often.
40		so I hope it happens to you too.
41	Brandon:	rubber wallets?
42	Lydia:	Henry still today kids me about *rub*ber wallets.
43	Ned:	I don't remember.
44	Lydia:	I wouldn't *buy* the boys little leather wallets
45		when they were little.
46		and he calls them *rubber*,

47	Sherry:	{chuckles}.
48	Lydia:	because he thinks his mother's
49		such a terrible cheapskate.
50	Brandon:	Henry?
51	Lydia:	oh yes.
52		he never lets me forget that.
53		rubber wallets {laughing}.
54	Ned:	{laughs}.
55	Lydia:	and I know the exact little wallet he's talking
56		about. I can *see* it as if it were yesterday.

Lydia not only declares Sherry "the coupon lady," but also rehearses a brief humorous story about her coupon use in lines 10–14. Lydia comments on the tale up by calling it "the cutest thing I'd ever heard," thus focussing on the child, but the underlying message of thrifty coupon utilization comes through as well. Initially it comes as something of a surprise that Lydia feels free to tell the coupon story at all, since it depicts an embarrassing event for Sherry, indeed an event which Lydia did not herself witness first hand. In my data, conversationalists usually tell embarrassing personal anecdotes only about themselves, but a mother-in-law cum grandmother can probably be forgiven for reproducing such anecdotes, particularly when they so nicely demonstrate both a thrifty daughter-in-law and a precocious grandchild.

Brandon immediately responds to the tenor of Lydia's anecdote by suggesting that Sherry report a more recent parallel incident. His question "did you hear the one the other day?" in line 15 shows that he assumes Sherry might already have related the event, presumably since it clearly represents one sort of family story appropriate in this group. In particular his phrase "the one" signals his evaluation of the story in question as another of the same type as Lydia told. Brandon even repeats this phrase at line 16 in his explicit request to Sherry to "tell the one about you in the grocery store." And Sherry's story does in fact parallel Lydia's in multiple ways. In both, Sherry's daughter Elizabeth asks her mom a question which reveals a regular pattern of behavior on Sherry's part, and in both the behavior corresponds with frugality, namely saving coupons and looking for good prices. Moreover, Sherry's second story has precisely the desired effect on Lydia, who laughingly characterizes the incident as "embarrassing" at line 27.

Once Sherry has finished, Lydia makes reference in line 37 to "rubber wallets" in a way that makes it clear she expects her hearers to identify the family story she has in mind. Again the story revolves around thrift, namely

Lydia giving "the boys" rubber wallets instead of the more expensive leather ones they desired. The boys in question are Ned, who is present, and the third, older brother Henry, who is not. Lydia even describes the ongoing consequences of the past event alluded to with "Henry still today kids me about *rub*ber wallets" in line 42. Thus Henry would certainly identify the allusion to rubber wallets and know the story, but neither of the two sons present seems to. Brandon asks rather bewildered: "rubber wallets?" at line 41. And Ned says explicitly that he does not remember in line 43, though it seems he recognizes himself to be one of "the boys" mentioned. We see here that even a presumed family story can backfire when one member presupposes shared memories which others fail to exhibit. What Lydia takes to be an event familiar at least from the telling of others turns out to have been an event she shares only with her oldest son, Henry. Where we expect signs of recognition and co-narration, we get instead befuddled questions and confessions like "I don't remember." Consequently, too, the story never really gets told at all: Lydia concentrates on the results of her "scrounging cheap" purchase rather than on the events of the story itself.

This description brings us back to the markers of a shared story we identified above. Everything that goes wrong here reveals a potentially positive function of familiar stories when they work as they should. After two stories about Sherry, Lydia apparently wants to return to her own thrift and to sum up this whole series of narratives. Parallel to the stories about Sherry's embarrassment by her daughter Elizabeth, this story would feature Lydia being embarrassed about something her son said with regard to her frugality. A familiar family story with Lydia at the center would have accomplished all this quite nicely. Furthermore, the story Lydia chose brings the only absent child, Henry, into this family setting. The story fails not because it is no family story at all, but because the current constellation of family members do not recognize it as a tale they were involved in. Here in **Rubber Wallets** the relevant family member is missing, so that collaborative narration never has a chance and the tale remains inchoate.

Conclusions

Consideration of twice-told tales, of narrative events built around stories already familiar to the participants, offers a special perspective on conversational storytelling, because it emphasizes those aspects of narration beyond information, problem solving and so on. In particular, we have seen that familiar stories are tellable under different circumstances than original stories. In free conversation, a new story is tellable if the narrator can defend it as relevant and newsworthy.

The tellability of familiar stories depends not on their newsworthy content, but on the dynamics of the narrative event itself: It is precisely the familiarity of story content which offers the opportunity for significant co-narration. Retold stories are typically prefaced in ways which label them as unoriginal, which, however, incites participants to involvement rather than cuing them to question the relevance or originality of the narratives.

We identified structural markers of retold tales such as prefaces including definite descriptions with the phrase "the story about" and questions with the word "remember." Participants typically check their own recollections of the story with open-ended statements containing indefinites like "or something" and requests for confirmation in the form of explicit questions and statements with question tags; they engage in substantial co-narration, contributing details and dialogue.

We saw that retelling can serve an informing function even when the story is known to the participants, since both the primary teller and the others often gain insight into the events related through the dynamic give-and-take of co-narration. Retelling a particular story or a type of story helps coalesce group perspectives and values. Further, co-narration modulates rapport in multiple ways, first because it allows participants to re-live common experiences, second because it confirms the long-term bond they share, and third because the experience of collaborative narration itself redounds to feelings of belonging.

Elicited retellings

Elicited stories and retellings can be suggestive and valuable for purposes of comparison with naturally occurring narratives. They may exhibit structures not commonly encountered in naturally occurring narratives, as is the case in the parallel tellings below. These passages nicely exemplify digressions and the distinction between local and global evaluation, allowing clearer explication and differentiation of these features than I have found elsewhere in my data or in the relevant literature.

As a methodological tool, I have collected story tellings from my students for several years now. In the first session of a term, I get my students together in groups of no more than ten with the tape recorder running and visible. We all take turns telling stories till we have two or three narratives from each student. I then ask the students to write out the same story at home that evening to be handed in the next class session. Along toward the end of the semester during a class session, but with no advance notice, I ask the same students to repeat one or two of the stories they told during the first session. In the following, I present and compare one such elicited set of three stories, consisting of two oral versions, performed thirteen weeks apart, along with a written version produced the evening after the first oral performance. We have already inspected the first oral version of the story as an example of an elicited narrative in chapter one.

Comparing oral versions of an elicited story

Tammy, as I call the woman who told (and wrote) the stories below, had already performed a narrative from her youth, relating to the animals on her farm and expressing her affection for dogs in particular. The importance of animals for Tammy and her father makes the story of the barn burning all the more poignant.

Barn Burning (first oral version)
"The Night The Barn Burned" (Student's own title)
 1   I guess the only time
 2   I've ever really seen my father cry
 3   was when I was a child,
 4   and it was August
 5   and it was very hot and dry.
 6   and we had the family habit of every night
 7   uh we'd drive into town to the Dairy Queen
 8   and get a special treat.
 9   and this particular night
10   as we were driving home,
11   we could see the glow in the western sky
12   and it shouldn't have been there.
13   and the closer we got to home,
14   the more we realized
15   that there was an awful big fire someplace.
16   Uh, that big fire turned out to be our barn
17   which was a humongous affair.
18   it- it housed the kennels,
19   it housed ah cattle
20   and horses and a couple of sheep
21   and all kinds of things
22   as well as the equipment.
23   and by the time we got there
24   the thing was engulfed in flames.

25 um, the animals were still in it.
26 and there was one act of tremendous kindness,
27 a a stranger from off the highway,
28 who was driving by
29 happened to see the flames.
30 and he had gone in
31 and gotten the horses out
32 and gotten one dog out,
33 but we had to listen to all those other animals die.
34 and I was so interested,
35 the fire was all gone,
36 and nothing but ash and the foundation left
37 to see my dad sit out on the porch and weep.
38 ah, I think that
39 was one of the most heartrending things
40 I'd ever seen.
41 somehow, when your father cries
42 it's ten times worse tragedy
43 than when somebody else does.
44 and, I think that still sits very strongly in my mind.

I propose to analyze this initial telling with the categories developed so far in this study as follows. Recall from chapter two that I distinguish background from both the general frame, valid for the whole story, and the narrow frame, which holds for just a single clause or event. I would like to recognize a further distinction operating in this narrative between local evaluations of persons, actions and events at various points in the story as such, from the generalizing global evaluation at the end, which compares the story and its local evaluations to other stories. Typical for local evaluations are the comment "it shouldn't have been there" with reference to the glow in the sky mentioned in line 12 or the characterization "act of tremendous kindness" in line 26. What I propose to call global evaluations, by contrast, involve generalization and comparison like the two judgments expressed just before the coda: "I think that was one of the most heartrending things I'd ever seen. Somehow, when your father cries it's ten times worse tragedy than when somebody else does." I also label one section of the story digression, a notion I define below. The narrative elements making up the main action are labeled A–F.

Abstract
> I guess the only time
> I've ever really seen my father cry
> was when I was a child,

General frame
> it was August
> and it was very hot and dry.

Background
> and we had the family habit of every night
> uh we'd drive into town to the Dairy Queen
> and get a special treat.

Narrow frame
> and this particular night
> as we were driving home,

Main Action

A   we could see the glow in the western sky

Evaluation
> and it shouldn't have been there.

Main Action

B   and the closer we got to home,

C   the more we realized
> that there was an awful big fire someplace.

D   that big fire turned out to be our barn

Background
> which was a humongous affair.
> It housed the kennels,
> it housed ah cattle
> and horses and a couple of sheep
> and all kinds of things
> as well as the equipment.

Narrow frame
> and by the time we got there

Main Action

E   the thing was engulfed in flames.

Background
> um, the animals were still in it.

Digression
> and there was one act of tremendous kindness,
> a a stranger from off the highway

who was driving by
happened to see the flames
and he had gone in
and gotten the horses out
and gotten one dog out

Main Action
F   but we had to listen to all those other animals die.
Result
and I was so interested
the fire was all gone
and nothing but ash and the foundation left
to see my dad sit out on the porch and weep.
Global evaluation
ah, I think that was one of the most heartrending things
I'd ever seen.
somehow, when your father cries
it's ten times worse tragedy
than when somebody else does.
Coda
and, I think that still sits very strongly in my mind.

First of all, I should motivate my classification of the narrative elements. Though the A-clause contains a phrase with the modal verb *could*, it seems to me equivalent to "we saw," so that I count it as a narrative element. My next two elements appear in the story in a formulaic unit: "the closer we got to home, the more we realized." This might be seen as excluding them from the narrow definition of narrative clauses, though we can easily analyze the formula into the pieces: "we got closer, we realized," which seem impeccable. Again in clause D, the verb form "turned out to be" might fail to qualify, because it is stative, though we can paraphrase the whole construction with another statement like: "we realized the fire was our barn." The same goes for the next clause, which could be rendered as "we realized the thing was engulfed in flames." Clause F again contains a modal construction "had to listen," though I feel the "had to" serves only as an expressive element, leaving the unexceptionable "we listened." In addition, one might view the construction "I was so interested ... to see my dad sit out on the porch and weep" as narratively equivalent to something like: "I watched my dad sit out on the porch and weep," with simplex past-tense narrative clause structure. Given the way it loops back to pick up the father's weeping from the abstract, I prefer to classify it as result.

Turning now to the chunk labeled as digression in the story analysis above, we can see that although it functions within the main story as background information, it has an internal structure of its own. This structure consists of an abstract along with the legitimate past-tense narrative clause A, the complete past-perfect clause B, and the two elliptical past-perfect clauses C and D.

Abstract
    And there was one act of tremendous kindness,
Main action
A   a stranger from off the highway
     who was driving by
     happened to see the flames
B   and he had gone in
C   and gotten the horses out
D   and gotten one dog out

The use of the past perfect tense here signals that the action described in the digression took place outside the time scheme of the main narrative. Tammy herself did not witness these actions, but rather she must have heard about them second hand. The structural distinctions nicely reflect these cognitive differences.

Thirteen weeks separate the initial version of **Barn Burning** from the performance transcribed below. Tammy's introductory question comes in response to a request to re-tell one of the three stories she had produced the first time around. Tammy starts off uncertainly, but she gathers momentum rapidly. She spreads a kind of Abstract over three separate elements, "I suppose that would be the more vivid in my thinking, because that is the only time I can remember seeing my dad cry. Uh, it was when our barn burned," then proceeds into a telling which parallels her initial performance quite closely.

Barn Burning (second oral version)
1   The story about the barn burning?
2   I suppose that would be the more vivid in my thinking,
3   because that is the only time
4   I can remember seeing my dad cry.
5   uh, it was when our barn burned.
6   it was in the late summer,
7   and it was August,
8   and it was very hot,

 9 and very muggy,
10 and it was our custom every night in the summer
11 that our family would get up after supper
12 and go to town to the Dairy Maid
13 and have a special cold treat,
14 and come back home,
15 and this particular night,
16 we were driving back home
17 and you could see this red glow on the horizon,
18 and it shouldn't have been there.
19 and the further we drove out of town,
20 the more we realized
21 that it was an awfully big fire someplace.
22 and when we got within a half a mile or so
23 we could tell it was our barn that was burning.
24 and by the time we got there,
25 the whole thing was engulfed in flames.
26 and the neighbors were there
27 but there was this one stranger,
28 who had spotted the fire
29 from way off on the highway
30 and had come over
31 to see if he could help.
32 and he had managed to get a couple of animals out uh,
33 but the flames were such
34 that he just couldn't continue,
35 his hands were cut from the effort.
36 we had to sit there all night,
37 what seemed like an all night thing,
38 and listen to those animals die.
39 I can still see my dad
40 just sitting on that porch
41 with the tears rolling down his face.
42 I think that's the hardest thing in the world
43 for a kid
44 is to see their very strong father crying.
45 And I suppose that's why
46 it's so vivid in my memory.

Analyzing this telling on the pattern of the one above reveals just how much the two tellings have in common. Again I label the narrative clauses A–F, and I label Digression as a single unit to receive separate treatment later.

Abstract
> I suppose that would be the more vivid in my thinking, because that is the only time
> I can remember seeing my dad cry.
> uh, it was when our barn burned.

General frame
> It was in the late summer,
> and it was August,
> and it was very hot,
> and very muggy,

Background
> and it was our custom every night in the summer
> that our family would get up after supper
> and go to town to the Dairy Maid
> and have a special cold treat,
> and come back home

Narrow frame
> and this particular night,
> we were driving back home

Main action
A   and you could see this red glow on the horizon
Evaluation
> and it shouldn't have been there.

Main action
B   and the further we drove out of town,
C   the more we realized
> that it was an awfully big fire someplace.

Narrow frame
> and when we got within a half a mile or so
Main action
D   we could tell it was our barn that was burning.
Narrow frame
> and by the time we got there,
Main action
E   the whole thing was engulfed in flames.

Background
    and the neighbors were there
Digression
    but there was this one stranger,
    who had spotted the fire
    from way off on the highway
    and had come over
    to see if he could help.
    and he had managed to get a couple of animals out uh,
    but the flames were such
    that he just couldn't continue,
    his hands were cut from the effort.
Main action
F   we had to sit there all night
    what seemed like an all night thing,
    and listen to those animals die.
Result
    I can still see my dad
    just sitting on that porch
    with the tears rolling down his face.
Global evaluation
    I think that's the hardest thing in the world
    for a kid
    is to see their very strong father crying.
Coda
    and I suppose that's why it's so vivid in my memory.

Instead of stressing the really quite substantial correspondences between the two tellings, which the reader can easily work out based on the parallel analyses, I would like to point out a few interesting differences. First, the high degree of overlap in the two stories derives not only from shared vocabulary and constructions, but also from close paraphrase. On the one hand, there is verbatim repetition, for instance: the evaluation "and it shouldn't have been there" and the complex sentence "and by the time we got there, the (whole) thing was engulfed in flames," but for the adjective *whole* in the latter version. On the other hand, we find narratively equivalent phrasing such as clause D: "uh, that big fire turned out to be our barn" in the first version versus "we could tell it was our barn that was burning" in the second. The codas in the two versions provide another case in point: "and, I think that still sits very strongly in my mind" versus "and I suppose that's why it's so vivid in my memory."

Second, there are differences in the details reported. In her first telling, Tammy describes the weather as "very hot and dry," while she terms it "very hot and very muggy" in the second. Although the precise meteorological conditions are irrelevant, they must fit the general frame provided by "August." In the first version, Tammy calls the ice cream vendor a "Dairy Queen," whereas she shifts to the name "Dairy Maid" the second time around. Again, the exact designation of the ice cream franchise is immaterial, so long as some appropriate name appears. Such differences from one version to the next reveal how tellers reconstruct events from their past, as opposed to simply recalling them from memory as a piece. The differences in the details reported in the two digressions are particularly instructive.

Background
    but there was this one stranger,
Main action
    who had spotted the fire
    from way off on the highway
    and had come over
    to see if he could help.
    And he had managed to get a couple of animals out
Evaluation
    but the flames were such
    that he just couldn't continue
Result
    his hands were cut from the effort.

First of all, this digression exhibits no abstract like the heavily evaluated one in the first version: "there was one act of tremendous kindness." Nevertheless, it does begin with a characteristic story opener: "there was this one stranger." The relative clause which follows I label as a narrative clause, inasmuch as it parallels the A-clause in the first version digression; in addition, Chafe maintains that this use of "who" is equivalent to "and he." The other narrative clauses in the two versions focus on different actions, though it is easy to view them as describing the same events. In any case, Tammy herself must have heard these events reported second hand. As pointed out above, the use of the past perfect tense marks the events as taking place outside the time scheme of the main narrative. Interestingly, the detail Tammy adds here, namely that the stranger's "hands were cut from the effort," is the sort of observation she either made herself once she reached the scene of the fire or heard reported by some other witness.

Comparing oral and written versions of the story

Turning now to the version Tammy wrote at home the evening after telling the story in class, we are struck by its brevity. A simple word count yields 275 and 296 for the first and second versions respectively, but only 178 for this written version.

The Night the Barn Burned
(Student's own title; Written version)

```
 1   I saw my father cry only once- — the night our barn burned. It
 2   is still a very vivid memory. It was our family's custom to
 3   drive into town after dinner to go to the Dairy Queen for a
 4   treat. As we drove home, we could see a red glow in the
 5   western sky. The further we drove, the brighter the glow
 6   became until we could see the flames. It was our barn! A
 7   stranger who had seen the fire from the highway had tried to
 8   rescue some of the animals from the barn and had succeeded in
 9   rescuing our two horses, a couple of dogs and sheep. We
10   arrived in time to hear the rest of the animals dying in the
11   blaze. The next morning, when all that was left were ashes, I
12   saw my father sitting on the front porch crying. Somehow
13   seeing my father cry was the most frightening experience I had
14   had. Other people cry, but when a father does, it has a great
15   impact upon a child.
```

The analysis below reveals some important differences between this written version and the two oral versions, besides the fairly obvious similarities.

Abstract
    I saw my father cry only once — the night our barn burned.
Evaluation
    It is still a very vivid memory.
Background
    It was our family's custom to drive into town after dinner to go to the Dairy Queen for a treat.

Narrow frame
> As we drove home,

Main action
A   we could see a red glow in the western sky.
B   The further we drove,
C   the brighter the glow became
D   until we could see the flames. It was our barn!

Digression
> A stranger who had seen the fire from the highway had tried to rescue some of the animals from the barn and had succeeded in rescuing our two horses, a couple of dogs and sheep.

Main action
E   We arrived in time to hear the rest of the animals dying in the blaze.

Narrow frame
> The next morning, when all that was left were ashes,

Main action
F   I saw my father sitting on the front porch crying.

Global evaluation
> Somehow seeing my father cry was the most frightening experience I had had. Other people cry, but when a father does, it has a great impact upon a child.

The comparative brevity of this version results from its reduction of all kinds of elements, not in any specific areas. Thus, Tammy reduces the orientation, writing nothing about the time of year or the hot weather. She skips the local evaluation, "it shouldn't have been there," we found repeated verbatim from the first spoken version to the second. The other nearly verbatim repetition missing constituted a narrow frame and a narrative clause, namely "And by the time we got there, the (whole) thing was engulfed in flames." Tammy also leaves out the coda, which was represented by very similar clauses in the two oral versions. I consider it quite surprising that elements repeated verbatim or as close paraphrases in both oral performances are missing in the written version. Tammy apparently relies on very different narrative strategies in speaking versus writing.

The digression, too, is shorter here than in the two oral versions. It consists of a single compound sentence with a relative clause containing background information about the subject. Thus, it lacks both the evaluative Abstract of the first example and the closing detail about the stranger's cut hands from the second. The analysis below represents my attempt to stress the similarities rather than the differences between this digression and the previous ones.

Background
    A stranger who had seen the fire from the highway
Main action
A   had tried to rescue some of the animals from the barn
B   and had succeeded in rescuing our two horses, a couple of dogs and sheep.

Conclusions

To summarize this section, in the case of Tammy, the written narrative differs from both spoken narratives more than either spoken narrative differs from the other. In particular, the spoken narratives exhibit several instances of verbatim or nearly verbatim repetition and paraphrase of passages missing entirely from the written version. It seems clear that Tammy interpreted the task of writing down her oral narrative as a very different matter than the telling itself. This may simply show that doctoral students in English are inappropriate people to ask for written renderings of their oral stories. But it also points to different cognitive strategies in written and oral production of narrative generally.

    It is not my primary purpose here to investigate differences between written and spoken versions of the same story, but only to glean what insight I can from narrative reproductions of any kind. On this front, I feel the analysis of elicited stories can provide us with a large repository of data exemplifying a wide range of narrative styles. It also provides a testing site for our hypotheses about narrative structures and production strategies. The particular stories analyzed here, for instance, offer clearer examples of variation in digressions and the distinction between local and global evaluation than anything I have been able to find in naturally occurring conversational narratives.

CHAPTER 5

Narrative Contexts

I fear I did not give my meaning clearly.
A little story may help.
Herman Melville, *The Confidence-Man*

Introduction

In the two preceding chapters, we have concentrated on the internal structure of conversational narratives, without much attention to such questions as what occasions storytelling, how and why conversationalists become storytellers, who tells stories to whom, in which contexts, with what sorts of responses and what interpersonal consequences. This focus is necessary for the complete description of conversational storytelling outlined in chapter one: It represents the next step in developing a rhetoric of conversational storytelling, including teller strategies in contexts which occasion stories and the effects they have on the surrounding interaction. We will investigate story prefaces and responses with regard to their structures and their interpersonal significance. We shall also continue to separate the stable, remembered elements of narratives from the contextually variable elements, as we investigate how stories fit into concrete contexts. Tellers adjust their perspectives and the points of their stories to the current topic to render them more relevant to the concrete context. This is particularly true for stories one participant tells in response to a story by another. Tellers must also navigate around listener questions and comments, gauging the interests, attitudes and background knowledge of their audience. Consequently, we will explore both familiar and new stories — even a collaborative fantasy where participants negotiate a fictional story line.

Tellability and telling rights

According to Labov & Fanshel (1977), a would-be narrator must be able to defend a story as relevant and newsworthy to get and hold the floor and escape censure at its conclusion. Sacks (1974, 1992) observes that stories must be "tellable" in order for their tellers to justify the extended turns they require. Conversationalists preface their stories so as to argue their tellability and to signal the sort of response they expect. Telling a story without a currently relevant point constitutes a loss of face for the teller (Polanyi 1979). By contrast, Ochs et al. (1989), Blum-Kulka (1993) and Blum-Kulka & Snow (1993) have presented data from family dinner-table talk showing that children routinely tell familiar stories and relate unnewsworthy tales at the request of their parents as a part of the socialization process. My own recent work (Norrick 1997, 1998a), moreover, demonstrates that conversationalists often tell stories familiar to some or even all their listeners. Familiar stories receive prefaces marking them as known, yet they are told and co-told anyway. Indeed, the tellability of familiar stories rests not on any newsworthy content, but on the dynamics of the narrative event itself. Story content need not be relevant or newsworthy if co-narration holds the promise of high involvement. Thus, the tellability of a story is a matter for negotiation. It hinges on social and contextual factors, rather than following from some single rule.

Further, tellability is tangled up with the notion of telling rights à la Shuman (1986) and Blum-Kulka (1993). After all, a potential teller must assure listeners not only that a story counts as tellable, but also that she or he is the proper one to tell it. Telling rights depend in large part on knowledge of the events related. Labov & Fanshel (1977) distinguish three relevant types of events. *A-events* are those known only to the primary story teller. Last night's dream is accessible only to me. It thereby constitutes an A-event par excellence, and I am the only rightful teller of it. *A–B events* are those known to the teller and one other participant in the conversation. Last summer's vacation spent with a partner present in the room constitutes an A–B event. If I begin to tell a story about our doings during that vacation, my partner shares telling rights and may rightfully bid to join me as a co-teller. Thirdly, *O-events* are those known generally to members of a group or culture. Last year's family reunion presumably constitutes an O-event for many or all members present at this year's reunion. Not only those events in which all present interlocutors took part, but well-known local happenings familiar from the media fall into this group as well. Blum-Kulka & Snow (1993) and Blum-Kulka (1993) further recognize *F-events*, those shared by the members of a family. F-events constitute O-events of a special kind. Since family events such as how Grandmother met Grandfather are passed on to younger family members primarily through storytelling, the notion of the F-event suggests a distinction between ways of acquiring knowledge of an event. Clearly, we may have direct knowledge of events through first-hand experience as well as vicarious knowledge through stories by others. A narrator with first-hand experience of an event will generally have a better claim to storytelling rights regarding the event than another participant who learned about the event only from the accounts of others. Nevertheless, a professor might retell a success story heard from a graduate student for an audience of other professors even in the presence of the student. In the same way, a grandmother might repeat a story from her son about his daughter — that is her grand-daughter — even when the son was present, say for an audience of her own neighbors. In both these contexts, the senior participants seem to have more right to tell a story to their peers in praise of a junior person than do the younger people themselves, especially since self-praise is generally frowned upon. These examples go beyond the usual contexts considered in discussions of storytelling rights, but they raise issues we must ultimately address. Storytelling rights depend on many contextual factors besides the matter of who has knowledge of the events reported.

Who tells which sorts of stories to whom and about what are just a few of the issues dealt with below. What counts as tellable in a given context, and how one conversationalist signals the desire to tell a story, let alone who has the 'right' to tell this particular story or any story at all are difficult matters to generalize about. In the following pages, I will present examples of conversation-al storytelling with an eye to exploring how conversationalists negotiate such matters in what I hope are representative contexts. We can approach these questions both by considering narrative passages as special sorts of turns in conversation with their own characteristic conditions on sequentiality, and by considering such contextual matters as power versus solidarity and the alignment of the participants in the particular interaction.

Sequentiality

Early in the development of the sociological approach which has become generally known as Conversation Analysis, sequentiality was a primary concern. Sacks, Schegloff & Jefferson (1974) sought to describe the system by which conversationalists know whose turn it is to speak. So long as each turn has recognizable sentence structure and makes a single proposition or consists of a simple back-channel like *m-hm* or *wow*, interlocutors have plenty of cues to determine where each successive one will end; but if turns can encompass any number of sentence-like units, as, for instance, most stories do, then would-be tellers must provide special cues when they wish to take a longer turn, and listeners must key their behavior to them. Then, just as single-sentence turns like questions herald particular responses like answers, so, too, certain sorts of stories expect particular hearer responses. And tellers must signal these features of their stories as well. We first investigate the place of story prefaces in this process of coordinating tellers and their audiences, so that stories can be performed and received appropriately. Then in the following section, we will examine the responses these same stories elicited. Finally, we consider response stories, that is stories told as direct rejoinders to foregoing stories and exhibiting parallels with them.

Prefaces

Conversationalists who want to gain the floor to tell a story must signal their intention to the others present. Moreover, they must enlist the interest of these potential auditors to convince them to listen. They generally accomplish this through a story preface which either announces a story appropriate to the current topic of conversation or promises a story which is particularly newsworthy or of special importance otherwise. In the first storytelling passage below, we will investigate a typical example of the latter sort of story preface, namely one which bids to change the current topic of talk with a new story of particular interest. Then we will inspect a narrative with a preface designed to connect it to foregoing talk.

Since conversationalists tend to expect topical talk, stories on new topics routinely exhibit prefaces constructed to sell them as particularly interesting. Highly evaluative and emotionally loaded words and phrases fill this need, as we see in the introduction to the story I call **Hunter** below. After a brief lull in general talk about cooking turkey, Jean prefaces her topic-changing story with the phrase "wasn't that awful," following this with a summary abstract, "the guy that went hunting and killed his son."

Hunter

1	Jean:	wasn't that awful
2		about the guy that went hunting
3		and killed his son,
4	Annie:	oh, hooh.
5	Jean:	and then he killed himself.
6		he didn't- he shot him by mistake.
7		he thought he was a deer,
8		coming, y'know, coming in the woods.
9		shot the kid.

10		when he went to check,
11		because he thought he shot a deer,
12		he found he shot his son.
13		dead.
14	Helen:	oh my God.
15	Jean:	and he turned the gun on himself,
16	Helen:	oh, how tragic.
17	Jean:	and he killed himself.
18		because he probably couldn't,
19		he probably knew he couldn't face his wife,
20		and whatever, y'know.
21	Annie:	first time he took his son, too.
22	Jean:	yeah, that's why today's paper said,
23		"make Orange Legal."
24	Annie:	yeah, you have to.
25	Jean:	"make them wear the orange."
26		that red and black check,
27		you can't see that,
28		when it blends in with everything.
29		and y'know I think it's just like a reaction.
30		if they hear or see something
31		through the corner of their eye,
32		moving,
33		and they just shoot,
34		without waiting to see what it is.
35		that was sad.
36		I don't know how old the kid was.
37	Chorus:	eighteen. {at least three separate voices}

The word *awful* performs multiple tasks: In expressing strong evaluation, it generates hearer interest, and it helps justify the telling of the story; it indicates Jean's attitude about the event related, and it signals to the hearers what kind of story to expect and, hence, what kind of reaction will be appropriate. The whole introductory sentence, "wasn't that awful about the guy that went hunting and killed his son," counts as an abstract, evaluating and summarizing the gist of the story. Since Jean identifies the incident and her attitude toward it, other participants familiar with the story might simply move into a general discussion immediately, rather than allowing Jean to tell it and express her opinion about the matter. Nevertheless, Jean's auditors are clearly willing to attend her telling,

although the story is familiar to most of them, as evidenced by the fact that three
different voices respond in chorus with "eighteen" when Jean wonders about the
son's age at the conclusion of the story.

Consider now an example of a preface designed to relate a story to preceding topical talk. In this excerpt, Lydia picks up Brandon's single-word turn
"coupons," relating it first to Sherry, then introducing a story about coupons,
Sherry, and Sherry's daughter Elizabeth. Thus can a teller select a single topic or
theme in an ongoing conversation and transform it into a story preface. Again a
salient adjective, this time *cute*, indicates an attitude, helps justify the telling,
signals the sort of story to expect and is repeated in the the coda, "I thought that
was the cutest thing I'd ever heard." In this example the preface leads directly
into the storytelling performance itself. The telling really illustrates only a brief
run-through for an audience already familiar with the basic story, as we saw in
chapter four, but it leads to a second story with an interesting preface of its own.

Coupon Lady (from Rubber Wallets)

1	Frank:	we don't tear out coupons.
2	Brandon:	I think you've got to enjoy the process.
3	Frank:	we don't.
4	Brandon:	*I* don't,
5	Frank:	so,
6	Brandon:	she does.
7		she's religious about it.
8	Sherry:	what, hon. {just tuning in to this conversation}
9	Brandon:	coupons.
10	Lydia:	how I know she's the coupon lady.
11		I've told the cute story about Elizabeth saying
12		when her mom's ready to go out to the store,
13		"got the coupons Mom?"
14		I thought that was the cutest thing I'd ever heard.
15	Brandon:	did you hear the one the other day?
16		tell the one about you in the grocery store Sher.
17	Sherry:	I was- I saw this *new* yoghurt.
18		that had only fifty calories.
19		and you know they have the Yoplait
20		that's a hundred and fifty,
21		and the other is ninety,
22		and Weightwatchers has a ninety calorie one-
23		this one was *fifty* calories

24		and I just looked at it and I went- wow.
25		and Elizabeth said, "what.
26		did you see a really good price Mom?" {laughs}.
27	Lydia:	isn't that em*bar*rassing {laughing}.
28	Sherry:	{laughing} and I just started *laugh*ing and laughing.
29		and I hugged her.
30		and she was saying,
31		"well, was it?
32		was it?"
33		said "no honey," uh
34	Lydia:	maybe you'll have the joy
35		of having *your* children tell *you*
36		what I've had them say to me
37		about my uh rubber wallets?

Notice how Brandon picks up the whole complex introduced by Lydia in mentioning another story about Sherry, Elizabeth, shopping and frugality. Brandon's two successive mentions of "the one" suggest that he sees significant topical overlap between the foregoing story and the story requested from Sherry.

Brandon: did you hear the one the other day?
            tell the one about you in the grocery store Sher.
Sherry: I was- I saw this new yoghurt... .

With these two sentences, Brandon both receives Lydia's first story and segues into a second one by Sherry. By requesting a second similar story, Brandon signals his judgment that this sort of story is appropriate in the current context and his expectation that everyone present will appreciate other stories of the same kind. Considerations like this move us into the area of audience response, which is properly the province of the next section.

Responses

The story **Hunter** in the previous section opens with the preface "wasn't that awful," which makes signs of outrage or distaste relevant as responses. Though, as noted above, several auditors show previous familiarity with the story in their rapid response to Jean's uncertainty about the son's age at the end of the story, everyone seems prepared to let Jean tell it nevertheless. Instead of the co-narration which often accompanies the performance of familiar stories, the other participants this time respond with appropriate comments practically from the beginning at intervals on to the end. Right after Jean delivers the abstract, Annie initiates the feedback at line 4 with a high-pitched "oh, hooh," which apparently signals her recognition of the story. Helen produces two appropriate evaluations of the events described: "oh my God" in line 14 following "he found he shot his son. dead," and "oh, how tragic" at line 16 following "and he turned the gun on himself." These comments indicate that at least Helen is hearing the story for the first time. Once Helen has commented and Jean seems to have finished, Annie offers an additional detail in line 21 which confirms her familiarity with the story: "first time he took his son, too."

This storytelling, then, allows Helen to respond in such a fashion that she can agree with Jean. It allows Annie to show that she already knows the story and also shares their opinion. All participants have an opportunity to register recognition and to agree with each other, as well as with the opinion associated with the newspaper which carried the story. The preface and the summary prepare the way for this cohesive response, which solidifies group rapport.

Recall now the second passage in the preceding section. Brandon suggested to Sherry that she tell "the one just the other day," in response to a story about stopping and their daughter Elizabeth. Here the other participants will assume that this story, too, will revolve around Sherry shopping frugally and Elizabeth acting cute. Indeed, in her response to the story of the new yoghurt, Sherry again describes a cute question by Elizabeth which reveals her mother's frugal shopping habits.

This consideration of the relationship between an initial story and a story told in reply to it naturally carries us into the subject matter of the next section on response stories.

Response stories

We turn now to a special sort of audience response to a story, namely the construction of a second story parallel to the first. Sacks comments on second stories at various points in his lectures (1992), and Ryave's (1978) work on achieving a series of stories is significant here as well. They show how carefully response stories are constructed to demonstrate understanding of their predecessors and to comment on them. Sherry's story about the new yoghurt performed in reply to Lydia's lead story about Sherry as the coupon lady provides a good illustration of this kind of response story. Not only does the second story imitate the first in its cast of characters, namely Sherry and her daughter Elizabeth, it mirrors the first with regard to the action portrayed, namely shopping for groceries. There are thematic parallels as well. In both stories, bargain-hunting plays a role: coupon use in the first story and a child assuming her mother was searching for low prices in the second. In both stories, Elizabeth asks a question of her mother which at once shows off her precocious awareness of shopping skills and her mother's frugal habits. Hence the simultaneous viability of comments on cuteness vis-à-vis Elizabeth and embarrassment vis-à-vis Sherry. Brandon recognizes the close parallels between the two stories, and this prompts him to suggest that Sherry tell the second in response to the first. Sherry understands Brandon's request, and she constructs the new story so as to mesh with the initial one in all the ways mentioned. Lydia further receives Sherry's story as an appropriate response, as indicated by the fact that she laughs along with Sherry and comments upon the story immediately after its completion, as we have seen. Finally, Lydia goes on to tell yet another story regarding children and embarrassment about frugality in **Rubber Wallets**, an example we investigated above. We return to the interpersonal meaning of all this congruency between initial and response stories in chapter four.

The following excerpt contains a second example of a response story for comparison. It begins with the final segment of a long account of an automobile accident the previous night by Marsha, then segues into the response story of a near accident by her sister Amy. Again in Amy's storytelling we can observe a close thematic relation to the foregoing story: Both stories involve cars skidding on ice and attempts to control the skids. Patricia has already suggested several potential codas to end Marsha's story, namely the final-sounding evaluation "it happened. it's over" in lines 14–15, the hopeful claim that memory cannot serve to add more details "you never do, because it takes seconds for it to happen" in lines 22–23, and the blatant urging "well the only thing you can both say is thank God you're safe. that's all" in lines 27–29. Yet Amy clearly wants to keep the story on the floor so that she can introduce her own story about skidding as an appropriate response; and she takes this last strategic opportunity to place her question, "did he hit the brakes at all?" in line 30 in order to establish a link to a new story of her own.

Spin Out

1	Ralph:	so how many cars spun out there,
2		[counting you.]
3	Marsha:	[three.]
4		three while we were there. (2.0)
5		and Brad says
6		"that's the only thing I have in my defense
7		that I wasn't driving too fast."

8	Amy:	yeah that's probably the only thing
9		that's keeping him,
10	Marsha:	because he does,
11		he blames himself because-
12	Patricia:	oh, it's so foolish to blame yourself
13		and think about it afterwards.
14		it happened.
15		it's over.
16	Marsha:	and then he said he was coming over.
17		he said "I can't get it out of my mind."
18		he said "I just keep playing it
19		over and over and over in my mind."
20		he said "I can't get it out."
21		and he doesn't remember too much about it.
22	Patricia:	you never do,
23		because it takes *seconds* for it to happen.
24	Marsha:	he- I can-
25		he fought the car for a good ten, fifteen seconds
26		before we lost total control.
27	Patricia:	well the only thing you can both say
28		is thank God you're safe.
29		that's all.
30	Amy:	did he hit the brakes at all?
31	Marsha:	no.
32		he didn't touch the brakes.
33	Amy:	now see what-
34	Patricia:	that's where I make *my* mistake.
35	Amy:	see, I slid a couple times
36		but I *pumped* the brakes.
37		that one time, I was coming down a *hill*.
38		and there was a car stopped at a red-light.
39		and when I hit the brakes the *first* time,
40		I slid.
41		and I was only less than a car-length away from him,
42		so I just started *slam*ming them down.
43		and I stopped within inches of his bumper.
44	Ralph:	that doesn't do any good.
45		slamming them down isn't going to do you any good.
46		you're going to-

47	Amy:	yeah but it was=
48	Ralph:	=it's going to throw you into another skid.
49	Amy:	yeah, but it was pumping them
50		and it got me *stopped*.
51		I mean,
52		as long as I didn't hit him into the intersection.

This response story by Amy, and response stories generally, accomplish more than simply demonstrating understanding of the foregoing story. They lay claim to parallel experiences, and often to shared values and feelings as well. Amy tells her skidding story to document her own experience with the hazards of winter driving. And response stories typically function in this way to ratify the second teller's membership in the same group as the previous teller.

To this point in the chapter, we have seen that tellers preface their stories in distinct ways, so that their auditors will recognize their desire to hold the floor long enough to complete a storytelling performance, but also so that they will know how to respond appropriately. Tellers often provide an abstract of their story with a synopsis of the content alongside an evaluative comment. The abstract allows potential hearers to identify the story, while the evaluative comment signals the teller's attitude toward the events depicted. Together they prepare hearers for the performance to come. Moreover, we have investigated audience responses to the stories so introduced to see how they are tailored to fit the telling. The most meticulously fitted reply to a story, however, consists in the performance of a response story, which depicts the new teller in parallel circumstances, demonstrating parallel behaviors, and felling parallel judgments. Clearly, appropriate responses to conversational storytelling, especially full-blown response stories, align interlocutors and enhance rapport between them — matters to which we now turn in more detail.

The interpersonal dimension

In order to maintain the coordinated give-and-take of spoken interaction, interlocutors send and receive cues about their understanding of the dynamic context, about the purpose and direction of the conversation, and about their interpersonal relationship. While such matters as age, family and social position are given, their significance and practically every other aspect of the relationship between participants in a conversation is open to negotiation from one turn to the next. The choice of topic and the sort of contribution to make, who has the right to tell a story, of what kind, to whom, and just where are questions which conversationalists must resolve for themselves in the real-time arena of everyday talk. The negotiation of these matters allows participants to align themselves in various ways in the course of conversation. In this section we investigate how conversationalists align themselves through cues about the teller's stance in the process of storytelling, and how response stories work to align participants.

When conversationalists are on the same wave-length, picking up each other's cues, meeting each other's expectations and sharing each other's judgments, they are enjoying high involvement in the sense of Tannen (1989), and this redounds to rapport. We have seen in the preceding sections how participants in conversation cue story beginnings and responses, how they signal attitudes toward ways of telling and the events depicted. In the sections to come, we will observe how participants come to enjoy high involvement and to enhance rapport through the co-narration of familiar stories and through participation in the creation of a story-like fantasy. At the same time, co-narration highlights the negotiation of the perspective and the point of a story. In vying to determine the point of view and the significance of a story, co-tellers demonstrate various methods of presentation. As they check their details and alternately propose potential conclusions for a story, they illustrate how tellers cobble together a coherent version for remembering and retelling.

Alignment

In the presentation of a conversational story, the teller often bids to win the audience over to a particular point of view about the events predicted. Tellers typically seek to achieve this end by means of evaluative comments around and within the story itself which convey their stance toward its characters and content. At the same time, hearers may explicitly align themselves with the teller through their responses. In the following section, we will investigate narrative passages which illustrate the use of stance markers to align auditors on the side of the teller, and also observe how auditors signal their agreement with tellers.

Alignment and stance markers. One obvious way tellers sway their audience is through clear identification and motivation of their own stance toward the events described or the point illustrated in their story. As an initial example, let us consider the conversational excerpt below in which Lydia sets up her story at great length in order to insure that her sons, Brandon and Ned, and her daughters-in-law, Sherry and Claire, understand not only the thrust of her story, but also her point of view and her motivation for it. The excerpt concludes with a fairly lengthy comment by daughter-in-law Sherry, which shows how well the connected themes of Lydia's story come across to her auditors. In the strict sense, Lydia's story consists only in the three clauses:

A   I was embarrassed when the girls from town came.
B   and saw my mother's patched washcloths.
C   I tried to hide them really fast.

Her several turns leading up to the story are occupied with establishing her frugality and the background for it in her childhood. Lydia marks her stance toward her little story very thoroughly, addressing a relevant question explicitly to Claire. Her strategy appears to work, since we see both her daughters-in-law vying for opportunities to align themselves with her. At the same time, the men align themselves opposite the women in their sarcastic dismissal of both frugality and embarrassment for it.

Patched Washcloths

1	Frank:	Grandma Imhof,
2		she was the stingy one.
3	Ned:	Claire has *darned* dish towels.
4	Frank:	*her* mother did it.
5		sure.
6	Lydia:	well see I said
7		if you grew up in a house
8		where your mother [patched washcloths].
9	Ned:	[remember darning, Sherry?]
10	Sherry:	I was going-
11		"what are *darned* dish towels."
12	Ned:	well.
13		it's when you don't want to say
14		*damn* dish towels.
15		{General laughter}
16		don't you call that process darning?
17	Lydia:	but my mother just
18		put them under the sewing machine
19		and took two washcloths and made one.
20		and *patched* the middle of a washcloth
21		when it was worn out.
22	Ned:	your mother didn't invent that. {laughing}
23	Lydia:	and I said

24		when you grow up like *that*
25		it's hard to get with this world
26		that throws things away.
27	Claire:	{arriving} here are darned dish towels.
28	Sherry:	{laughing} *darned* dish towels.
29	Lydia:	but were you ever embarrassed, Claire?
30		when you invited *friends* to your house,
31		did you ever have to be embarrassed?
32		I was embarrassed
33		when the girls from town came.
34		{Laughter from Sherry, Brandon and others}
35	Ned:	our mother was embarrassed?
36	Lydia:	and saw *my* mother's patched washcloths.
37		I tried to hide them really fast.
38		{Sherry and Lydia in a two-party conversation
39		from here on}
40	Sherry:	we had a-
41		my mom always had
42		like a dish cloth that had holes in it?
43		and I always still get holes in them
44		before I throw them away.
45		and he's like going,
46		"don't you think we need a new dish towel?"
47		and she always had an old *green* pad
48		that she used to scrub the pans with.
49		and we always called it that ratty green pad.
50		and so in my mind
51		it's *supposed* to be like really awful and ratty.
52		before you throw it away {laughs}.
53		and once a year I buy two new dish cloths
54		whether I need them or not. {laughs}
55	Lydia:	{laughs}

Lydia first introduces the topic of patched washcloths, and hence her frugal upbringing, in line 8, and forges ahead with it in lines 17–21 in spite of interruptions. She then offers a clear motivation for her frugal ways in lines 23–26: "and I said when you grow up like *that* it's hard to get with this world that throws things away." In lines 29–33 Lydia clearly marks her stance, producing no fewer than three tokens of the lexeme "embarrass" with regard to herself and her daughter-in-law Claire. Lydia seems very eager to impress upon her daughter-in-law that she prizes frugality for herself now, though her mother's frugality embarrassed her as a girl.

Moreover, frugality is somehow not sufficient in itself; one has to suffer embarrassment for it vis-à-vis "the girls from town" in line 33. In the current setting, Lydia's husband Frank and her son Ned represent those who scoff at frugality, calling Grandma Imhof "the stingy one" and making light of the darned dish towels Claire keeps for later use. Indeed, everyone present seems to find Lydia's embarrassment about her mother's patched washcloths funny rather than painful. Certainly Claire has received the message about frugality already, and she produces the darned dish towels to prove it. Further, Claire's husband Ned — Lydia's own son — laughs at her for darning dish towels. Sherry chuckles about the notion of darned dish towels as well, though she may still just be savoring Ned's joke about *darned* versus *damn* dish towels in lines 13–14.

Nevertheless, Sherry apparently also feels the need to ratify her group membership by producing a lengthy comment about frugality and kitchen cleaning habits. She seems to want to construct two separate stories, one about her mother's ratty green pad and another about her own kitchen towels, as well as covering the themes Lydia stresses in her story, namely that the frugality she learned from her mother embarrassed her as a young girl, though she values it highly as an adult. However, Sherry's use of generalized past tense clauses and her shifting point of view from her mother to herself and back prevents her comment from taking proper narrative shape. Notice first the cut-off and restart in lines 40–42 where Sherry says, "we had a- my mom always had like a dish cloth that had holes in it?" which changes the focus from Sherry to her mother. Like Lydia, Sherry also learned frugal habits with kitchen cloths from her mother. Also like Lydia, she suffers embarrassment for it. Moreover, Sherry maintains her frugal kitchen cleaning habits even today. Finally, Sherry makes light of her own behavior, using a somewhat formulaic frame for her conclusion in lines 53–54, "once a year … whether I need them or not," which elicits laughter from Lydia, thereby completing the parallelism between their two contributions, since Lydia also evoked audience laughter with the initial tale of the patched washcloths.

As a second example for purposes of comparison, let us consider the conversational excerpt below in which the description of background and attitude looms larger than the story itself. This sort of narrative was described as a 'diffuse story' by Polanyi (1985: 66 ff.). The initial storytelling evokes a response story from the hearer, which is included here, but does not come in for detailed investigation till later.

Brianne and Addie are close friends, meeting in their home town for the first time in several months after both spending the fall term at separate universities. We examined a story by Brianne about the nude model sighted downtown in chapter three, but here she is telling Addie about a romantic relationship which never quite materialized. Brianne terminated a long-standing relationship at the end of the summer; she returned to college unattached, yet wary of entering into a new relationship. Brianne is clearly at pains to explain that she could be "going out with" a guy, but that all sorts of considerations led her to avoid becoming involved. Indeed, explanation in the form of background information and evaluation occupies most of the talk in the first fifty lines of the excerpt, while the story itself is fairly brief. The bare skeleton of the story which Brianne relates in the first third of this excerpt can be represented as follows.

A   and for a while there was like this big, I don't know.
B   for a while I kind of was starting to think that something was gonna happen,
C   and then, "oh my god, I don't want to deal with that either," (I didn't want to get into it.)
D   so I kind of like told myself to shut up. and don't even think about it.

Brianne seems at once both reticent and eager to talk about her present situation, though Addie provides her with an ideal listener. Moreover, because Brianne has apparently not resolved this situation for herself, no clear stance emerges from her explanations, so that Addie must tread carefully in her response. Note especially the frequent back-channels and supportive comments Addie supplies, while letting Brianne take all the time she needs to tell her story. The density of the interaction is characteristic for talk between close friends about troubles, and appropriate to this dialogue on unsuccessful personal relationships.

Mutual Friend

1	Brianne:	and for a while there was like this big,
2		I don't know.
3		it's well, he,
4		he's like our mutual friend Peter, okay?
5	Addie:	aha, m-hm.
6	Brianne:	and then, that was why.
7		he's our mutual friend of all our friends, y'know?
8		and I don't know.
9		for a while, um,
10		I kind of was starting to, y'know?

11	Addie:	m-hm.
12	Brianne:	maybe think that something was gonna happen
13		or that y'know I kind of liked him.
14		because y'know we're ju-,
15		we're always together,
16		always with them and stuff like that,
17		and he's a nice guy {giggling}.
18	Addie:	m-hm, m-hm.
19	Brianne:	{laughing} and y'know.
20		but, then I- I just had to stop myself,
21		because I- I just didn't even want to deal with it.
22		because things- it was so stupid in a way.
23		because, I don't know, if it was more like just
24		because, well he was there,
25		or if I really would have picked him out, necessarily.
26	Addie:	m-hm.
27	Brianne:	but um,
28		because there had been something going on,
29		nothing like they weren't going out or anything.
30		but I mean, y'know, some sparks between him and
31		Christina
32	Addie:	ooh, yeah.
33	Brianne:	like a few months ago.
34		and then, I'm like
35		"I don't want to deal with that either" y'know
36		and Christina has a boyfriend of course, y'know.
37	Addie:	oh yeah.
38	Brianne:	but um,
39		she had kind of a crush on Peter.
40		I, I didn't want to get into it.
41		so I kind of like told myself to shut up.
42		and like don't even think about it.
43		don't even because y'know,
44	Addie:	oh yeah.
45	Brianne:	I just, I don't think it would work anyway,
46		in that situation.
47	Addie:	that's fairly prob- Yeah.
48	Brianne:	so it didn't work out either.
49	Addie:	m-hm.

50	Brianne:	like y'know, we still hang out sometimes.
51	Addie:	that's good.
52	Brianne:	yeah.
53		see this is one of those things,
54		you just get-
55		it comes over you and then it {giggles} goes back
56		and you forget that it ever [happened at all. {laughs}]
57	Addie:	[oh, {laughing} I know.]
58		I know.
59		it happened.
60	Brianne:	{giggles}
61	Addie:	yeah, it happened to *me*,
62		this year with, um, a different guy.
63		um, my friend Tom has a, and I have-
64		well, Tom's friend Chris,
65	Brianne:	m-hm.
66	Addie:	is a pretty cool guy
67		and I sort of fell for him ear- earlier.
68	Brianne:	m-hm. {laughs}
69	Addie:	and uh y'know we had a little something started.
70		and then after that
71	Brianne:	m-hm. {giggling} I know.
72	Addie:	{giggles}
73	Brianne:	{giggles} it's so funny.
74	Addie:	and then after that he jus-
75		it was like he didn't want to
76		and I was like y'know,
77		I, I still wanted to go out with him.
78		but he didn-
79		he didn't seem to show any indication that he wanted
80		to, so then I got,
81		and I just gave up. [{giggles}]
82	Brianne:	[yeah,] m-hm right.
83	Addie:	I don't know if it's over yet.
84	Brianne:	{laughs}
85	Addie:	but I, I guess it is.
86		I mean, I, I could probably be persuaded.
87	Brianne:	right. [{laughs}]
88	Addie:	[y'know,] if he wanted to go out with me

89		I would figure, y'know,
90		I would be happy.
91		I would probably go out with him,
92		but if he doesn't
93		then I don't think that's the way I want to go.
94	Brianne:	sure, m-hm.
95	Addie:	because y'know I mean I can't force it.
96	Brianne:	um, the thing that makes me mad is that,
97		y'know, I mean, I-,
98		if we went out it wouldn't be like a serious
99	Addie:	uh-huh.
100	Brianne:	I would be,
101		I think, we would be like really good friends.
102	Brianne:	uh-huh.
103	Addie:	but, you know, not like we're gonna get engaged
104		or anything like that, [y'know.]
105	Brianne:	[m-hm] m-hm.
106	Addie:	just forcing each other, y'know.
107	Brianne:	uh-huh.
108	Addie:	but, um,
109	Brianne:	that's okay.
110	Addie:	it kind of makes me mad.
111		{giggling} y'know, because he's all of our friends
112		[and things.]
113	Brianne:	[oh yeah.]
114	Addie:	because I know that if he wasn't like,
115		if he was just my friend, say,
116		I know I would go out-
117		{laughing} be going out with him.
118	Brianne:	yeah, that would be kind of bad.
119		aggravating.
120	Addie:	but because it's nothing that's- that's- so intense,
121		or deep.
122	Brianne:	uh-huh.
123	Addie:	it's not worth m- messing with.
124		do you know what I mean?
125	Brianne:	yeah, kind of.
126	Addie:	if it was just me,
127		there would be nothing to, worry about messing up.

128   because we would go out or whatever.
129   but since, like,
130   he's friends with my friends,
131   and my friends are his friends, and all this,
132 Brianne: yeah, if everything got, eh, complicated then.
133   I know there is a trouble there,
134   because girls and boys can get close-
135   can be friends.
136   and then if there's something more in the middle of it,
137   then are you still friends with all those same people
138   [if it doesn't work out?]
139 Addie: [yeah, exactly.]
140   exactly.
141 Brianne: or if it hurts somebody else?
142 Addie: yeah, I know.
143 Brianne: and, y'know, he's close to Christina,
144   you know what I mean.
145 Addie: yeah, you live with her.
146 Brianne: I live with her.
147 Addie: {laughing} I know.
148 Brianne: if we have problems.
149   what if he, he, y'know,
150   they're good friends,
151   what if he wants to talk to her about it?
152   y'know?
153 Addie: right.
154   you don't want to hear about that, right?
155 Brianne: yeah.
156 Addie: yeah.

It takes some time for Brianne to get into her story at all. The situation appears so complicated that she cannot decide where to begin. When she does seem ready to begin in line 6, her statements are conditional and heavily hedged: "and I don't know. for a while, um, I kind of was starting to, y'know? maybe think that something was gonna happen or that y'know I kind of liked him." Then she breaks off giggling at line 17, finding it hard to get started again. All the false starts and back-tracking give the impression that Brianne has not yet made up her own mind about how to evaluate the circumstances she describes. Furthermore, Brianne's feelings for Peter are ambivalent. As she says in lines 23–25:

"because, I don't know, if it was more like just because, well he was there, or if I really would have picked him out." She apparently desires to maintain her emotional distance from the topic of the potential new relationship, just as she avoided the interpersonal committment itself.

Addie reacts to this ambivalence and restraint on Brianne's part with steady, frequent back-channels, showing constant interest without creating the appearance of trying to interfere. She can align herself with Brianne only by being a patient listener, since Brianne presents no clear stance. Then Addie responds in the best way possible with her own story of an inchoate affair once Brianne has finished: When the first story has clearly arrived at an unmistakable stopping place with the proverbial sounding construction, "it comes over you and then it goes back and you forget that it ever happened at all" in lines 55–56, Addie segues naturally into a response story to demonstrate understanding and parallel experience. And this consideration of a response story itself naturally segues into the next section.

Alignment and response stories. Conversationalists routinely align themselves through matching their response stories with foregoing ones. These response stories may go far beyond simple thematic or structural parallels to depict the successive tellers in similar situations, performing similar actions, registering similar feelings and passing similar judgments. In the paired stories from the passage **Mutual Friend** in the previous section, we see a beautifully coordinated transition from an initial story to a response story.

As described above, Brianne concludes her story of a relationship which could not thrive because she and Peter were best friends of best friends with the epigrammatic: "It comes over you and then it goes back and you forget that it ever happened at all" (lines 55–56). Then her auditor Addie picks up the phrase "it happened," using it first as a comment in ratification of Brianne's assessment: "oh, I know. I know. it happened" in lines 57–59. Once Brianne has giggled in reply, Addie subtly shifts the sense of *happen* from this fatalistic resignation to a report about her own similarly unfulfilled romantic relationship with: "yeah, it happened to *me*, this year with, um, a different guy" in lines 61–62.

Further, in Addie's case, too, the affair failed to blossom because of complex involvements with friends of friends. Addie also introduces her story with apparent confusion about where to start and what point of view to adopt in lines 63–67: "um, my friend Tom has a, and I have- well, Tom's friend Chris, is a pretty cool guy and I sort of fell for him ear- earlier." Notice here also the hedges *pretty* and *sort of* to parallel those in Brianne's story, as well as *a little something* in line 69: "and uh, y'know, we had a little something started." Also

like Brianne, Addie repeatedly stresses that she would presumably be going out
with Chris if it were not for all their mutual friends, for instance in lines 111,
130–131, 136–137 and further on. In a final parallel with Brianne's initial story,
Addie reports that she gave up on her relationship in line 81, though she remarks
in her very next turn: "I don't know if it's over yet" (line 83), and then "but I,
I guess it is. I mean, I, I could probably be persuaded." She thus aligns herself
with Brianne as disappointed that mutual friendships stood in the way of
romantic involvement, but at the same time unsure about just where things stand.
We should note that Brianne begins receiving Addie's response story in the same
almost giddy frame of mind with which she closed her own: Her first two
responses are a giggling "m-hm. I know" and "it's so funny" in lines 71–73. The
response story then appropriately flows back into talk about the topic of friends
and romantic relationships. The whole exchange illustrates not just two closely
connected stories, but highly involved talk conducive to enhanced rapport.

Rapport

Conversationalists signal and enhance rapport in various ways. Enjoying familiar
stories through communal retelling provides multiple opportunities for building
rapport, as does the collaborative construction of narrative-like fantasies. In
retelling familiar stories, conversational partners demonstrate shared knowledge,
usually of joint experience, which ratifies their membership in the same group,
while the co-invention of plots and characters in a fantasy presupposes parallel
thought patterns. In both cases, however, participants work in unison to create a
coherent text, agreeing on point of view and details of description. This process
is highlighted in a collaborative fantasy, where participants negotiate an original
fictitious story line. If the participants also coordinate their contributions at the
micro-level of conversational organization, completing descriptions and sentences
for one another, then this further modulates rapport. We will examine examples
of both types in the paragraphs to come.

Co-narration of a familiar story. As we saw in chapter four, conversationalists
retell familiar stories for various reasons. Though past research such as Labov
(1972), Labov & Fanshel (1977), Sacks (1974, 1992) and Polanyi (1979, 1981)
had suggested that only new stories can gain the attention of hearers, our
examples demonstrated that familiar stories not only interest auditors, but can
also entice them to participate and even to become full-fledged co-narrators. The
passage below contains another example of co-narration, this time by four family
members who were all involved to some degree in the events described. More-

over, the initial phrase, "the story about you and the little chipmunk," suggests that the group members recognize the story as a piece of their family lore. Family lore often includes a set of stories which are recalled and repeated spontaneously during regular interaction between members. Although such stories may be retold primarily for amusement, they function simultaneously to inform or remind members, most especially children, of a common past and shared values, so that they enhance feelings of a family's identity as a group.

The family members are Patricia and Ralph, the parents of two college-age daughters Amy and Marsha, who are home for the long Thanksgiving break. These are the same interlocutors involved in telling the paired stories entitled **Spin Out** about winter driving in chapter four. The family has remained sitting at the kitchen table after supper. Patricia has been describing a party she attended where she related this same story for the amusement of outsiders, but here the story is told as one familiar to those present.

Chipmunk

1	Patricia:	and I told the story
2		about you and the little chipmunk
3		out in the garage.
4	Marsha:	oh. {laughing}
5	Amy:	I kept- I kept-
6		I was just thinking about that the other day.
7		that thing scared the *heck* out of me.
8	Patricia:	with all with all the
9	Amy:	it was twice.
10	Marsha:	{laughs}
11	Amy:	it was twice.
12		and the first time,
13		"there's a rat in there,
14		there's a big mouse in there.
15		I saw it."
16	Marsha:	{laughs}
17	Amy:	"no, there's nothing in there."
18		"yes, I *saw* it."
19	Marsha:	I wouldn't believe her.
20	Patricia:	well I went out.
21		remember,
22		and set the bag-
23		it was a bag of *cans*.

24		that was when we were looking for the golf ball,
25		cause you hit the ball in the can.
26	Amy:	yeah and then you found its little cubby holes
27		in a box or something.
28	Patricia:	well, what- what-
29	Marsha:	you found all the *seeds*, didn't you?
30	Patricia:	all the seeds.
31	Ralph:	all the seeds in a plastic bag.
32	Patricia:	right by the wood out there.
33		and when we moved the wood to clean it
34		there was the whole thing.
35		it must have sat against the wood
36		and then ate all the {laughing} [sunflowers.]
37	Ralph:	[all the] sunflower seeds.
38		all the shells were in [the bag.]
39	Patricia:	[there were] shells everywhere.
40	Amy:	yeah and you guys wouldn't believe me.
41	Marsha:	well I guess there *was* [something there.]
42	Patricia:	[well I didn't] the first time
43		but the second time I did.
44	Amy:	scared me both times. {laughing}
45	Marsha:	{laughs}
46	Amy:	and of course it happened to *me*.
47		you know, nobody *else*.
48	Patricia:	little sucker was living in the garage
49	Ralph:	living it *up*.
50		[and living high on the hog.]
51	Patricia:	[had it *made*.]
52		he was in out of the *cold*
53		and he had something to *eat*.
54		and, and by the way,
55		we have to get a bird feeder.
56		I'll have to talk to ma
57		and go to that Audubon place.

All the features I have found typical of collaboratively constructed familiar stories are present here. First, there are explicit markers that the story is already known to at least some of those present. Thus Patricia prefaces the passage with a definite noun phrase, "the story about you and the little chipmunk," which presupposes identifiable reference for members of the immediate family; and she says *remember* as she gets into the actual story at line 21. Participants also check on the accuracy and completeness of their own recollections with open-ended statements like Amy's "and then you found its little cubby holes in a box *or something*" in lines 26–27 or with explicit questions, often in the form of a statement plus a tag as in Marsha's "you found all the *seeds*, didn't you?" at line 29. Conversely, participants confirm each other's statements, as does Amy in beginning two contributions with "yeah and" in line 26 and line 40.

Second, there is substantial co-telling. Amy immediately ratifies the familiar character of the story by claiming that she had been thinking of it just the other day. At the same time, she makes a bid to become co-teller of the story. After all Patricia has identified Amy as the human protagonist, and Amy wastes no time in trying to place her emotional response at the center of interest in the story. Participants demonstrate knowledge of the story and hence group membership, particularly through addition of details. Ralph speaks little overall, but when he does, he contributes salient details, first that the seeds were "in a plastic bag" at line 31 and then that "all the shells were in the bag" in line 38.

Third, there is often disagreement about details and especially about the point of the story. As a consequence of differential memories and points of view, participants correct each other's accounts and vie for the right to formulate the story's point. This is typical of what Polanyi (1985:92 ff.) describes as a 'negotiated story'. When Amy says, "yeah and you guys wouldn't believe me" at line 40, Patricia objects, "well I didn't the first time but the second time I did." Amy seeks to construct the story around her fright and her indignation at failing to convince the others of her credibility, but Patricia and Ralph conspire to focus the story on the chipmunk's successful survival strategy: Their joint assessments to this effect stand unchallenged as the final evaluation of the story following Amy's last gasp with "and of course it happened to *me*. y'know, nobody *else*" in lines 46–47. Again Ralph's contribution is short on words but long on meaning because he casts it in idiomatic and proverbial language: "living it up. living high on the hog" in lines 49–50. And Patricia makes a final determination that the story was about animals in winter by moving to the related topic of feeding birds. Agreement on the final point of a story enhances rapport, and serves to fix the story in the minds of participants for future tellings.

Familiar stories are tellable under different circumstances than original stories. Retold stories are typically prefaced in ways which label them as unoriginal, which, however, incites participants to involvement rather than cuing them to question the relevance or originality of the stories. Structural markers of retold tales include prefaces with uniquely identifiable referents like "the story about" and questions with the word "remember." Participants typically check their own recollections of the story with open-ended statements containing indefinites like "or something" and requests for confirmation in the form of explicit questions and statements with question tags; they engage in substantial co-narration, contributing details and dialogue. Despite disagreements about facts and competition in determining the point of view, participants frequently confirm each other's statements and negotiate agreement on the final point of the story. This communal storytelling thus clarifies details and stabilizes the story for the participants. The competition to determine point of view and the final significance of the story highlights processes involved in verbalization.

Collaborative fantasy. The collaborative invention of a narrative-like fantasy accentuates the negotiation of story line and perspective all the more, because the participants are not bound by jointly remembered events. Proposed details and events are subject only to the whim of the co-tellers. Consequently, collaborative creation of a fantasy is very conducive to rapport. An example provides the best explanation of what I intend to demonstrate here. Jacob and Erik are brothers who share an apartment with a third student Mark, who has left for the afternoon. The two brothers are engaged in a discussion of cloning when the exchange below takes place.

Clone Mark

1	Erik:	perhaps I'll do some rudimentary experiments,
2		on my own.
3	Jacob:	yeah, Mark, we could probably, y'know,
4		uh get one of Mark's hairbrushes
5		and get started. {chuckles}
6	Erik:	isn't that uh,
7		somehow you have to increase the metabolism rate
8		to have it grow?
9		what would, what would they-
10		that would automatically uh multiply the cell growth
11		to the age of nineteen,
12	Jacob:	and then, we could then,
13		we could then try it, though.
14		so it would be better than Mark, y'know,
15		his personality- we could kill Mark off,
16		and then we'd have a better roommate to live with.
17		and nobody'd ever know the difference.

18	Erik:	okay, yeah, let's see,
19		what do we want-
20		what do we want to do to the new Mark.
21		okay.
22		we don't want to make one
23		that's so quite so arrogant.
24	Jacob:	okay.
25		not quite so arrogant.
26		more subservient.
27	Erik:	yeah, ahuh yeah.
28		he should have to give us more things.
29	Jacob:	yeah, he's got a lot more things
30		jammed in his room
31		than I've got in here.
32	Erik:	he should um, perhaps,
33		sleep out in the hallway more often.
34	Jacob:	y'know, or, like you could probably blast out-
35		look, you could um,
36		you could divide this room right in half,
37		and blast out Mark's wall,
38		and then we could just have two rooms,
39		two big rooms.
40		and Mark could sleep in the hallway closet
41		or something.

Though collaborative fantasies like this are fairly common in my conversational data, they have received no attention in the literature on conversation or narrative. Of course, they fail to meet the regular conditions for narrative in several important ways. Most obviously, they delineate fictional events placed into an alternate world or into the future, rather than describing events in the past. They share this fictional textual mode with much narrative literature. Still, unlike literary fiction which pretends to describe the so-called real world, or at least some real world, usually in the pure past tense, conversational fantasy repeatedly marks the irreality of the constructed world with the modal verbs *could* and *would*. Further, since the collaborators generally project their alternative reality into the future, the events described need not follow each other in chronological order. Instead, participants tend to develop their fabrication, as new ideas come to them, and to play off suggestions from the other participants in no strict order. If anything, Erik and Jacob are more careful about their causal relationships here than conversationalists generally tend to be, since they have been thinking in terms of scientific experimentation and consequences: hence the frequency of sequences built around the formula "we could ... , then we could ..." One attempt to impose a logical order on **Clone Mark** might yield the following pseudo-narrative, which differs significantly from the order of the relevant clauses in the passage above.

A   We take hair from Mark's brush.
B   We produce a clone of Mark with different characteristics.
C   We increase the metabolism to make the cloned Mark nineteen years old.
D   We kill off the old Mark.
E   We divide the living-room in half.
F   We blast out Mark's wall.
G   We make the cloned Mark sleep in the hallway closet.

Clearly, the participants in a collaborative fantasy intend to amuse themselves and share high-involvement talk, rather than to engage in a logical exercise. Cleverness and creativity take precedence over consistency and credibility. With no specific remembered events to verbalize, co-tellers are free to develop any sort of plot they can agree on. Still, the sequence of the clauses Erik and Jacob articulate apparently represents a logical temporal sequence for the actions they describe: By imposing sequentiality, the co-tellers free their collective imagination to create scenarios.

Conclusions

The foregoing description of storytelling contexts complements the analysis of the internal structure of narratives in the preceding chapters as a major element in a complete account of conversational storytelling. We have seen how tellers preface their stories in distinctive ways in order to gain the floor for a storytelling performance, but also to signal what sort of response is expected. Tellers may also provide an abstract for a story which summarizes and evaluates its content. Together they prepare hearers for the performance to come. We found that prefaces need not establish tellability qua originality or even topical relevance, if they only announce a story of current interest like **Hunter** or a familiar story offering the possibility of co-narration like **Chipmunk**. A preface may also pick up a particular *motif* latent in topical conversation, as in **Coupon Lady**. Indeed, we observed how conversationalists manipulate topical talk and even stories in progress to segue into their response stories, for example in **Spin Out** and **Mutual Friend**. Audience responses to the stories so introduced revealed how they were tailored to fit the context. Our examination of storytelling in real conversational contexts revealed different conditions on tellability than postulated in much of the earlier research based on elicited stories.

We further investigated how conversationalists align themselves through cues about the teller's stance in the process of storytelling, and how response stories work to align participants. A typical response story depicts the new teller in similar circumstances, demonstrating similar behaviors, and arriving at similar conclusions. Such response stories can be painstakingly fitted to the foregoing story; conversely, because response stories demonstrate a particular understanding of their predecessors, they determine what these predecessors are taken to mean.

We have also observed how participants enjoy high involvement and enhance rapport through the co-narration of familiar stories and through collaborative participation in the creation of a story-like fantasy. Co-narration throws into relief the negotiated character of conversational storytelling. As co-tellers interact to determine the details, the perspective, the conclusion and the point of a story, they illustrate how narration balances memory and context to generate a coherent, understandable performance. Narrative-like collaborative fantasies bring out the negotiation of story line and perspective even more clearly, since the participants need not rely on remembered events, yet even here temporal sequencing appears.

CHAPTER 6

Varieties of Conversational Narrative

There are several kinds of stories, but only one difficult kind — the humorous.
Mark Twain, *How to tell a story*

Introduction

This chapter expands the catalogue of conversational storytelling types and
addresses the problem of the transition from non-narrative talk to narration
proper. It describes the macro-structures and conventions conversationalists key
on in responding to the various types of stories. We will survey personal stories
of past experience, dream tellings, third-person stories, generalized recurrent
experiences, collaborative retelling and collaborative fantasy as well as diffuse
stories which flow and ebb during topical conversation. In exemplifying these
types of stories, I will be concerned to present some more problematic and
marginal examples. My inclusion of these materials represents an attempt to
counterbalance the tendency to concentrate on well-organized, single-teller and
interview-style stories in work by Labov & Waletzky (1967), Hymes (1985),
Bauman (1986), Linde (1993) and others. Research on oral storytelling began
with elicited narratives, often from practiced storytellers. It borrowed terminology
and preconceived ideas about the form of narrative from literary theory. The
standard definition of narrative in terms of temporally ordered clauses excluded
several narrative-like genres from research programs. These influences are still
evident in our thinking on conversational storytelling. Examination of this wider
range of storytelling types reveals different kinds of teller strategies, interpersonal functions and listener input. Polyphonic and diffuse stories test listeners'
abilities to reconstruct a coherent narrative and to respond appropriately. Hence,
these storytelling types provide a testing ground for the analytical methods
developed so far.

Of course, some scholars have considered emergent and polyphonic
narratives. Sacks and other practitioners of Conversation Analysis have always
oriented themselves entirely to spontaneous narratives, documenting the influence

of active listeners and co-tellers (Sacks 1992; C. Goodwin 1986; Schegloff 1992 and others). Tannen (1978) examined an unsuccessful narrative, which failed to match listener expectations. Falk (1980) treated two-party narration. Michaels & Cook-Gumperz (1979), Boggs (1985), Ochs, Taylor, Rudolph & Smith (1992), Blum-Kulka (1993) have described the interaction of children with adults to create coherent narratives. Polanyi (1985) discusses both negotiated and diffuse stories as special types, but really in spontaneous conversation all stories are diffuse and negotiated to a greater or lesser degree. Chafe (1997) investigates marginally narrative passages of conversation. The influence of these researchers will be evident in the following discussion.

Personal narratives

Conversationalists tell stories for all kinds of reasons. The examples below illustrate four typical kinds of personal narratives. In the first section, we inspect narratives which enhance the reputation of the teller: A college student tells a story about putting down an older person, and a man tells a story of an encounter with a film personality. In the second section, we turn to stories about events which embarrassed the teller. As told by adults about their childhood, such stories also tend to enhance personal image through a special sort of covert prestige, but also through their humor. In the third section, we investigate two stories told to relate troubles and hence to elicit understanding and commiseration. Finally, we also consider dream tellings which take narrative form in conversation.

Self-aggrandizement

While most storytellers in my corpus avoid manifestly boastful stories about their own victorious exploits, the students — most especially the male students — often tell self-aggrandizing tales in which they get the better of their fellows or older people. This jibes with what Johnstone (1993) has written about gender and storytelling in conversation. The first passage cited below illustrates the explicit self-aggrandizing type well. Storytellers may, however, boast more covertly, for instance through name dropping and other apparently casual references to prestigious places and activities. The second passage below shows how one speaker presents himself in a rather flattering situation in a story told as an appropriate contribution to the ongoing topic of conversation.

In the first example, Chad and Wayne are sitting and talking to George,

who has a recorder set up in his apartment. They have been swapping stories of
their successes, when Chad introduces a narrative in which he puts down an
older person. The story presents Chad in a particularly positive light, since he
serves as a referee for high school basketball games on a voluntary basis, while
the coaches often have baser motives. Chad may be especially concerned about
self-presentation in his narrative, because he is aware of addressing a potential
audience beyond those present, as shown by his asking George whether he can
freely cite "the exact words" the coach used.

Basketball Referee

1	Chad:	some parents take it offensive though.
2		and- and- ah th- like this past weekend
3		this this *one* coach.
4		I called a flagrant foul.
5		on his fifth and sixth grade team.
6		three weekends ago.
7	Wayne:	flagrant P F. {i.e. personal foul}.
8	Chad:	flagrant was-
9		okay, this was the situation.
10		there is a kid, dribbling down the court
11		and he has a wide-open lay-up.
12		his- his- the kid on his team,
13		was right behind him, okay?
14	Wayne:	uh-huh.
15	Chad:	and my instinct when I'm an official
16		I always say, "let 'em go"
17		y'know, lay off them
18		so that they don't do something stupid
19		y'know hit them in the back and hurt them.
20		I always say just let ['em go.]
21	Wayne:	[you can talk] to them during the game?
22	Chad:	I just pull the whistle on them.
23		I just yell at them.
24		the official can say anything.
25		no one hears it except- you know, the players.
26		I'm like let 'em go, let 'em go.
27		well this *kid* trips over his own two feet.
28	Wayne:	{laughs}
29	Chad:	and as he's falling,

30		he grabs onto the back of the player
31		holding uh carrying the ball.
32		and he pulls down his jersey
33		and pulls him down.
34		and I was like "whoa, all right,"
35		I had a decision to make.
36		obviously it was-
37		it wasn't with the intent to hurt him,
38		because he tripped.
39		but then again he *did* obstruct him
40		from getting a wide-open lay-up.
41		so I ju- I was like, "well, you know,"
42		I called the flagrant,
43		which is the arms crossed.
44		if you want to call a flagrant with aggression,
45		with the intent to hurt,
46		you have the arms crossed,
47		then you've got to *swing* them down.
48		like really, really hard.
49	Wayne:	{sniffs}
50	Chad:	then you know it's like
51		that was a really serious foul.
52		and that's a technical
53		and you can get kicked out of the game
54		for doing something like that.
55	Wayne:	m-hm.
56	Chad:	I just called the simple flagrant.
57		the coach went *nuts*,
58		he went nuts.
59		so this past weekend I'm officiating this game,
60	Wayne:	uh-huh.
61	Chad:	not- not- not even close to the same situation,
62		I officiate the entire game,
63		everything went so smoothly.
64		he didn't say two words to me
65		other than, you know,
66		he warned me about
67		one of his players almost getting hurt,
68		I'm like, "whatever."

69		you know you just- you blow it off.
70		you completely look through him,
71		you say thank you sir, you know,
72		I'll look into that,
73		and you walk away.
74		well at the end of the game,
75		he came up to me,
76		and his exact words were
77		I don't know if I should *bleep* this out or anything,
78	George:	nuh.
79	Chad:	the exact words were,
80		he came- he came up to me and said,
81		"you mother fucker.
82		you're holding a grudge from three weeks ago."
83		and I'm just sitting y'know
84		and I'm like, "oh my God."
85		right?
86		and my first reaction was to say to him y'know
87		something very sarcastic about his mother?
88		considering he brought that into effect?
89	George:	m-hm.
90	Wayne:	{laughs}
91	Chad:	but I thought,
92		this guy paid money to be in this tournament.
93		and I said, "sir, I'm in college,
94		I can't re*mem*ber three weeks ago,"
95		and I walked away.
96	Wayne:	{laughs}
97	Wayne and George:	{laugh for 2 seconds}
98	Chad:	that's what I said to him,
99		[and I walked away.]
100	Wayne:	[that's funny.]
101	Chad:	and he went *straight* to my coach.
102		and said "this tournament's this and that
103		and da da da da da.
104		yadda yadda yadda."
105		and my coach just *laughed* when he heard what I said?
106	Wayne:	{laughs}
107	Chad:	{laughing} he just laughed,

108		he came up to me,
109		he was like, "that was *great*."
110		I was like, "well, y'know."
111		that guy was such a jerk.
112	Wayne:	that's good.
113	Chad:	oh I hate that guy.

The teller is in a very strong position in any case, since he does this refereeing voluntarily. Note how he makes a special point to cite the response of his coach, also an adult, who not only supports him, but compliments the humor of his remarks.

Consider first the function of the verb *say* in the unit "I always say, 'let 'em go,' y'know" in lines 16–17. *Say* is hardly literal here; Tannen (1989), Mayes (1990) and Chafe (1994) all comment on the constructed nature of reported speech and its special functions. The phrase "I always say" here describes an attitude or an "instinct," as Chad calls it, and "let 'em go" sums up his philosophy of officiating. "Let 'em go" has a proverbial quality even the first time Chad cites it, but it acquires additional resonance through repetition. After explaining the phrase, Chad repeats the whole unit, "I always say just let 'em go" at line 20. This spontaneous formula then conveniently serves to bridge the digression introduced by Wayne's question at line 21: "you can talk to them during the game?" Once Chad has answered the question, he paraphrases: "I'm like let 'em go, let 'em go" (line 26). Not just this formulaic phrase, but also the central dialogue between Chad and the coach sound as if they had taken on permanent form through retelling. He twice claims to be citing the "exact words" of the coach (lines 81 and 82). Anecdotes and jokes often turn on the exact duplication of dialogue, and this put-down story seems to work the same way.

In the next excerpt, family members are discussing how celebrities suffer for the loss of privacy. Brandon introduces a story about the actor Jack Nicholson, as an illustration of the public harrassment of stars. He mentions himself only as an observer to authenticate the story, but, of course, his presence at the theater in question suggests that he engages in the same activities as the celebrity, and this potentially enhances his reputation. Thus can the careful insertion of topically relevant stories serve as covert self-aggrandizement when the stories present the teller in enviable circumstances.

Jack

1	Ned:	and Sean Penn.
2		but other than that.
3	Brandon:	I was in New York a couple of months ago.

4		and I was seeing a show called M. Butterfly
5		with John Lithgow in it.
6		it's gotten pretty good uh reviews.
7		and one of the people in the crowd
8		to see this show
9		and to see John Lithgow
10		was Jack Nicholson.
11	Lydia:	uh.
12	Claire:	*oh.*
13	Brandon:	and Jack Nicholson was *houn*ded and *hass*led
14		and *spot*lighted and *dealt* on
15		by everybody in that movie theater,
16	Frank:	yeah.
17	Brandon:	by probably thirty-five photographers outside th-
18		movie theater um um *the*ater,
19		was completely public property.
20	Frank:	yep.
21	Brandon:	and to see a person,
22		with two body guards to protect him,
23	Lydia:	wow, to think [of it.]
24	Brandon:	[to see] a person in that position,
25		where just because he wants to go see a buddy of his in
26		a well-respected play in New York,
27		to have to put up with that aggravation,
28		I can understand why Sean Penn
29		has shoved a camera into a cameraman's face
30	Frank:	oh.
31	Brandon:	I can understand why,
32		when the thirty-fifth guy
33		has jumped over the back wall of his home
34		and into his backyard
35		to take a picture of his wife
36		at the swimming pool
37		that a person would get a little,
38	Frank:	yes.
39	Brandon:	testy.
40	Lydia:	but Jackie Onassis …

Brandon tells his story in defense of Sean Penn, who has acquired a bad reputation for overreacting to pressures from the public and, in particular, from the press. He is very careful to insert his story at an appropriate point in the conversation, and to draw out the consequences of the story for his argument about Sean Pean, although the story concerns Jack Nicholson. Moreover, he barely mentions his own presence as an observer in the story. Nevertheless, the story serves to place Brandon at the theater in New York with John Lithgow on the stage and Jack Nicholson in the audience, not to mention thirty-five photographers outside. Whether Brandon intends it or not, this story redounds to his personal image as a man of the world who visits New York City, and goes to the sort of play where Jack Nicholson turns up.

Two other observations about this story are worthy of discussion, both of them regarding repetition. The first case occurs in lines 13–15, where Brandon uses parallel phrasing to underscore his argument. The repetitive pattern of syntax and intonation in "Jack Nicholson was *houn*ded and *hass*led and *spot*lighted and *dealt* on" nicely emphasizes Brandon's point about the ongoing pressure of public attention. The second case of repetition concerns the number thirty-five, which crops up in lines 17–18 with reference to the "thirty-five photographers outside th- movie theater um um *the*ater," and then again in line 32 with reference to "the thirty-fifth guy" who has jumped over the wall of Sean Penn's home. Now, while it is presumably possible that Brandon counted and committed to memory the number of photographers outside the theater, and that he read and recalls the number of the wall-jumper who incurred Sean Penn's wrath, it is certainly more likely that both numbers are approximate reconstructions. The recurrence of the number thirty-five may reflect a telling strategy: Once a specific number has been mentioned, it is convenient to use it again, especially since the exact figure is irrelevant. Nevertheless, I am enough of a Freudian to believe that the number thirty-five has a special significance for Brandon generally or at least in relation to this story. Either way, the recurrence of numbers is another sort of repetition which may contribute to the recollection and production of stories.

Embarrassment

Most storytellers in my data shy away from explicit tales of personal aggrandizement; in fact, they are much more likely to tell humorous stories about embarrassing events, often from their fairly distant past. Still, a kind of covert prestige attaches to having overcome foolish mistakes in the past. In addition, the ability to laugh at one's own foibles and errors demonstrates a sense of humor, which also counts as a virtue. Far from resulting in a loss of face, the telling of stories about personally embarrassing moments actually ends up working as covert self-aggrandizement. Furthermore, this sort of self-aggrandizement is unassailable, since it poses as self-deprecation.

Consider as an example the story of the finger caught in the hole in the excerpt below. Here a woman relates an embarrassing story from her childhood to a group of her fellow graduate students. As her introduction indicates, other speakers had already told stories of "stupid things" they did in their youth. Thus Iris offers a safe contribution to an established topic, rather than risking a new type of story. This strategy practically ensures that her embarrassing tale will elicit laughter and understanding.

Finger Caught

1	Iris:	Ginger's story reminded me of
2		well I don't know,
3		speaking of stupid things you did in your youth.
4		{General laughter}
5		I went to the orthodontist one time.
6		and they had just gotten-
7		they had just redone the whole office,
8		it was really nice.
9		and they had put in these new *cab*inets
10		that had all the tools and stuff.
11		and I always- when I was young
12		I'd always like y'know
13		mess around with things, and stuff.
14		and so I y'know put my finger in this-
15		there was like this little *hole* in this cabinet
16		{teller laughter followed by audience laughter}
17		and I put my finger in there.
18		and all of a sudden I'm like,
19		and I can't get my *fin*ger out. {Audience laughter}
20		so I kind of start panicking
21		because I'm kind of like,
22		"what am I going to do?"
23		and I didn't want anybody to see it of course.
24		so I'm kind of like
25		trying to avoid being seen y'know.
26		but, as I'm trying to pull it out,

27		my finger starts swelling.
28	Ginger:	oh.
29	Iris:	so then I get really sort of panicky.
30		and I'm sitting there
31		trying and trying to get it out
32		and trying to disguise it at the same time.
33		and finally the lady
34		uh one of the {clears throat}
35		dental hygienists
36		I mean whatever you call them,
37		uh came up and she realized what I'd done.
38		so she brought me some some vaseline,
39		and put that on
40		and helped me try to get the finger out,
41		and about five minutes later we got it out, y'know
42		{laughing} and then and then she says to me,
43		"now don't do that again." {General laughter}
44		so I was afraid they were going to
45		have to cut open their new cabinets. {More laughter}
46	Ellen:	or cut open your finger.
47	Iris:	well no I wouldn't have let them do *that*.

Iris demonstrates particular telling strategies in this story. In her orientation, she self-corrects twice. The first time in lines 6–7 "And they had just gotten- they had just redone the whole office" introduces the general frame. The second time at line 11–13 "And I always- when I was young I'd always like y'know mess around" presents background information. Two indefinite extender phrases occur in the orientation as well: "all the tools and stuff" at line 10 to describe the contents of the cabinets, and "mess around with things, and stuff" at line 13. These phrases gain planning time for the teller, while they serve to engage the imagination of the listeners.

Notice also two uses of repetition. First, Iris repeats the phrase "put my finger in" from line 14 again at line 17 to bridge an episode of laughter. Second, she paraphrases the clause "so I kind of start panicking" from line 20 again in line 29 "so then I get really sort of panicky" to mark a further stage in the main action.

In a group where participants are "speaking of stupid things you did in your youth," Iris acquits herself nicely with a story which elicits a great deal of laughter. Recounting one's own mistakes and problems humorously, and laughing about them with others accrues to covert prestige within the group for the teller.

Troubles

In this section, we will explore two examples of stories about troubles or problems the teller is going through. Such stories may arise during troubles talk or they may crop up in the course of any conversation, say in explanation of particular behaviors or attitudes. In the first passage below, Addie and Brianne are commiserating with each other about various troubles they have been experiencing lately.

Fitted

1	Addie:	and they said "well then we can go shopping."
2		{chuckles} and I said "sure."
3	Brianne:	I know.
4		I'm so tired.
5		we were all over Rockford shopping today.
6	Addie:	oh yeah.
7	Brianne:	bopping around.
8		I had to uhm to get fitted for my bridesmaid's dress.
9	Addie:	oh.
10	Brianne:	oh God.
11		I was like ready to tell Elinor
12		I couldn't be in her wedding.
13	Addie:	{laughs}
14	Brianne:	I swear.
15		The dress- it looks really bad on me... .

The marginal narrative really just consists of the two clauses A–B below, where the initial clause labeled O counts as orientation.

O   we were all over Rockford shopping today.
A   I had to get fitted for my bridesmaid's dress.
B   I was like ready to tell Elinor
       I couldn't be in her wedding.

It is little more than a report of the day's activity, but it contains plenty of evaluation in the phrase "oh God," and in the suggestion that Brianne might refuse to participate in the wedding. This brief story serves not only to let Addie know why Brianne was shopping, but also to introduce the whole problem of the upcoming wedding of a friend, in particular the trouble and expense Brianne has already endured as a bridesmaid.

The next excerpt was recorded at a technical school in Chicago. The story about a car accident arose during a conversation between an instructor and a student she knew rather well, following a discussion of a writing assignment. Rita is a Hispanic woman who grew up in Chicago, went to work after high school, and returned to school only recently.

No Car

1	Rita:	yesterday,
2		it was two weeks ago,
3		I got in a car accident.
4		I was going to work
5		and I hit this lady that was turning.
6		and I didn't see her,
7		so I hit her.
8		and she happens to be my aunt.
9	Elaine:	oh. {laughing}
10	Rita:	and then I hit her
11		and then this other car hit me-
12		this big truck hit me in the back.
13		so my car got sandwiched.
14		and now I don't have no car,
15		my boyfriend brings me,
16		and I'm, I'm looking for a new car and everything.
17		so I'm like, no car.
18	Elaine:	okay.
19	Rita:	but I just got whiplash and that's it.
20	Elaine:	that's it?
21	Rita:	yeah.

Here again we see repetition used as a bridging device to overcome the brief interruption and get back into the story. After revealing that the person she hit was her aunt and eliciting listener laughter, Rita repeats the phrase "I hit her" from line 7 at line 10. Rita also repeats "no car" from the result in line 14 again at line 17, where it takes on the function of an evaluative coda.

Dream tellings

Reports of dreams enjoy a venerable history in literature and science. Freud (1950) and Jung (1985) are the classical sources to consult on dream telling; Ferrara (1994) devotes an interesting chapter to dream reports. As she states, "A complete theory of narrative will have to recognize dream tellings as a special type of personal experience narrative. A study of dream tellings can increase our understanding of the structure of personal experience narratives" (85). Of course, dream reports may occur in therapy sessions and other settings besides conversation. Moreover, they certainly need not assume the form of narratives; indeed, Ferrara herself presents several non-narrative examples. In the present study, however, dream tellings concern us only insofar as they actually occur in natural conversation couched in narrative syntax. When dreams are reported in narrative form, they naturally count as personal experience stories, as Ferrara argues (94–104). Hence, they deserve representation as a special type in this present section.

The passage below contains two reports of dreams by Paula, the secretary in charge of a large university program. Two co-workers, Belinda and Leona, sit together off to one side of Paula at desks of their own. When Belinda mentions dreams in their talk about playing the lottery, Paula announces her first dream report with what must be the most formulaic preface for this sort of story: "you know what I dreamt last night?" The discussion following the dream report breaks off because of an interruption from a graduate assistant working in the adjacent office. Then after an intervening telephone call, Paula returns to the topic of dreams by reporting a particularly fascinating one from her fairly distant past.

Dreams

1	Belinda:	you might win.
2		it wasn't in my dreams.
3		{General laughter}
4	Paula:	you know what I dreamt last night?
5	Belinda:	what?
6	Paula:	I {laughing}
7		I dreamt that I had congestive heart failure
8		and had to have an operation {laughs}
9	Leona:	does that mean [something?]
10	Paula:	[we were going-] see,
11		I don't remember exactly.
12		but we were going to the hospital
13		to see someone else.
14		and it turned out
15		the doctor took a look at me {laughing}
16		and said and said something about I didn't look well
17		and that I had congestive heart failure

18		and had to have surgery.
19		so then they were getting me all ready for surgery.
20		and then I woke up. (1.5)
21		and I thought of you {laughing} and *your* dreams.
22	Belinda:	{laughing} my dreams. {Paula and Belinda laugh}
23	-----Talk from adjoining room and telephone call intervene-----	
24	Paula:	well I dreamt-
25		when I was pregnant with Nat,
26		I dreamt that I gave birth to a fox.
27	Leona:	{laughs}
28	Belinda:	oh my God.
29	Paula:	and I can still picture this.
30		and there was a fox in the waiting room,
31		running around in circles
32		because he was so happy because I had a fox
33		{General laughter}
34	-----Telephone rings---------------------------------	

As pointed out above, the first dream report begins with a formulaic preface reminiscent of other types of conversational storytelling we have inspected. Then comes a summary abstract in lines 6–8, "I dreamt that I had congestive heart failure and had to have an operation," which differs from those in stories about objective past events only in its explicit reference to the dream context with "I dreamt that." Again in the second report, this explicit reference appears — indeed, it appears twice in lines 24 and 26. Further, in the first report, Paula states "I don't remember exactly" at line 11, and records her inexact memory of the doctor's words in line 16 with "and said something about I didn't look well." The explicit mention of memory, "and I can still picture this," in line 29 in the second report may also emphasize the dream context. In general, conversationalists are especially careful to characterize dream reports as such, just as they are assiduous in marking fantasies as irreal, as we saw in chapter four.

One dream report makes any other topically relevant in conversation, even if the dreams concern very different events. Apparently, when other conversationalists talk about their dreams, it jags our memories to recall our own. Thus, successive speakers may sometimes report their last night's dreams in series. However, Paula's two dream tellings display significant thematic overlap. Both dream reports place Paula in the hospital as the one in need of attention, so it is easy to see how the first might suggest the second on thematic grounds alone.

Third person stories

All the stories so far in this chapter, indeed the vast majority of the stories in this book and in my data as a whole, represent personal narratives, that is stories in the first person in which the teller is the central actor or affected participant. The sorts of storytelling considered in the preceding sections naturally revolved around personal experiences. Stories for personal aggrandizement, those which describe embarrassing scenes from the past, those which relate troubles from one's own past, and, of course, dream tellings all presuppose first-person narration.

The two narrative passages below differ in that they are third person stories, told not from events remembered first-hand but about someone else. They are further of interest because they are topically connected, illustrating an initial story and a corresponding response story, as described in chapter five. This response story is particularly worthy of attention, because it remains incomplete, prompting the listener to request further information. The two young men in this excerpt have been discussing how dangerous rough-housing can become, when Mark recalls an accident story his aunt told him, and this story in turn reminds Jason of an accident reported about his own aunt. Mark's story was considered in chapter three as an example of repetition used to stress evaluation; in particular, Mark evaluates his story three times with "horrid" in lines 19–20 and 23, then switches to the synonym "terrible" in line 28.
then repeats his original rhetorical question.

Accidents
```
 1   Jacob: we've kept everything pretty much under control
 2          [though this year.]
 3   Mark:  [that's right,]
 4          you can't wrestle around
 5          or bad things will happen.
 6   Jacob: yeah, Roger got [his nose]
 7   Mark:  [you know what] happened
 8          to my one of my aunt's friends out in Iowa?
 9          like when- when she was younger,
10          she had a headgear from braces,
11          and these two girls were wrestling around
12          just playing around, wrestling.
13          and one girl pulled her headgear off her mouth
14          and let it snap back.
```

15   and it slid up her face
16   and stuck in her eyes
17   and blinded her.
18 Jacob: wow.
19 Mark: isn't that horrid?
20   that's horrid.
21 Jacob: [when my-]
22 Mark: [blinded her] for life.
23   isn't that horrid.
24   that's just- I mean just from goofing around,
25   just from screwing-
26   a little bit of screwing around.
27   and if- and another thing,
28   it- it- it's terrible the things that can happen.
29   that's why I don't like people
30   screwing around with swords
31   and trying to throw people in the showers
32   and stuff like that,
33   and everything like that.
34 Jacob: you know what happened to my aunt Florence
35   when she was a little girl?
36 Mark: ooh what happened.
37 Jacob: she was like screwing around
38   like around Christmas time?
39   and like she,
40   I- I guess this was like
41   when they had candles on trees?
42   she lit her hair on fire.
43 Mark: oh wow.
44 Jacob: you met her.
45 Mark: but did anything happen?
46   she get a burned head or something?
47 Jacob: uh I don't know,
48   maybe you could shave her
49   and look for scar tissue.
50 Mark: oh I don't want to shave your aunt Florence's head.
51   does your aunt Florence have like
52   spinalbiffera or something like that?
53 Jacob: I don't know... .

Besides the formulaic repetition of "horrid" already mentioned for Mark's story, we should note particularly the way Jacob picks up Mark's phrase "screwing around" at line 37 in the orientation to his attempted response story. Mark produced three tokens of *screwing* in the evaluative talk following his story: two in the self-correction "just from screwing- a little bit of screwing around" in lines 25–26 and a third at line 30.

The phrase "screwing around" provides an obvious link to Jacob's attempted parallel response story. Jacob begins with a standard abstract in lines 34–35: "You know what happened to my aunt Florence when she was a little girl?" But he apparently lacks the details to reconstruct an incident he knows about only second-hand. He puts together three clauses, one element each for an orientation, background information and main action, as shown below.

A   she was like screwing around like around Christmas time?
B   I guess this was like when they had candles on trees?
C   she lit her hair on fire.

The incompleteness of the story provokes Mark to ask the obvious question: "but did anything happen? she get a burned head or something?" in lines 45–46. This inchoate storytelling also lacks evaluation, and leaves a disconnected impression unlike the personal involvement characteristic of first person stories.

Generalized recurrent experience

The passage below illustrates a fairly common type of narrative-like representation of a recurrent shared past experience in generalized form without reference to any specific instance. Although the clauses match the temporal order of the events they describe, they are not cast in the preterite, as stipulated for narrative elements. Instead, these generalized collaborative exchanges thrive on verb phrases with *would* and *would be -ing* along with *used to* forms.

Like the two connected stories in the preceding section, this passage concerns primarily a person somehow related to the teller rather then the teller herself. As such, it also counts as a third person account. However, in this case the teller places herself in the story as an observer, much as Brandon did in the story **Jack** in the introductory section of this chapter. Though Ellen appears briefly in the story as someone living in the same house as an undergraduate, she makes no pretense of real familiarity with the women pool players. In fact, Ellen distances herself from the women, noting that "they'd wear, what I thought was kind of sleazy clothing" in lines 9–10, and makes a point of revising her initial formulation "to pool halls" as "to bars really" in line 12. The generalized report format, further, matches Ellen's approach to the women here, since it allows her to produce a description of a pattern of behavior, as opposed to a specific instance, which would have required her own presence in the bar. This format is typical for reports of information learned second hand, much like gossip.

Ellen and Stuart are students of English in an office Ellen shares with other graduate students in the Department of English. Stuart has told a longish tale about playing pool, which suggests to Ellen a generalized story about a woman she knew in her undergraduate days.

Pool hall
```
 1   Stuart: it's just like I don't know,
 2           it's not my thing it's just my hobby.
 3   Ellen:  no [I understand.]
 4   Stuart: [it's just a pastime.]
 5   Ellen:  I had a
 6           there was a girl in my house
 7           when I was an undergraduate
 8           and she, and her friend used to get dressed up
 9           and they'd wear,
10           what I thought was kind of sleazy clothing.
11           and they'd go um to pool halls,
12           or to bars really-
13   Stuart: uh-huh.
14   Ellen:  and they'd play a couple games
15           and they wouldn't play very well.
16           and so guys would want to come up and bet them
17           and then and uh so they'd lose the first game
18           and they'd jerk them for the next three.
19           they were so good.
20           but I think the dress
21           and the uh the being w- women
22           had a lot to do with
23           being able to draw the [the guys in.]
24   Stuart: [yeah.]
25   Ellen:  the guys thought
26           they were going to be making easy money
27           and [then they-]
28   Stuart: [yeah I've] got a good friend Sheree
```

29   who works down at The Den.
30   she's really good.
31   she even has a shark,
32   a little shark on her poolcase.
33   Ellen: really? {laughing}
34   [people still don't get it?]
35   Stuart: [{and when she closes the thing-}]
36   *no*, they don't *get* it.
37   *it*'s terrible.
38   but she's good.
39   and she doesn't have to hustle anybody.
40   Ellen: {laughing} well that's funny.
41   it's funny-
42   Stuart: tricks of the trade.

If we analyze the passage according to the methods developed for narratives above, we see that it has the same basic structure.

Background
    there was a girl in my house
    when I was an undergraduate
Main action
A   and she, and her friend used to get dressed up
Evaluation
    and they'd wear,
    what I thought was kind of sleazy clothing.
Main action
B   and they'd go um to pool halls,
    or to bars really
C   and they'd play a couple games
Background
    and they wouldn't play very well.
Main action
D   and so guys would want to come up and bet them
E   and then so they'd lose the first game
F   and they'd jerk them for the next three.
Evaluation
    they were so good.

Global evaluation
>   but I think the dress
>   and the being women
>   had a lot to do with
>   being able to draw the the guys in.

Coda
>   The guys thought they were going to be making easy money

Ellen seems to be formulating a coda in this last line, when Stuart introduces a narrative-like response of his own, so that she trails off. The remainder of her report follows the pattern of conversational stories like **First Job** in chapter two, where background and evaluation interact with narrative clauses describing the main action. One could easily transform Ellen's report into a particularized story by rendering all the verb phrases in the pure past tense. Indeed, the initial clause in lines 6–7 already displays the simple past tense, and might stand unaltered as the introduction to a typical story: "There was a girl in my house when I was an undergraduate." However, the presence of *would* and *used to* throughout obliterates any possibility of distinguishing between narrative elements and narrow frames. This lack of distinction helps account for the somewhat undifferentiated structure of the passage.

Collaborative retelling

We examined collaborative retelling for fun in chapter four based on the story **Change**, but here I would like to comment on collaborative narration of a familiar story to ratify group membership and modulate rapport. Then we will compare another excerpt which illustrates co-narration of a story for a third party unfamiliar with its content.

Co-narration to ratify group membership

We have already inspected the introductory passage of **Poodle** as representative of formulaicity in story openings in chapter three, but here group dynamics assume center stage.

Poodle
1 Jean: Annie gave me a permanent once, too.
2 Louise: Annie did?

3	Jean:	once and only once.
4		{General laughter}
5		I would never allow her to touch my hair again.
6	Louise:	well remember the time-
7	Jean:	*yoooh.*
8		talk about afro
9		when afro wasn't even in *style.*
10		my God.
11	Annie:	well see I *start*ed [something.]
12	Jean:	[frizz ball.]
13		I was a frizz ball.
14		it wasn't even afro.
15		I was just *frizz.*
16	Louise:	remember [when-]
17	Jean:	[it was] *terr*ible.
18	Louise:	Jennifer, the first time Jennifer had a perm
19		when she came home.
20		it was the funniest thing.
21	Jean:	she put something on her head,
22		a bag or something?
23	Louise:	she wore her-
24	Annie:	{laughs}
25	Louise:	well she wore her-
26	Helen:	"hair ball, hair ball."
27		yeah, because she-
28	Annie:	she just always had this *hood* on.
29		and she ran right upstairs,
30	Louise:	*no.*
31		*first* she *threw* her bag up the stairs,
32		almost *hit* me.
33	Annie:	oh yeah.
34	Louise:	then "*bang.*"
35		the door slams.
36		and I'm like- I was on the *phone.*
37		I was like "ah I don't know.
38		my sister just walked in.
39		I think something's wrong."
40		and [then she ran up the stairs.]
41	Annie:	[oh that's it.]

42		"I look like a damn *poodle*."
43		{General laughter}
44	Louise:	like *sob*bing,
45		"I look like a poodle."
46	Helen:	aw {laughing}
47	Annie:	then she came down to eat
48		and she'd *wrapped* a towel around her head.
49	Helen:	aw {laughing}
50	Louise:	she barricaded herself for a while in her room.
51	Jean:	*my* hair takes like *this*.
52		I mean.
53	Annie:	yeah.

Louise first announces her story with: "well remember the time-" at line 6, before Jean will let her have the floor. As we saw in chapter two, the preface with *remember* provides a way of explicitly marking a story as familiar to at least some participants. When Jean again seems to have finished, Louise reiterates her *remember*-preface at line 16, and allows Jean one final evaluative comment before plunging into the story about Jennifer's first perm. Even when Louise has begun her story, Jean waits only till the first pause before contributing a detail in lines 21–22, albeit in the form of an uncertain request for confirmation: "she put something on her head, a bag or something?"

Both Annie and Helen are involved in co-telling the story as well. Helen adds only a bit of dialogue at line 26, and sympathetic *aw*s at lines 46 and 49, but she makes the most of this contribution, since, as Tannen notes, animating dialogue illustrates shared experience (1989: 11). By contrast, Annie makes extensive contributions but receives corrections from Louise on almost every detail she adds. Thus Annie's description "she just always had this *hood* on" at line 28 is allowed to stand, but her following statement that "she ran right upstairs" elicits a prompt *no* from Louise, who proceeds to place herself in the center of the story's action. Again when Annie attempts to add a piece of dialogue: "I look like a damn *poodle*" at line 42, Louise objects to her tone, saying it was "like sobbing." She renders Jennifer's statement as sad rather than angry, deleting the *damn*. Finally, even Annie's statement beginning "then she came down to eat" at line 47 displeases Louise, who insists that Jennifer first "barricaded herself for a while in her room." Although Louise has a hard time getting started and has difficulty responding to Jean's query about what Jennifer wore on her head, she controls the story through to the end, as becomes quite clear in Annie's acquiescent responses to Louise's corrections: "oh yeah" at line 33 and "oh that's it" at line 41.

Even without a final coda expressing agreement on the evaluation of a past event or on the point of the story about it, collaborative narration serves to ratify group membership and modulate rapport in multiple ways, first because it allows participants to re-live salient common experiences, second because it confirms the long-term bond they share, and third because the experience of collaborative narration itself redounds to feelings of belonging. Moreover, collaborative narration helps fix the verbal form of a shared experience for the participants.

Co-narration for a third party

The next story **Up and Over** illustrates not only co-telling, but also a third person narrative like those in the foregoing section. As pointed out there, the first person perspective is much more usual for the conversational storytelling in my corpus. Here Patricia and her husband Ralph collaborate in telling a story both of them had read in the local newspaper, and perhaps had heard reported on the radio or television as well. Their audience consists of their two daughters Marsha and Amy, both home from college for the long Thanksgiving weekend. A mention of a particular intersection in a previous story about a neighbor provides the occasion for this storytelling. It is also Patricia's reference to the fateful intersection which finally closes the story and the topic. I include the transcript of the discussion following the story proper to show how it weaves its way in and out of the discussion. Talk of slow clocks intervenes, but the topic of the accident remains viable till Patricia officially closes it down.

Up and Over

1	Patricia:	but she found a different place
2		because she said
3		she doesn't like to go over on Flavey Road.
4		(1.7) Flavey Road is where that
5	Ralph:	truck
6	Patricia:	truck went over the
7	Ralph:	m- car
8	Patricia:	car killing three people from Grant Lake.
9	Marsha:	what do you mean the truck went over?
10		over what?
11	Ralph:	[guy from Atlanta]
12	Patricia:	[guy] drove all the way over from Atlanta

13		without a s- without making a rest stop.
14		he had- he didn't have any sleep.
15	Ralph:	amazing.
16	Amy:	so?
17	Ralph:	then he r- then he ran into a car,
18	Patricia:	got off-
19	Ralph:	I think he burst into flames, didn't he?
20	Patricia:	m-hm,
21		ca- the truck ran right over.
22	Ralph:	ran right over him.
23	Patricia:	right up and over
24		and killed three young people.
25	Marsha:	up and over what?
26	Ralph:	[a *car*.]
27	Patricia:	[a *car*.]
28	Ralph:	[at an exit ramp.]
29	Patricia:	[with three young] coup- three young people in it from
30		the Grant Lake Naval Base.
31	Ralph:	wow.
32	Amy:	you just kept saying "up and over,
33		up and over,
34		up and over."
35	Ralph:	forget it.
36	Marsha:	[did the truck driver die?]
37	Ralph:	[just call me if you get too much news.]
38		what?
39	Amy:	just kidding.
40	Marsha:	they should shoot him.
41	Ralph:	hoh {with strong exhalation}.
42	Marsha:	well, that's what he deserves, isn't it?=
43	Patricia:	=well, he certainly deserves to go to jail.
44	Marsha:	[did he?]
45	Amy:	[were all three people killed?]
46	Patricia:	ha, you never read a follow-up.
47	Amy:	all three people were killed?
48	Patricia:	yeah, they were all like y'know
49		twenty-one, twenty-two.
50	Ralph:	yeah, they were about the same.
51	Amy:	what would you charge him with.

52	Marsha:	with three counts of manslaughter.
53	Ralph:	probably manslaughter.
54		(3.2) {clock strikes in hall}
55	Amy:	[I think that reckless driving would be-]
56	Marsha:	[reckless driving,]
57		three counts of manslaughter.
58		whole tons of things.
59	Patricia:	he *was* probably [asleep.]
60	Ralph:	[your clock's slow too.]
61	Patricia:	hm?
62	Ralph:	your clock's slow, too.
63		oh you took the battery out.
64	Amy:	what kind of truck was he driving?
65	Patricia:	yeah, but I fixed them, after.
66	Ralph:	that one, too?
67	Patricia:	probably.
68		Amy and I did it.
69	Amy:	what kind of *truck* [was he driving.]
70	Ralph:	[that one is five minutes slow.]
71	Amy:	so was your truck *driver.*
72	Ralph:	because your VCR is slow.
73	Marsha:	mm.
74	Ralph:	like [almost thirty- fifteen minutes.]
75	Amy:	[obvious that you killed somebody]
76		if it went up and over.
77	Marsha:	I know, its-.
78	Patricia:	but Flavey Road,
79		there's been a lot of accidents at Flavey Road
80		because it's …

The introductory sentence offers a classic example of joint production between two speakers in close synchrony with each other. At barely perceptible hesitations from Patricia, Ralph inserts *truck* and then *car* almost seamlessly at lines 5 and 7. Then in response to a question from Marsha, he and Patricia begin in lines 11 and 12 what seem intended as essentially interchangeable statements — so much so that Ralph simply stops, letting Patricia take over. Ralph appears willing to return to the status of auditor, offering only the comment "amazing" at line 15. But when Patricia fails to continue, Ralph proceeds: "Then he r- then he ran into a car" at line 17, and asks Patricia to confirm his statement that the truck burst into flames. This motivates Patricia to resume the story. When Marsha interrupts to ask "Up and over what?" at line 25, Ralph and Patricia again respond in tandem: "A *car*." Then again they resume in tandem, and again Ralph lets Patricia take over. Once Patricia finishes her thought, the story proper is done as well. Hence, Ralph returns to the role of commentator in line 31, remarking "wow."

If we amalgamate and streamline the contributions of the co-tellers, Patricia and Ralph, adhering to the logical order of events, we come up with something like the following basic narrative. This skeleton represents an attempt to meld the contributions of both tellers into a single coherent narrative structure, as a listener might.

A   Guy drove all the way over from Atlanta without a rest stop.
B   He got off at an exit ramp.
C   He ran right up and over a car.
D   He killed the three young people in it.
E   He burst into flames.

When Amy criticizes their joint storytelling technique in lines 32–34, Ralph offers to end the topic with "Forget it," and again in line 37 with the sarcastic remark, "Just call me if you get too much news," suggesting that the girls would know the story if they paid attention to the local news media. But Amy and Marsha find the topic too interesting to let it drop. They continue to ask questions and speculate about the legal ramifications of the case. This discussion brings out further details of the accident, for instance the ages of the young people killed and the conjecture that the truck driver was asleep, but they do not alter the basic narrative structure.

Ralph loses interest in the whole matter, and broaches a new topic regarding slow-running clocks in line 60 and again in line 62. Amy never receives an answer to her question about the kind of truck involved at line 64, because Ralph insists on talking about clocks running five minutes slow. Amy makes a sarcastic remark about the truck driver running slow as well at line 71. Then she and Marsha exchange sarcastic messages about their parents' inadequate narrative skill, with special reference to the recurrent phrase "up and over" in lines 75–77. Ralph seems oblivious to this undercurrent, but mother Patricia addresses their comments indirectly in her return to the original topic of the intersection at Flavey Road in line 78.

Co-narration in collaborative fantasy

We saw in chapter five with regard to the story **Clone Mark** how two students who share an apartment created a fantasy about replacing their third apartment-mate with a more subservient clone. Such fantasies construct a fictional world, by contrast with typical conversational stories, which recapitulate events in the experienced past. But they also differ from literary fictions. Both conversational storytelling and literature generally purport to describe events in the real world, or at least in some potentially real world in the past tense, while collaborative fantasies typically display their irreality with conditional clauses and verb phrases with the modals *would* and *could*. Sometimes conversationalists constructing a fantasy follow standard narrative practice in paying considerable attention to chronological order, as we saw in **Clone Mark**, but in the passage below the participants rather spin out their ideas and elaborate suggestions from each other as they come. Collaborative fantasies represent high-involvement talk in its pure form, where interpersonal interaction prevails over believability and sequentiality.

Shelley and Cal are two students involved in a long-term romantic relationship. They are sitting in Cal's car outside a fast food restaurant, talking about their unwelcome week-long separation over the Thanksgiving break. Shelley will return home the next day, while Cal will stay in his apartment near the university to work. Their collaborative creation of a fantasy about guardian angels allows them to express feelings they might have trouble discussing otherwise.

Guardian Angel

1	Shelley:	{laughs} I guess I better go.
2	Cal:	you don't have to.
3	Shelley:	na, I don't have to,
4		but if I want to get up tomorrow morning I do.
5		guess *oh* I couldn't believe it,
6		I was so happy.
7		I wanted to go home Friday morning, right?
8		this guy's leaving early early Friday morning.
9		well I have an eight o'clock class
10		that I don't want to miss because
11	Cal:	it got canceled.
12	Shelley:	{whispered} right.
13		the one day I'm like "bless you,"
14		I it must be *des*tined for me to go home.
15	Cal:	someone's looking out for, looking at you.

16	Shelley:	*and* I found someone to work for me right away,
17		and Julie's going to Finite even,
18		so she's going to take notes for me
19		so I have the whole day covered.
20	Cal:	you probably have some guardian angel
21		that doesn't want to see you die
22		and I'm going to die in some firey explosion
23		that [you won't be in.]
24	Shelley:	[don't you dare] say that.
25	Cal:	{laughs}
26	Shelley:	don't you dare.
27	Cal:	I just want that on record
28		so that if it's true,
29	Shelley:	{laughs} well what if it is-
30		was because it's my time to go?
31	Cal:	oh and that I was there in place of you.
32	Shelley:	no.
33		n- n- no,
34		what if it's my time to go
35		and it's I'm going to die on my way home.
36	Cal:	so you're going to die with him.
37	Shelley:	yeah.
38	Cal:	so,
39	Shelley:	or maybe not with him
40		or maybe at at home or something.
41	Cal:	you better *not* die with him.
42	Shelley:	no, aw, no.
43	Cal:	{laughs} ug.
44	Shelley:	you never know {sing-song}
45	Cal:	yeah.
46	Shelley:	oh well.
47	Cal:	well okay.
48		well see I was looking at it
49		as a positive on your end.
50		that you've got a guardian angel
51		and that=
52	Shelley:	=and that you *don't*? {tsk}
53		everybody has a guardian angel.
54	Cal:	I don't know,

55		he hasn't been helping me that much lately.
56	Shelley:	well that's because
57	Cal:	I feel like I'm on my own.
58	Shelley:	well, when you feel *alone*,
59		that's when he's with you the most,
60		so, do you know that?
61		probably not.
62	Cal:	naw I just=
63	Shelley:	=because=
64	Cal:	=like to wallow in my self pity.
65	Shelley:	ri- that's that's that's right.
66		we all do it.
67		I do it all the time.
68		*all* the time... .

In this collaborative fantasy, no real narrative-like progression can take hold, because the participants continually revise each other's proposed scenarios. Thus, when Cal suggests that he is "going to die in some firey explosion" without Shelley (lines 21–23), she objects "don't you dare say that." Again when Shelley suggests that it is her "time to go" and that she will die on her way home (lines 34–35), Cal's response induces her to revise. When she attempts a very open scenario in lines 39–40 with "or maybe not with him or maybe at at home or something," Cal makes his objection explicit: "you better *not* die with him" (line 41). With no remembered structure to fall back on, this collaborative fantasy drifts into speculations.

Diffuse stories

In the longish passage below, we see two examples of inchoate narratives, stories which never actually take shape, though interested listeners can certainly reconstruct the events from the fragments produced by two or more speakers. In each case, following a legitimate story preface, a diffuse story emerges from the surrounding talk, if we are prepared to construct it from the pieces supplied.

Sybil and Tom are graduate students living together in a house owned by a professor on research leave. Tom's parents, Yvonne and Lester, have just arrived to spend the weekend with them. As she enters the kitchen where Tom has set up a cassette recorder, Yvonne unveils a pineapple upside-down cake baked according to a new recipe. Talk about the cake suggests to Tom and Sybil a conversation they had the previous evening, and together they almost tell a story about it. They also play on the taste adjectives they had bandied about in that conversation, which here again take on a formulaic feeling.

Cake

1	Yvonne:	I found this recipe,
2		has zero fat in it.
3	Tom:	wow.
4	Sybil:	wow.
5	Yvonne:	it's probably no good.
6	Tom:	it looks good.
7		looks moist and juicy, cool and fresh.
8	Sybil:	moist and crispy.
9	Tom:	crispy,
10		no it's not [crispy.]
11	Sybil:	[we were] trying to define-
12	Tom:	was that just [last night?]
13	Sybil:	[some aspects] of healthy food.
14	Tom:	no it was not,
15		well, yeah it was,
16		[I was just, I was in the mood for,]
17	Sybil:	[you wanted something fresh and crispy,]
18		but then you realized it wasn't just fresh and crispy
19		because that could have been crackers.
20		it was moist and crispy like an apple.
21	Tom:	right.
22		but, but don't crackers seem kind of stale
23		and [crispy?]
24	Lester:	[yes they do,]
25		at night especially.
26	Sybil:	so you wanted an apple
27		and then ah-
28	Lester:	yep.
29	Tom:	o- or like a tomato or some lettuce,
30		[I would have been happy with some lettuce]
31	Sybil:	[which wouldn't have been crispy,]
32		a tomato wouldn't be crispy, though,
33	Tom:	no.
34	Sybil:	so maybe moist and fresh are the two characteristics.

35	Tom:	yeah right,
36		but crispy was what I was more in the mood for
37		[actually.]
38	Lester:	[crackers] are a noontime thing,
39		not a nighttime thing.
40	Tom:	no.
41		but crisp, and fresh, and juicy, and moist,
42		those are all nighttime things,
43		like an apple.
44	Lester:	we- well, not always.
45	Tom:	no.
46		so- sometimes yes.
47	Lester:	sometimes it has to be something else, yeah.
48	Tom:	salty and hot and fatty.
49	Lester:	that's right.
50	Yvonne:	that's the best.
51	Sybil:	{laughs}.
52	Yvonne:	anytime, anywhere.
53	Lester:	piece of pie.
54	Sybil:	hm hm hm.
55	Yvonne:	[that's not too bad]
56	Lester:	[with a lot of] lot of ah syrup in it.
57	Tom:	{laughing} like a cherry pie.
58	Lester:	exactly.
59	Tom:	right.
60	Yvonne:	oh did I tell you-
61	Tom:	oh by the way, sorry.
62	Yvonne:	my boss had a bag of
63		I think they're like mini-rice cakes.
64	Sybil:	[oh yeah.]
65	Yvonne:	[and he said] have- [have]
66	Lester:	[piece of cardboard]
67	Yvonne:	have a-
68		oh that's what it was.
69		"an apple flavored piece of cardboard."
70	Sybil:	oh ho ho. {sadly}
71	Yvonne:	and, they were pretty bad.
72	Tom:	yeah.
73	Yvonne:	they were not really even apple flavored.

74 Lester: {laughs}.
75 Yvonne: plus they were,
76   I don't know,
77   so hard to chew.
78 Sybil: m-hm,
79 Yvonne: [anyway,]
80 Tom: [Sybil] had some of those mini-rice cakes.
81 Sybil: yeah, I had some of them.
82   I had like honey-nut rice [cakes.]
83 Tom: [yeah,] and ah actually hers were really good,
84   when you put, uh, some butter and honey on them.
85 Lester: yeah. {laughing}
86 Yvonne: yeah {laughing} yeah.
87 Sybil: yeah.
88   that's what you did with them, wasn't it.
89 Tom: yeah, actually those were really good
90   with butter and honey on them,
91   they were little [crackers.]
92 Yvonne: [did you] defeat the purpose? {laughing}
93 Tom: well, the purpose was,
94   maybe at the time just a medium.
95 Yvonne: {laughs}.
96 Tom: so um uh so I don't actually have to just uh,
97   dig my hands into honey and butter, and,
98 Sybil: and just eat it off your fist.
99 Yvonne: it's just so funny, though.

The first diffuse story begins in lines 11–13 with an utterance by Sybil which could function as an abstract: "we were trying to define some aspects of healthy food," though Tom disturbs it with his question: "was that just last night?" Tom negates Sybil's assertion, then accepts it, then proposes a modified reading in lines 14–16: "no it was not, well, yeah it was, I was just, I was in the mood for," but Sybil completes his thought for him — and with it what might count as a minimal narrative, as outlined below.

Trying to Define (Outline)
A   we were trying to define some aspects of healthy food.
B   Tom was in the mood for/wanted something fresh and crispy.
C   then he realized it wasn't just fresh and crispy:
    It was moist and crispy like an apple.

Presumably the collaborative attempt to define just what Tom wanted either led to or followed his realization that he really wanted something "moist and crispy like an apple." Hence, the order of the clauses above does not match the logical chronology of the reported events. Still, the two clauses B–C reflect the order of the events they report, so that we might allow **Trying to Define** as a minimal narrative. This diffuse story segues into more talk about foods to which the predicates in question apply.

Then at line 60, Yvonne produces a very recognizable story preface: "oh did I tell you-." Tom begins just after Yvonne to introduce a new topic of his own with: "oh by the way." When Tom realizes he has interrupted Yvonne, he says "sorry" to signal that she should procede. Yvonne starts over with an orientation clause in line 62: "my boss had a bag of I think they're like mini-rice cakes." However, when she begins another narrative element describing the main action, her hesitation and repetition of *have* prompt her husband Lester to fill in the phrase "piece of cardboard" at line 66. Yvonne improves upon Lester's suggestion with a simulated boss's voice: "an apple flavored piece of cardboard" at line 69. Then in lines 71–77, she produces three back-to-back evaluations without a second narrative element: "they were pretty bad... they were not really even apple flavored... plus they were, I don't know, so hard to chew." Now, any listener can retrieve the information that Yvonne must have tasted the proffered rice cake in order to have arrived at her evaluations, but the clauses she actually produces never come together into a narrative on the narrow definition. Compare the proposed analysis below.

Rice Cakes (Analysis)
Preface
    oh did I tell you-
Orientation
    my boss had a bag of mini-rice cakes.
Main action
    and he said have an apple flavored piece of cardboard.
Evaluation
    and they were pretty bad.
    they were not really even apple flavored.
    they were so hard to chew.

If we allow for 'zero clauses' which listeners retrieve as logical or social consequences from the foregoing talk, for instance that Yvonne accepted a rice cake from her boss and tried it, then the analysis above naturally expands to a complete narrative. This sort of potential narrative almost but not quite material-izing in talk, complete only for listeners prepared to fill in the conveyed informa-tion, is precisely what I identify as a diffuse story. This notion of the diffuse story allows us to talk about emergent narratives in natural conversation.

Conclusions

This chapter as a whole represents an attempt to broaden the basis of what receives attention in the study of narrative. The materials analyzed exemplify many different interpersonal functions of storytelling in conversation. Conversa-tionalists tell stories of personal experience to inform each other about them-selves and their values. In doing so, they may align themselves with members of the group present or with the whole group. When evaluations coincide and response stories demonstrate parallel experiences, storytelling enhances rapport between participants. At the same time, personal stories serve to entertain listeners, especially when they are funny. Narrative-like accounts of recurrent experiences share personal experiences in similar ways. We have also seen how conversationalists use stories for argumentation or to illustrate a point. Finally, they tell third-person stories to inform one another of events and to express their feelings about them.

   In everyday conversation, stories and narrative-like structures bubble up and recede back into turn-by-turn talk. It is often difficult to decide exactly where a conversational story begins and ends. Sometimes two or more participants collaborate in producing a story, so that it becomes impossible to say just who is the teller or even the primary teller. Nevertheless, participants as listeners can distill a coherent story from the talk which allows them to respond appropriately — sometimes with parallel stories of their own. Indeed, listeners are also perfectly capable of recognizing incompleteness and incoherence in narratives and formulating appropriate questions to fill in the missing information, as we have seen here as well. Problematic and marginally narrative passages provide a testing ground for our analytic methods, but they also show us listeners respond-ing in ways which shed additional light on the data. Finally, teller strategies like repetition, formulaicity, disfluencies and constructed dialogue remain quite constant across the types of storytelling explored.

CHAPTER 7

Extensions of the Approach

Clov: What is there to keep me here?
Hamm: The dialogue. [Pause]
           I've got on with my story. [Pause]
           I've got on with it well. [Pause. Irritably]
           Ask me where I've got to.
Samuel Beckett "Endgame"

Introduction

In this chapter, I propose to extend the methods elaborated to this point for the analysis of conversational narratives to the description of other types of discourse, in particular to the internal structure and the contextual integration of jokes and to literary representations of storytelling. Applying the account of conversational storytelling developed in the foregoing chapters to these related genres serves both to test and to refine its conclusions. I hope to show that the methods and results of the foregoing analysis extend naturally, and that they shed light on jokes and literary narratives, thereby demonstrating the more general value of the present study to a broad range of narrative genres.

   Joketelling is an obvious place to begin, because jokes are typically narrative in form and arise naturally in conversation. Since conversational storytelling also often aims at humor, an investigation of narrative structures and strategies in joketelling performances will certainly be instructive. Then I turn to the rendition of storytelling in drama, choosing examples from both an older play and a fairly recent one, namely Shakespeare's "Romeo & Juliet" and Beckett's "Endgame" respectively. I will seek to show how the account of conversational narratives developed in this book can inform our assessment of meaning in literary texts, and also how the analysis of humorous conversational narrative can enrich our understanding of literary humor.

Jokes as narratives

Of course, many jokes are not narrative as such. Knock-knocks and riddle jokes, for instance, have a non-narrative structure. However, narrative jokes are probably the largest and most typical genre of conversational joketelling, so that it is natural to investigate how narrative strategies intertwine with the structures of humor in jokes.

My approach to the internal organization of jokes owes much to Hockett (1960), who developed convincing structural analyses of various joke genres. Hockett showed that jokes must consist of a 'build-up', which comprises the body of the joke, and a 'punchline', which structurally closes the joke. At the same time, the punchline semantically reverses the sense we would expect from the build-up, and forces an unexpected sense to our attention. Hockett showed that we can often recognize a 'pivot' as well, that is a word or phrase around which the dual meaning potential revolves. His extended treatment of joke structures grew out of his earlier work on slips of the tongue. While his main thrust was taxonomic, Hockett discussed constraints on tellability for jokes, and he stressed the importance of context as well. Concerning the performance of narrative jokes, Hockett hypothesized that tellers memorize only the punchline and perhaps a few key parts verbatim, while they recall only a bare skeleton form for the body of the joke, which they flesh out in the actual performance. This notion of the skeleton to be fleshed out in performance recalls the basic narrative crytalized from the storytelling performance, as described in the foregoing chapters.

My analysis of verbal humor combines frame theory and the notion of bisociation. According to Koestler (1964) and his followers, humor arises from the perception of a single event "in two self-consistent but habitually incompatible frames of reference." While this cognitive state lasts, the stimulus "is not merely linked to one associative context, but *bisociated* with two" (1964: 35 ff., italics in original). This cognitive state leads to a release of psychic energy in the form of laughter. I interpret Koestler's frames of reference as equivalent to the semantic frames described in chapter one. Raskin (1985) formalizes the same idea in his notion of the semantic script, so that his treatment of jokes as evoking a clash between opposed semantic scripts parallels this analysis. Furthermore, I have argued (Norrick 1986, 1993b) that the basic tenets of the bisociation theory of humor subsume and synthesize the apparently disparate approaches of Bergson (1900), Freud (1905), Fry (1963), Bateson (1953) and others.

Before we enter into the analysis of narrative jokes in conversation, I would like to demonstrate the frame-theoretical bisociation analysis of verbal humor.

This demonstration provides a convenient place to point out that some so-called one-liners exhibit narrative structure, though we usually assign them to a separate group all their own. Thus, the classic one-liner below certainly must count as a narrative.

> A panhandler came up to me today and said he hadn't had a bite in weeks, so I bit him

This joke consists of three past tense clauses in the same order as the events they depict, relating the story of a panhandler and a victim who apparently misunderstood his plea for a handout as a request to be bitten.

A   A panhandler came up to me
B   He said he hadn't had a bite in weeks
C   I bit him

This one-liner is briefer than most narrative jokes, but it exhibits the two parts necessary to any joke: a build-up, which consists of the orientation and much of the complicating action, and a punchline, which concludes the joke. Clearly, the build-up consists in clauses A–B in the panhandler joke, while clause C represents the punchline. Furthermore, the frame in force in the build-up, namely a panhandler seeking a handout from a passer-by, vanishes in the punchline. Here a new frame takes hold in which the victimized passer-by becomes the attacker, while the panhandler becomes the victim. The ambiguous phrase which serves as the justification for the frame switch is the marginally ambiguous phrase "have a bite," and this frame constitutes the pivot of the joke. We can schematize this breakdown as follows, where "had a bite" belongs structurally to the build-up, while functioning semantically as the pivot.

BUILD-UP   A panhandler came up to me today and said he hadn't
Pivot   *had a bite* in weeks,
PUNCHLINE   so I bit him

This parsing intertwines with the narrative structure to yield a story with a final humorous twist. On reflection, we realize that the final twist was already latent in the pivot. It is, of course, characteristic for jokes that the punchline constitutes the final line. For most narratives, a denouement follows the climax, often including a resolution, evaluation and a coda. Semantically, the punchline of a joke serves as its resolution, even though jokes characteristically resolve themselves in unexpected ways. Thus, the presumed victim biting the panhandler reverses the roles of the participants and switches the sense of "have a bite," but it does resolve the situation and lead to a conclusion.

Analyzing conversational joketelling

In the following, we will investigate three conversational excerpts containing narrative jokes. As in previous chapters, we will explore both their internal structure and their contexts. Sacks (1974) demonstrated how conversation analysis can apply to the telling of jokes in natural conversational contexts. I followed him in my own work on conversational humor (Norrick 1993a), in which I sought to develop a comprehensive account of jokes and joking in everyday conversation. I investigated a large body of conversational joking to show how conversationalists weave wordplay into their talk, but also how they interrupt the flow of topical talk and get the floor to perform funny stories and jokes. I further explored how speakers use puns, banter and sarcasm, but also personal anecdotes and narrative jokes to align themselves together, to present a personality, and to build rapport. I will proceed in much the same way in the following to lay out the internal structure of the joke text and to demonstrate the interactional significance of the joke performance.

In particular, I hope to show how studying both successful and unsuccessful narrative joke performances can help us better understand narrative processes generally. To this end, the first joke to be considered is carefully prefaced and set up to achieve the desired effect of making the audience laugh. The second joke falters at the beginning, but smoothes out as it progresses. The third joke never gets on track at all. The teller begins with an allusion to a joke, which fails to elicit laughter from one hearer, motivating the teller to repetitions and explanations, which, however, remain unhelpful.

Drunken Irishmen

Several graduate students are telling jokes after class. Ellen has just finished a joke which elicited no laughter. Grant and Robert explained that they knew versions of the joke Ellen told, but Ginger gave no reason for not laughing. Robert wonders whether Ginger ever laughs at jokes in the initial turn in this example; and Ginger is responding to Robert's question in the first part of her turn, "I don't, actually I don't," which overlaps with Grant's initial preface, while her "no" comes in direct reply to the preface.

Grant clearly wants to make quite sure his joke is not familiar to Ginger, as we see from his second preface in which he more carefully describes the content of the joke. He apparently wants to test her propensity to withhold laughter in response to jokes: Notice his "see" once Ginger has laughed and commented positively on his performance, "that's cute." Notice also how Grant pauses after

Ginger's second confirming response with "okay, so," before launching into the joke proper.

Drunken Irishmen

1	Robert:	maybe you don't ever laugh at jokes
2	Grant:	do you- have you heard the drunken Irishman one
3		[that's making the rounds lately]
4	Ginger	[I don't, actually I don't.]
5		no.
6	Grant:	okay.
7		it's a *two* drunken Irishmen.
8		maybe maybe you know it now?
9	Ginger:	no.
10	Grant:	okay, so.
11		guy walks into a bar
12		there's there's a a drunken Irishman sitting at the
13		bar and another Irishman walks into the bar
14		and he is like,
15		"oh. h- how do you do?"
16		and the guy says "I'm doing just fine."
17		and so he says, "well, let's have a drink."
18		and then so they have a drink.
19		and then eh {Audience laughter} he says,
20		"well, where are you from?"
21		and he goes, "I am from Dublin."
22		he goes "well, imagine that,
23		I'm from Dublin as well."
24		so they have another drink.
25		and then he says,
26		"well, where did you go to school in Dublin?"
27		and he says "oh, I'm from-
28		eh I went to St. Mary's down in"
29		and he- he gives a street address.
30		and then so like,
31		"what a coincidence this is so odd,
32		I went there, too."
33		and they have another drink.
34		"so let's let's drink to St. Mary's."
35		and they have another drink.

36		and then the guy says,
37		"well, what year did you graduate?"
38		he says, "well, I graduated back in seventy-two."
39		and he goes,
40		"now this is getting downright perplexed
41		because I graduated from seven-
42		in seventy-two just as well."
43		and so they were like
44		"let's have another drink."
45		so they have another drink
46		and another guy walks into the bar
47		goes there to the bartender and asks,
48		"what's up?"
49		and he says
50		"oh, nothing,
51		just the O'Malley twins getting drunk again."
52	Robert:	{laughs}
53	Ginger:	{laughs} that's cute.
54	Grant:	see.
55	Robert:	{laughs}

The joke-telling frame is already in force, so that no special prefacing must occur in order to announce or justify the telling of a joke. Grant begins the joke text in characteristic conversational narrative fashion with a sentence which breaks off and requires patching together. Grant discards the whole initial phrase from line 11, "guy walks into a bar," and restarts, though not without some backtracking, "there's there's a a drunken Irishman sitting at the bar and another Irishman walks into the bar." Now, "guy walks into a bar" is of course a classic joke introduction, particularly due to the bare noun *guy* with no article. Moreover, this introduction comes close to providing an appropriate expository statement even here, so that Grant may be excused for beginning the joke this way. Indeed, the classic opener may even set the mood for the joke to come better than the proper introduction alone. We cannot reasonably exclude the possibility that Grant begins the joke this way on purpose.

In any case, it remains for the 'correct' introduction in lines 12–13 to set up the premise of the joke: "there's a a drunken Irishman sitting at the bar and another Irishman walks into the bar." This sentence also functions as a misleading garden path, since it suggests a state of affairs which turns out not to hold. Granted that the phrases "a drunken Irishman" and "another Irishman" do not logically exclude the possibility that the two Irishmen are related or even brothers or even twin brothers, they nevertheless conversationally impel us to conclude that the two are unrelated.[1] Even the punchline discloses the contrivance of the joke, since it indicates that the bartender knew the two were twins. In responding, "oh, nothing, just the O'Malley twins getting drunk again" in lines 50–51, he suggests that their relationship is trivial, general knowledge. Despite its rather transparent subterfuge, the joke works quite well, and it elicits a fair amount of laughter in a context where participants have been claiming they never laugh and withholding laughter to spite the teller as part of the competitive atmosphere.

Talk show hosts

Consider now a second conversational excerpt where two male undergraduate students are telling jokes. I include the preceding riddle joke, which is *not* a narrative joke, for purposes of comparison, but also to give some of the flavor of the context. Since the joke-telling frame is already established in this case as well, no special joke introduction is required. Yet here again the participants take their joking seriously as a kind of competition, and they are extremely concerned that no one should tell an 'old joke'. Thus, Erik responds almost bitterly, "that's right, no laughter, Jacob knew it" in lines 23–25, when Jacob immediately provides the correct answer, "decaffeinated," to his riddle joke. Just before, Jacob had objected to the traditional-sounding introduction, "well there was this" in line 1, before Erik could even properly start what seems to have been a narrative joke. Interestingly, Jacob introduces his own narrative joke about the talk show hosts with essentially this same formula in line 28, but he begins so suddenly that Erik has to ask him to repeat himself.

Two Jokes

 1 Erik: well there i- well there was this-
 2 Jacob: no no no see-
 3   that that's so unoriginal.
 4   what about something else.
 5 Erik: okay, how about ah,
 6   like there's all this new ah
 7   all this supreme court rulings
 8   and pro-choice and all
 9   I've got a pretty a pretty topical joke,
10   pretty uh current joke,

11		pretty important joke for the country to hear.
12	Jacob:	{inaudible: three syllables}
13	Erik:	huh?
14		you want to hear it?
15	Jacob:	do you care?
16	Erik:	no.
17		it was in my speech for sophomore year
18		in high school.
19		I remember it still.
20		what do you call a cow that has had an abortion?
21	Jacob:	decaffeinated.
22	Erik:	decaffeinated,
23		that's right,
24		no laughter,
25		Jacob knew it.
26		that was the only joke I could think of
27		off the top of my head.
28	Jacob:	okay, there was a guy driving down the road.
29	Erik:	a what?
30	Jacob:	there's a *guy* driving his car down the road, okay?
31		he was driving along.
32		and he's driving a nineteen-fifty-seven convertible,
33		T-bird.
34		and he sees uh Jay Leno
35		jogging along the side of the road.
36		and he goes, "I hate talk show hosts."
37		he swerves over and he runs him over,
38		kills him.
39		and he's driving,
40		and he turns a corner,
41		driving down the road a bit.
42		and he sees ah ah Johnny Carson.
43		and he says, "God, I hate talk show hosts."
44		he swerves over and he *kills* him.
45		then he- then he sees the uh his *mini*ster
46		hitchhiking on the side of the road. {tsk}
47		and he stops
48		and he says, "how's it going father,
49		do you need a ride?"

50   he's like "yes, my son, yes,
51   could you take me to the uh church?"
52   and they start driving along
53   he sees Oprah *Win*frey driving along-
54   y'know *jog*ging along on the side of the road.
55   and he goes, "God, I hate talk show hosts,
56   but I've got a minister here,
57   it's kind of risky to swerve over and kill her,
58   y'know?" {tsk}
59   so he goes,
60   "here's what I'll do
61   I'll pretend like I uh I *sneeze*
62   and I'll swerve by mistake."
63   so he is driving along.
64   when she comes up,
65   he sort of *sneez*es,
66   and he swerves over,
67   and he has his eyes closed,
68   and he goes, "Oh, my God,
69   I heard a *thud*.
70   did I *hit* her?"
71   and the minister goes,
72   "no, you missed her,
73   but I got her with the car door."
74   Erik: {laughs}
75   Jacob: I got a laugh.

Joke telling can become a rather competitive enterprise in certain circles, especially within what I described as 'joking relationships' in my monograph *Conversational Joking* (1993a), and as the foregoing passage demonstrates. Jacob not only prevents Erik from telling a joke he characterizes as "so unoriginal" in line 3, based on the first few words, he also knows the answer to Erik's riddle joke (line 21). What is even worse, he induces Erik to laugh at the joke *he* tells — a victory he revels in with the final remark, "I got a laugh."

Still, Jacob has trouble beginning his joke. Somewhat surprisingly, given the competitive nature of their joking session, Jacob includes no standard preface to determine whether Erik knows the joke. Instead, after a simple "okay," he rushes into the introductory sentence so fast that Erik must stop him to request clarification.

Jacob: okay, there was a guy driving down the road.
Erik: a what?
Jacob: there's a *guy* driving his car down the road, okay?

From the way Jacob stresses *guy*, and appends an impatient "okay" to his repeat, he sounds almost peeved at Erik for interrupting his joke. Then just when he seems to be back on track with the phrase "he was driving along" in line 31, Jacob falls into a rambling and superfluous description of the car: "and he's driving a nineteen-fifty-seven convertible, T-bird" (lines 32–33). This digression gives the impression that Jacob is buying time to organize his narrative, as if Erik's interruption truly had confused his telling plans. Jacob pauses briefly before producing "Jay Leno" as the name of the first victim in line 34, but once he recalls the key phrase, "I hate talk show hosts" (line 36), the text picks up speed. One can readily imagine Jacob accessing some skeleton form of the joke narrative with a few verbatim phrases, and fleshing it out as he goes. Especially in the case of a narrative joke segmented into three episodes like this one, parallel phrasing aids memory. Moreover, the recurrent phrasing here recalls the local formulaicity we have described in previous chapters. Parallel phrasing brings with it pitfalls of its own, however, as we see in the third episode, when Jacob describes Oprah Winfrey as driving as opposed to jogging: "he sees Oprah *Win*frey driving along- y'know *jog*ging along on the side of the road" in lines 53–54. The tension between repetition as mechanical reproduction versus repetition as clever variation underlies much joking behavior, and it reflects opposed principles in verbal humor, as I show in my article in the journal *Humor* 6 (1993b).

This joke exhibits classic three part structure, with the appearance of the minister before the third part adding a further complication. The first two episodes serve to establish a pattern which the third episode skews, thereby introducing the frame shift responsible for its humor. In jokes like this, it is the pattern created through repetition which functions as the pivot, rather than any specific verbal unit. Nevertheless, such tripartite jokes typically employ formulas and parallelism to reinforce the patterns, and, as we have observed, Jacob relies heavily upon repetition in his performance. Thus, although it is not a pivot as such, the first half of the final speech by the minister, namely "no, you missed her," slows down the action just before the punch-line proper, "but I got her with the car door." In this way, the teller briefly suspends our expectation that the driver will run down Oprah Winfrey, just as he has run down the first two talk show hosts. Instead, he suddenly holds out the hope that nothing adverse has happened to Oprah in spite of the thump — a possible resolution provided by divine intervention in the form of the minister — only to dash this hope with the now doubly unexpected action of the minister, who not only fails to save Oprah, but in fact contributes to her demise.

Singing telegram

Finally, let us examine a third conversational passage in which one participant alludes to a joke he assumes to be familiar to his audience. When one of his two listeners not only fails to recognize the joke allusion, but then fails to understand the complete joke once he reviews it, the teller resorts to explanations, which, however, seem also to miss the mark. All this results in a confused, repetitive joke performance, reminiscent of the inchoate telling of **Rubber Wallets** in chapter three, where the teller also incorrectly presumed her hearers to be familiar with her story.

The excerpt derives from a series of tapes Marsha recorded at her home over the Thanksgiving holidays. Ralph and Patricia are her parents, while Peter is the significant other of Marsha's sister Amy, who does not appear in this passage at all. Both Amy and Peter have objected to Marsha taping their conversation at various junctures. At the outset of this excerpt Marsha has again drawn Peter's attention to her recording, and elicited a derisive comment from him, because she has just replaced a full tape to insert a fresh one and to begin the recording process anew. This is a fairly typical example of one sort of recording effect described in chapter one. Ralph's decision to repeat the punch-line of a favorite joke represents an opposite sort of recording effect, where those present feel they must perform for the recorder.

Singing telegram

1	Peter:	oh no recording again.
2		how stupid.
3	Ralph:	oh yes,
4		we're going to have a singing telegram:
5		"*Fred* and the *kids* are *dead*."
6		{singing and clapping on stressed words}
7	Peter:	{laughs}
8	Ralph:	you ever hear that joke?
9	Marsha:	no. {laughing}
10	Ralph:	well, it was just one woman wanted a telegram?
11		she always wanted a singing telegram?
12		guy says,
13		"ma'am I don't think you want this

14		as a singing telegram."
15		"yeah, go ahead."
16		*"Fred and the kids are dead."*
17		{singing and clapping on stressed words}
18	Marsha:	{laughs briefly} I didn't get it.
19	Ralph:	you don't *get* it.
20		you don't sing a telegram about *death*
21		or anything bad news.
22	Marsha:	well, I lost the bad news part.
23		I never knew there *was* bad news.
24	Ralph:	Fred and the kids are dead.
25		opens up the telegram,
26		sings,
27		*"Fred* and the *kids* are *dead"* {singing}
28	Patricia:	that's an old *old* joke.
29	Marsha:	oh. {laughs}

Peter laughs at Ralph's joke allusion, but Marsha does not, and this motivates Ralph to ask her if she knows the joke in question. When Marsha denies that she knows the joke, Ralph tries a brief run-though, as though he thinks Marsha will recall the joke if he can offer the appropriate hints. The question intonation on his two introductory statements probably indicates that Ralph still expects Marsha to register recognition of the joke and stop him from retelling the entire text. Ralph's abbreviated version of **Singing telegram** between lines 10 and 16 neither prompts Marsha to recognize the joke, nor does it provide her with enough background information to understand it at line 18. She laughs more embarrassed than amused, and claims that she "didn't get it." Though one might imagine that Marsha intends her claim that she didn't get it as a negative comment on the joke, rather than an honest admission of failure to understand it, her father Ralph clearly does not hear it this way. After all, he proceeds to a serious explanation of the usual conditions surrounding singing telegrams. Moreover, Marsha responds to his explanation by saying she had missed the information that the message constituted bad news. At this point, Ralph carefully speaks rather than performing the punch-line, then produces a final brief version of the joke between lines 24 and 27 with another repetition of the punch-line. Even after all this, Marsha seems still not to understand.

A turn-by-turn analysis of Ralph's attempts to tell the joke may help us understand why Marsha fails to get the joke. Initially, Ralph furnishes only the sung punch-line and the information that it represents a singing telegram.

Actually, his overwrought singing and clapping performance of the telegram text about the death of family members is enough to elicit laughter by itself. In fact, even Peter may be laughing at the performance without knowing the joke. When Marsha does not laugh for whatever reason, Ralph produces the somewhat more complete version outlined below. (I add the "woman says" for clarification here, though Marsha must process the text without it, of course.)

A   one woman always wanted a singing telegram
B   guy says,
      "ma'am I don't think you want this as a singing telegram."
C   (Woman says,) "yeah, go ahead."
D   "*Fred* and the *kids* are *dead*."

Even this version adds precious little information for a hearer unfamiliar with the joke. For one thing, it does not spell out who the "guy" is, and for another, it does not clarify how the telegram message relates to the recipient. The A-clause acts as the orientation for narrative. But at the same time, it functions as the pivot for joking purposes, because it provides the explanation for the singing of the bad news. And this singing of bad news constitutes the clash of frames responsible for bisociation and humor in this joke. The clauses B–C represent the complicating action. They should help bring out the incongruency of the telegram text with the practice of singing telegrams. But Ralph is so eager to get to the punchline that he does not develop this action in sufficient detail for Marsha. Then Ralph has recourse to explaining the incongruency of the telegram in a general way, saying: "you don't sing a telegram about *death* or anything bad news" in lines 20–21. But Marsha can still object that she "lost the bad news part." In a different version of this joke, the sung text runs: "Your sister Rose is dead." This explicit characterization of the family relationship involved would perhaps constitute a better form to explicate the thrust of the joke for Marsha. At least it might clarify the point that the telegram constitutes bad news. As it is, Ralph seems unable to grasp Marsha's difficulty with the joke. In any case, he remains unable to produce any more cogent explanation than another repetition of the punchline, albeit pronounced slowly rather than sung, followed by an even more abbreviated version of the joke in lines 25–27:

A   opens up the telegram,
B   sings, "*Fred* and the *kids* are *dead*" {singing}

This time Ralph omits mention of the woman entirely, and describes only the actions of the *guy*, though even the guy is not explicitly named here. Curiously, Ralph instead supplies the rather superfluous information that someone —

presumably the guy — "opens up the telegram." This addition will certainly not improve Marsha's chances of comprehending the joke.

Once we spell out the information Marsha actually receives, it is hardly surprising that she does not get the joke. But Ralph's ineffectiveness also suggests a couple related points about telling and understanding jokes and narratives. As in the case of the abortive telling of **Rubber Wallets** reviewed in chapter three, when tellers allude to stories they presume familiar to their hearers, they find it hard to reconstruct a satisfactory complete version after the fact. Seen from the opposite point of view, once a hearer fails to recognize a story allusion, no haphazard accumulation of quick summaries and disorganized details seems to help them piece it together. Apparently retelling a story with different sets of clauses and collections of details is no substitute for one careful, complete narrative. This holds all the more true of jokes. As traditional lore on humor has it, if you have to explain jokes, they are no longer funny. By way of gratitude for all his trouble, Ralph's wife Patricia announces what "an old *old* joke" it was to begin with.

Patricia's comment leads us back to the importance of newness in jokes. We have seen that familiar stories may be welcome in conversation, because they offer an opportunity for co-telling. This co-telling, moreover, allows participants to ratify their membership in the group, to check on and corroborate their personal versions of the story, and to engage in high rapport talk, perhaps about pleasant, shared past experiences. But old jokes are simply old jokes. They hold out little possibility of renewed amusement, and they do not invite co-narration. Thus, conversationalists are justly wary of telling familiar jokes, and they have various means at their disposal for insuring that they can avoid telling them.

Literary storytelling in plays

In this section, I hope to demonstrate how the account of conversational narratives developed in this book can shed light on dramatic representations of storytelling. The idea of applying methods and results from the analysis of conversational storytelling to literary narrative is, of course, not original. The progression from conversational storytelling to literary narrative in Fludernik's (1996) so-called natural narratology follows this basic principle. Early on, Burton (1980) applied methods from conversation analysis to drama, using the framework of Labov & Waletzky (1967) to analyze narrative passages. The narratives Burton analyzed from plays by Pinter and Ionesco were not much like conversational stories. By contrast, I have purposely chosen for analysis a narrative passage which seems to thrive on conversational models, namely a humorous story told by the Nurse in Shakespeare's "Romeo & Juliet." I hope to show that Shakespeare explicitly drew on particular conversational characteristics for humor in this passage.

The Nurse's story in Shakespeare's "Romeo & Juliet"

The passage is a story Juliet's nurse relates in Act I, scene ii, just before Lady Capulet speaks to Juliet of an arranged marriage and sends her downstairs to the party where she is expected to interact with the intended future husband Paris.

The Nurse's Story ("Romeo & Juliet" I, ii)

1	Enter LADY CAPULET and Nurse	
2	LADY CAPULET	Nurse, where's my daughter? call her forth to
3		me.
4	Nurse	Now, by my maidenhead, at twelve year old,
5		I bade her come. What, lamb! what, ladybird!
6		God forbid! Where's this girl? What, Juliet!
7	Enter JULIET	
8	JULIET	How now! who calls?
9	Nurse	Your mother.
10	JULIET	Madam, I am here.
11		What is your will?
12	LADY CAPULET	This is the matter: — Nurse, give leave awhile,
13		We must talk in secret: — nurse, come back again;
14		I have remember'd me, thou's hear our counsel.
15		Thou know'st my daughter's of a pretty age.
16	Nurse	Faith, I can tell her age unto an hour.
17	LADY CAPULET	She's not fourteen.
18	Nurse	I'll lay fourteen of my teeth, —
19		And yet, to my teeth be it spoken, I have but
20		four —
21		She is not fourteen. How long is it now
22		To Lammas-tide?
23	LADY CAPULET	A fortnight and odd days.
24	Nurse	Even or odd, of all days in the year,
25		Come Lammas-eve at night shall she be fourteen.
26		Susan and she — God rest all Christian souls! —
27		Were of an age: well, Susan is with God;

28		She was too good for me: but, as I said,
29		On Lammas-eve at night shall she be fourteen;
30		That shall she, marry; I remember it well.
31		'Tis since the earthquake now eleven years;
32		And she was wean'd, — I never shall forget it, —
33		Of all the days of the year, upon that day:
34		For I had then laid wormwood to my dug,
35		Sitting in the sun under the dove-house wall;
36		My lord and you were then at Mantua: —
37		Nay, I do bear a brain: — but, as I said,
38		When it did taste the wormwood on the nipple
39		Of my dug and felt it bitter, pretty fool,
40		To see it tetchy and fall out with the dug!
41		Shake quoth the dove-house: 'twas no need, I
42		trow,
43		To bid me trudge:
44		And since that time it is eleven years;
45		For then she could stand alone; nay, by the
46		rood,
47		She could have run and waddled all about;
48		For even the day before, she broke her brow:
49		And then my husband — God be with his soul!
50		A' was a merry man — took up the child:
51		'Yea,' quoth he, 'dost thou fall upon thy face?
52		Thou wilt fall backward when thou hast more wit;
53		Wilt thou not, Jule?' and, by my holidame,
54		The pretty wretch left crying and said 'Ay.'
55		To see, now, how a jest shall come about!
56		I warrant, an I should live a thousand years,
57		I never should forget it: 'Wilt thou not, Jule?'
58		quoth he;
59		And, pretty fool, it stinted and said 'Ay.'
60	LADY CAPULET	Enough of this; I pray thee, hold thy peace.
61	Nurse	Yes, madam: yet I cannot choose but laugh,
62		To think it should leave crying and say 'Ay.'
63		And yet, I warrant, it had upon its brow
64		A bump as big as a young cockerel's stone;
65		A parlous knock; and it cried bitterly:
66		'Yea,' quoth my husband,'fall'st upon thy face?

67		Thou wilt fall backward when thou comest to age;
68		Wilt thou not, Jule?' it stinted and said 'Ay.'
69	JULIET	And stint thou too, I pray thee, nurse, say I.
70	Nurse	Peace, I have done. God mark thee to his grace!
71		Thou wast the prettiest babe that e'er I nursed:
72		An I might live to see thee married once,
73		I have my wish.

I do not intend to analyze this excerpt in detail, but rather to point out some of the questions it raises in the play and in the Shakespearean canon generally — questions for which sound methods of conversation analysis and suggestive examples from real natural talk offer interesting answers. To this end, then, I will compare the Nurse's story with a genuine conversational anecdote we looked at in chapter two, namely the story I call **Twins**.

First, is the passage from "Romeo & Juliet" really conversational? Would a nurse have told an anecdote like this in late 16th century England? Or is Shakespeare exaggerating for humor? It comes down to the question: Is this a realistic portrait of a funny storyteller or a broad parody of anecdote telling? Certainly repetition helps make the story funny and the nurse laughable, but does the nurse really repeat herself more than a normal conversational anecdote teller? Or is it funny only because everyday conversation comes off as repetitive and disorganized if accurately portrayed on stage? And consequently, how does this telling style serve to characterize the nurse? What is the purpose of all the repetition in the passage, particularly the second telling of the story? Does it make the nurse look ludicrous? Or does it bring out the growing embarrassment of Juliet and her mother at the frank sexual content of the story?

Critical opinion has been divided. On the one hand, Ferguson & Yachnin (1981) simply classify the Nurse as a typical low-comedy character, as did Kreider (1975), who views her garrulousness as interfering with the dispatch of business. Rees (1983) sees an element of parody in the story, but also notes the "splendid garrulity of Juliet's Nurse"(47). On the other hand, Brooke (1968: 92) calls the Nurse's speaking style "something altogether new ... in Shakespeare's output," and Everett (1972: 130) considers the Nurse's story "perhaps Shakespeare's first greatly human verse speech." What we need in order to decide the questions is enough research on anecdotes in everyday conversation to produce and describe a typical example of a conversational anecdote for comparison. The story **Twins** already analyzed in chapter two, transcribed as it is from spontaneous conversation, provides concrete evidence that Shakespeare's rendering of the

Nurse's story is really quite realistic, adhering to patterns still very common these four-hundred years later.

Twins

{Alice and Vivian looking at pictures of (grand)children}

1	Alice:	people have asked us, "are they twins?"
2		not just once.
3		{to Earl} how often have people asked us
4		if they're twins,
5		if our kids are twins.
6	Earl:	well.
7	Alice:	I mean seriously.
8	Earl:	fairly often.
9	Alice:	fairly often.
10	Earl:	more often than I would've imagined.
11		yeah, I consider it such a stupid question.
12		for me it's=
13	Vivian:	=when we moved to Pennsylvania,
14		Delbert and Earl walked to school by some neighbors,
15		and I met that lady one day
16		when we were very new,
17		and she said,
18		"oh, you're the one with the twins."
19		and I said,
20		"oh no,
21		maybe you mean my boys
22		that are a year and a half apart."
23		"oh no, they're twins."
24		{laughing} this lady was telling me,
25		"oh no, they're twins."
26		I said, "I have sons a year and a half apart."
27		"ah, well I think they look like twins."
28		and I could've just throttled that woman=
29	Earl:	=this was like the guy who said to me,
30		when I said Lilly has just turned three-
31		no, *she* said,
32		"oh, you mean four."
33	Vivian:	isn't that charming,
34	Earl:	I said,

35	Vivian:	when somebody tells the parents what-
36	Earl:	"she's my daughter.
37		she's three."
38	Vivian:	I could've just *kicked* that woman.
39		"oh, no, they're twins." {laughing}

In both stories women are recalling past times when their children were young. Both stories arise from and are tied to their immediate context thematically and interactionally. Both tellers laugh at their own stories: The Nurse says at line 61, "Yet I cannot choose but laugh," and she also laughs fulsomely while recounting the story in productions of "Romeo & Juliet"; Vivian laughs at both the initial and the third delivery of her punchline. Both stories are personal anecdotes, by which I mean funny narratives which reveal personal feelings and values. Consequently, both contain much evaluative talk, e.g. the Nurse says, "By my holidame" at line 53; "To see, now, how such a jest shall come about!" (line 55); and "I warrant, and I should live a thousand years,/I never should forget it." (56–57); while Vivian stresses, "This *la*dy was telling *me*" (line 24); "And I could've just throttled that woman" (28); and "I could've just *kicked* that woman" (38).

Finally, both stories contain copious repetition. The Nurse tells her story initially at lines 48–54, and repeats the whole story at lines 66–68. She also repeats the final question-answer sequence at lines 57–59, and the bare punch line at line 62. Labeling the clauses A–E in the first telling, then again where they reappear in the repetitions, reveals how the Nurse varies her story through the three verbalizations. Clearly the dialogue elements D–E constitute the stable center of the story, while the rest provides the variable background and complication.

A	For even the day before, she broke her brow:
B	And then my husband took up the child:
C	'Yea,' quoth he, 'dost thou fall upon thy face?
D	Thou wilt fall backward when thou hast more wit;
	Wilt thou not, Jule?'
E	And the pretty wretch left crying and said 'Ay.'
D	'Wilt thou not, Jule?' quoth he;
E	And, pretty fool, it stinted and said 'Ay.'
E	To think it should leave crying and say 'Ay.'
A	And yet, I warrant, it had upon its brow
	A bump as big as a young cockerel's stone;
	A parlous knock; and it cried bitterly:

C   'Yea,' quoth my husband,'fall'st upon thy face?
D   Thou wilt fall backward when thou comest to age;
     Wilt thou not, Jule?'
E   it stinted and said 'Ay.'

By comparison, Vivian produces her initial story at lines 13–23, then repeats the
punchline with an explanation in lines 24–25, and repeats the punchline a final
time in line 39. In addition, she repeats her evaluative comment from line 28 "I
could've just throttled that woman" again at line 38, changing only the verb
throttled to *kicked*.

As we noted in chapter two, Vivian's **Twins** shows greater stability in
dialogue and evaluation than in the order of narrative elements. And **Twins**
mirrors the Nurse's story in its stable repetition of dialogue surrounded by
variable background and narrative elements. The analysis of clausal repetition in
Twins from chapter two appears below for comparison.

A   when we moved to Pennsylvania, Delbert and Earl walked to school by
     some neighbors,
B   and I met that lady one day when we were very new,
C   and she said, "oh, you're the one with the twins."
D   and I said, "oh no, maybe you mean my boys that are a year and a half
     apart."
E   "oh no, they're twins." {laughing}

E   this lady was telling me, "oh no, they're twins."
D   I said, "I have sons a year and a half apart."
C   "ah, well I think they look like twins."

F   and I could've just throttled that woman=

F   I could've just *kicked* that woman.
E   "oh, no, they're twins." {laughing}

Shakespeare's deft manipulation of repetition with variation highlights the natural
conversational character of the Nurse's speech.

Considering the shorter overall length of **Twins**, the two telling performances have about equal amounts of repetition. Even if the nurse seems laughable due
to the repetition in her telling on stage, comparable repetition can be found in the
rendition of a humorous anecdote by a woman sharing fond memories where
they are topically relevant even today. Nor does this narrative style characterize
the speech of an uneducated servant class, since Vivian counts as a member of

the upper middle class, not just educated, but herself an educator at the second-ary level.

Still, in performance, representations of real conversation sound highly repetitive, poorly planned and, hence, uneducated, so that Shakespeare is characterizing the nurse as lower in class than Juliet and Lady Capulet. However, this distinction bears significance here, because the nurse represents the natural attitude toward sex and marriage by contrast with Lady Capulet's business-like perspective and Juliet's romantic ideal. Notice, moreover, that the Nurse speaks blank verse here and elsewhere with the other women, rather than the prose Shakespeare used for the ruffians in the "Public Place" at the outset of the play and for the simple servant delivering invitations in the immediately preceding scene. The Nurse herself speaks prose with Romeo and Mercutio in the street in II iv 108–232. Thus, in spite of the repetition, Shakespeare renders this narrative performance as a fairly well-organized speech.

Consequently, I feel we can confidently say that this is a realistic portrait of a funny storyteller rather than a broad parody of anecdote telling. Shakespeare wants the Nurse to sound real, down-to-earth vis-à-vis both Lady Capulet and Juliet. Though repetition helps make the story funny and the nurse laughable, I think we laugh about the nature of everyday conversational storytelling, rather than at the nurse personally, who finally does not repeat herself more than a normal conversational anecdote teller. Thus, real conversational evidence in conjunction with the analytical methods developed in the preceding pages clearly support the position of Brooke and Everett that the speech is a realistic portrayal of humorous storytelling as against the contention of Kreider, Ferguson & Yachnin, and Rees that the speech is a parody designed to characterize the Nurse as a low comedy figure.

If accurately portrayed on stage, conversation as such can be funny, because it appears repetitive and disorganized by comparison with normal dramatic prose or blank verse. Harold Pinter and Tom Stoppard have capitalized on this fact repeatedly. Beckett plays on conversational practices in other ways, as I will try to show in the next section. Here I hope to have demonstrated how linguistic analysis of everyday conversation can inform our study of meaning in literary texts, and in particular how the analysis of humorous conversational narrative can enhance our understanding of literary humor.

The Story of the Tailor in Beckett's "Endgame"

Consider now by contrast a narrative passage from Beckett's play "Endgame", namely the story of the tailor told by Nagg. A fresh look at this story in comparison with the narratives analyzed in the preceding pages, and employing the descriptive tools developed in the course of this investigation so far, can shed new light on this difficult passage.

In "Endgame" Nagg and Nell occupy adjacent dust bins, half full of sand, because they "lost their shanks" in an accident riding a tandem bicycle on their honeymoon years ago. Hamm seems to be their son, and Clov in turn seems to be his son, though we know only that they occupy a space together. Nagg tells the story of the tailor during a reminiscence in which Nell recalls her happiness during that honeymoon before the misfortune.

The dialogue in "Endgame" often diverges from everyday talk. Beckett revels in double meanings, vagueness and apparent dead ends. The dripping vein and, of course, vanity are recurrent themes in the play.

The Story of the Tailor

1	HAMM:	Perhaps it's a little vein.
2		(Pause.)
3	NAGG:	What was that he said?
4	NELL:	Perhaps it's a little vein.
5	NAGG:	What does that mean? (Pause.) That means nothing.
6		(Pause.) Will I tell you the story of the tailor?
7	NELL:	No. (Pause.) What for?
8	NAGG:	To cheer you up.
9	NELL:	It's not funny.
10	NAGG:	It always made you laugh. (Pause.) The first time I
11		thought you'd die.
12	NELL:	It was on Lake Como. (Pause.) One April afternoon.
13		(Pause.) Can you believe it?
14	NAGG:	What?
15	NELL:	That we once went out rowing on Lake Como. (Pause.)
16		One April afternoon.
17	NAGG:	We had got engaged the day before.
18	NELL:	Engaged!
19	NAGG:	You were in such fits that we capsized. By rights we
20		should have been drowned.
21	NELL:	It was because I felt happy.
22	NAGG:	(Indignant.) It was not, it was not, it was my STORY
23		and nothing else. Happy! Don't you laugh at it still?
24		Every time I tell it. Happy!
25	NELL:	It was deep, deep. And you could see down to the

26   bottom. So white. So clean.
27   NAGG: Let me tell it again. (Raconteur's voice.) An
28   Englishman, needing a pair of striped trousers in a
29   hurry for the New Year festivities, goes to his
30   tailor who takes his measurements. (Tailor's voice.)
31   "That's the lot, come back in four days, I'll have it
32   ready." Good. Four days later. (Tailor's voice.) "So
33   sorry, come back in a week, I've made a mess of the
34   seat." Good, that's all right, a neat seat can be
35   very ticklish. A week later. (Tailor's voice.)
36   "Frightfully sorry, come back in ten days, I've made
37   a hash of the crotch." Good, can't be helped, a snug
38   crotch is always a teaser. Ten days later. (Tailor's
39   voice.) "Dreadfully sorry, come back in a fortnight,
40   I've made a balls of the fly." Good, at a pinch, a
41   smart fly is a stiff proposition. (Pause. Normal
42   voice.) I never told it worse. (Pause. Gloomy.) I
43   tell this story worse and worse. (Pause. Raconteur's
44   voice.) Well, to make it short, the bluebells are
45   blowing and he ballockses the buttonholes.
46   (Customer's voice.) "God damn you to hell, Sir, no,
47   it's indecent, there are limits! In six days, do you
48   hear me, six days, God made the world. Yes Sir, no
49   less Sir, the WORLD! And you are not bloody well
50   capable of making me a pair of trousers in three
51   months!" (Tailor's voice, scandalized.) "But my dear
52   Sir, my dear Sir, look — (disdainful gesture,
53   disgustedly) — at the world — (pause) — and look —
54   (loving gesture, proudly) — at my TROUSERS!"
55   (Pause. He looks at Nell who has remained impassive,
56   her eyes unseeing. He breaks into a high forced
57   laugh, cuts it short, pokes his head towards Nell,
58   launches his laugh again.)
59   HAMM: Silence!
60   (Nagg starts, cuts short his laugh.)

The story of the tailor in Beckett's "Endgame" has spawned multiple, often contradictory interpretations, especially concerning three questions: (1) Does Nagg perform the joke well or poorly? (2) Who is the butt of the joke? (3)

Based in large measure on the answers to the first two questions, how does the story relate to the play as a whole?

For instance, Cohn (1969:52) asserts that "the joke is at God's expense." Kenner (1969) also sees God as the butt of the joke, calling the story, "a recitation, a vaudeville standby," which is "poorly performed" (1969:59). And Fletcher (1978:87) maintains that "Nagg's public house joke veers off into a full-scale onslaught on the Creator, and ceases to be a funny, if rather crude story." By contrast, Lewis (1989:62) argues that the joke performance is complete and polished, and "shows Nagg and Nell attempting to recapture the spirit of their past relationship"; furthermore, "it condenses Beckett's vision of a world poorly fashioned." In a similar vein, Acheson (1986:189) writes, "the tailor's story destroys the argument from an orderly universe to God's existence." Certainly, the story of the tailor cannot both deny the existence of God and make God its butt at the same time. Indeed, the tailor puts the Englishman down for his naive belief in God, and we laugh with the tailor not at God but at belief in a deity. In the English version of the story cited above, Nagg introduces the joke in a "Raconteur's voice," but it is suggestive that the original French version of the play instructs that Nagg put on an English face — "visage Anglaises" — underscoring the aggression directed at the Englishman as the apparent butt of the joke. Of course, our laughter at the Englishman may fade into existential angst at the realization that we are now left alone to face the messy world.

The joke is, of course, not original with Beckett. Reik in his *Jewish Wit* (1962) gives a version of the story as an example of "antithetical thinking" in Jewish jokes. In Reik's joke text, a Galician engineer instead of an Englishman comes to a Jewish tailor, and the process lasts seven years rather than the three months in Beckett's "Endgame" version. The tailor brings "his customer the trousers and receives the reply, 'God has created the whole world in seven days and you need seven years to make some trousers?' But the tailor gently stroking his work replies, 'Yes, but look at the world and then look at these trousers!'" (207). In spite of the differences between the two versions, the sarcastic put-down is the essence of both Reik's joke and the story of the tailor in "Endgame." The story of the tailor had special significance for Beckett over a long period of time. His "fondness for the joke is shown by the fact that he used it in 1945 also as an epigraph to an essay in French on the painters Bram and Geer van Velde" (Fletcher 1978:97). The story of the tailor is, then, not just an old joke, but a retold joke for Beckett, just as it is for Nagg.

The story thus represents a special type of put-down joke in which one attack, the Englishman's tirade lines 46–51, brings on a witty counter-attack lines

51–54 serving as the punchline of the joke. We may laugh at the chutzpa bordering on hubris displayed by the tailor, but clearly the Englishman receives the counter-attack, and hence must be the butt of the joke. We analyzed a conversational anecdote parallel to this story at the opening of chapter six, namely **Basketball Referee**.

Comparing Nagg's performance with the joke-tellings examined earlier in this chapter, we see how it approaches and diverges from conversational joke telling conventions. Beckett comes very close sometimes to everyday conversation in his plays, in "Endgame" closer than elsewhere in his drama. After all, in telling a joke, Nagg is doing something characteristic of everyday talk. Nagg produces a preface to the story similar in many respects to a joke preface in conversation, and he embeds the preface within a comment reminiscent of the sort of justifications for tellability one might hear in everyday joke telling. Just a few lines earlier Nagg asks Nell, "Are you crying again?": Her unhappiness would give Nagg a natural motivation for telling a story Nell had enjoyed in the past. Then he asks, "Will I tell you the story of the tailor?" at line 6 of our excerpt. The actual form Nagg chooses for his preface with "will I tell you" sounds rather odd,[2] and perhaps serves to set the telling off from the surrounding talk more clearly. Certainly "should I tell you" or "would you like to hear" would be more idiomatic phrases to suggest that he intends the joke to cheer up the crying Nell, as the following dialogue indicates. Since Nagg knows the story is not new to Nell, he does not try to justify its tellability on grounds of newness or topical relevance. Perhaps due to the odd preface, Nell rejects Nagg's offer to tell the story, saying "No. What for?" at line 7. This amounts to a demand for Nagg to justify the story's tellability, to which Nagg responds appropriately, "To cheer you up." Even this justification does not suffice for Nell, who questions the tellability of the story even on the grounds Nagg suggests, saying "It's not funny" at line 9. Nagg accepts her challenge, and argues from past performances that "It always made you laugh," indeed, "The first time I thought you'd die" (lines 10–11). In a real conversational situation, this much rejection and demand for justification would presumably dissuade the most arduous teller from carrying on with a joke. Recall how Erik dissuades his apartment-mate Mark from telling an unoriginal joke in the excerpt **Two Jokes** above.

Yet even the persistent Nagg cannot get the floor to tell his joke before Nell falls into a reminiscence: "It was on Lake Como … One April afternoon" in line 12. Nagg even engages in co-narration at line 17: "We had got engaged the day before," a sign of his sharing the fond memory with Nell. He had told Nell the story of the tailor that day, and Nell had laughed voluminously. At line 19, Nagg says, "You were in such fits that we capsized," still attempting to justify telling the story because it will make Nell laugh. Nell, however, counters that it was only "because I felt happy." With Nell in a reverie, Nagg finally begins his tale at line 27, though no one seems to be listening. Consequently, when Nagg has finished, no one laughs. Finally, to fill the glaring gap, Nagg breaks into a laugh himself. Even though Nagg produces the laughter expected at the end of the joke, his laughter is "cut short" by Hamm's command, "Silence!" at line 59. Of course, the word "silence" works not only as an imperative directed at Nagg, it also identifies the failure of this story to elicit laughter.

We miss Nell's involvement not only at the end of the story, but also during the telling. In a real conversational context, we would generally expect to hear interruptive laughter and comments from listeners, especially since Nagg enlivens his performance with dramatic voice switches, and he interlards his joke text with bawdy innuendo in phrases like "a snug crutch is always a teaser" in lines 37–38, and "a smart fly is a stiff proposition" in lines 40–41. Nagg further juxtaposes such phrasing with elegant variation, alliteration and rhyme. He also clearly marks his story into sections with the introductory phrase, "An Englishman, needing a pair of striped trousers" in lines 27–28, with switches from the raconteur's voice to those of the Englishman and tailor and back, and with repetitions of "good," formulas specifying time intervals like "ten days later," and wording within each segment. The phrase, "Well, to make it short" in line 44 in the raconteur's voice indicates that Nagg could choose to lengthen the tale by having the Englishman return more times and having the tailor botch the trousers in more ways; the fact that he opts for the shorter version shows that Nagg is in control of the telling despite his coy claims to the contrary. The absence of any involvement by the impassive Nell leaves spaces for Nagg to comment on his own performance with leading comments like, "I never told it worse" in line 42. Based on our analyses in the previous pages, we must view these comments as attempts to involve Nell actively in the performance, rather than Nagg's honest assessment of how well he is telling the story. Hence, neither Nell's silence nor Nagg's negative comments constitute grounds for considering the performance of the story poor. The highly poetic text of the joke is all the more noticeable for occurring in a play surrounded by language which comes as close as anything Beckett has written to everyday talk with its non-sequiturs, repetitions and misunderstandings. Hence Nagg's claim that "I tell this story worse and worse" in lines 42–43 serves only to highlight its careful construction.

In conclusion, we have seen that the careful construction and high poeticity of the story of the tailor set it off from the surrounding more colloquial talk. Clearly the performance must count as artful. The narrative has a classic put-down structure, in which the tailor betters the Englishman with witty repartee. To see God as the butt of the joke, as Lewis and others do, misses the richness of the story: We laugh at the tailor for his incompetence and his hubris; we laugh at the Englishman for putting up with the tailor, but also for his naive belief in a "creator" which renders him the helpless victim of the tailor's wonderfully profane counter-attack; and we laugh through our tears at the existential human condition which leaves us with no defense against inexorable fate besides our petty, if beloved, trousers and stories.

Conclusions

This chapter as a whole extends the categories and methods developed in the foregoing pages to the telling of narrative jokes in conversation, then to humorous stories in drama.

We found that jokes observe special conditions on tellability, and that they require special prefaces because of the high premium placed on newness. Jokes are not conducive to co-telling like many other types of stories we considered. Instead, joke-telling is often a competitive enterprise, albeit one with a payoff in enhanced rapport. We observed how joke structure intertwines with narrative structure to yield a story with a final humorous twist. Aside from particular wording for some pivotal element in the build-up and the often necessarily verbatim production of the punchline, the narrative structure of jokes can be fairly loose. We examined both successful and unsuccessful narrative joke performances in order to better understand narrative processes generally. When allusions to stories presumed familiar fail to secure understanding, tellers are often at a loss to produce a satisfactory version after the fact, and listeners seem unable to piece together a coherent narrative from ad hoc summaries and accumulated details. Allusions to jokes presumed familiar seem particularly susceptible to this liability.

We further saw how the analyses developed for conversational storytelling can shed light on narrative passages in drama. Based on what we have discovered about personal anecdotes and jokes in conversation, we investigated two humorous stories from plays: the Nurse's story from Shakespeare's "Romeo & Juliet" and the story of the tailor from Beckett's "Endgame." The Nurse's story appears to represent a fair portrayal of conversational storytelling practices rather than a parody of a low-class teller. Comparison with the parallel story **Twins** from my own corpus showed the two tellers utilizing the same strategies of repetition and variation. In both cases, we found nearly verbatim repetition of dialogue at the center of the story with variable evaluation, background and narrative clauses ranged around it. Shakespeare's skilled orchestration of repetition and variation underscores the natural conversational character of the Nurse's speech.

Finally, we determined that the story of the tailor from Beckett's "Endgame" belongs to the genre of put-down stories, and that the Englishman thus represents the butt of the joke. Our foregoing investigations of tellability, prefaces and responses in the negotiation of conversational narratives provided a background and methods for the description of the dialogue surrounding the story of the tailor in the context of the play. Comparison of the story with transcriptions of jokes from real conversation indicate that the performance must count as highly poetic and successful.

Thus, results from our foregoing description of conversational data suggest approaches to the classification and interpretation of narratives in literary texts. The extension of analytic procedures developed in the preceding chapters yields cogent answers to questions about the evaluation of narrative passages in drama. At the same time, this productive application of our methods to jokes and literary narratives demonstrates the broader significance of results obtained from the investigation of a broad range of conversational narrative data.

CHAPTER 8

Conclusions and Perspectives

I find all the world in the same story.
H. Brooke "Fool of Quality" I

In this chapter I would like to gather together the recurrent themes of this book and spell out their consequences, paying special attention to areas for future research in discourse analysis and narrative theory.

I first became interested in storytelling during my exploration of conversational humor. My investigation of jokes showed tellers delivering dialogue and punchlines surely and flawlessly, though they frequently hesitate and correct themselves in their introductions and build-ups. Apparently, tellers remember some portion of a joke verbatim and piece the rest together observing certain narrative strategies. Repetition and formulaic phrasing often serve to organize joke texts into convenient chunks. Personal anecdotes display similar features of composition, although they develop through telling over time, while jokes are heard from other tellers and repeated. Anecdotes, too, are organized around dialogue, with evaluative comments at strategic points. I naturally looked for these same traits in conversational storytelling generally — and I found them abundantly.

Yet my survey of research on storytelling turned up precious little about teller strategies. Instead, temporal sequence was elevated to the principal organizational property of narrative. Taking a sequence of narrative clauses as the form underlying any concrete narrative performance discounted the features I had found to be salient. In the integrated approach developed here, I view constitution of a basic narrative and isolation of a sequence of narrative elements describing the main action only as initial steps in analysis. The sequentiality represented in what I call the basic narrative reflects the coherent form a listener might construct from a diffuse, polyphonic conversational performance to serve as the basis for determining causality and forming an evaluation of the events described.

The next step in the analytic process required micro-analysis of the storytelling performance and its integration into turn-by-turn talk. Here Conversation

Analysis provided appropriate tools, though it viewed each storytelling performance as *sui generis*. This point of view would frustrate the search for any
underlying structure and render irrelevant the question of what tellers remember
versus what they reconstruct. Nevertheless, I clung to the goal of describing
conversational storytelling performances in such a manner as to reveal the
structures behind teller strategies and listener comprehension. Chafe's work on
discourse and consciousness and Tannen's research on the poetics of talk
convinced me that such structures were identifiable through careful investigation
of real conversational data.

While I sought to extend the framework proposed by Labov & Waletzky, I
ultimately rejected methods which pull stories apart or summarize them in favor
of an analysis which reflects the listener's task of reconstructing a coherent
narrative from the conversational performance. Such a reconstruction could serve
as the basis for remembering and later re-verbalization. I utilized the notions of
schematization and chunking from Bartlett (1932) and Miller (1956) along with
current frame theory to help describe strategies for recalling and verbalizing
stories. These include both relations between narrative units and macro-structures
for stories themselves. Repetition and formulaicity can signal openings, transitions and closings, as well as providing the principal image for developing a
narrative. A unit repeated at crucial points in a story can acquire local formulaic
resonance within the current performance. All these sorts of formulaicity have
obvious consequences for the organization, recall and later verbalization of stories.

Retellings provide a special perspective on conversational storytelling,
because they highlight the distinctions between a basic story and those aspects of
the narration tied immediately to the local context. I proposed several methodological tools for the analysis and comparison of successive tellings of a single
story in conversation. Immediate retellings provided natural evidence for
claiming that the two performances count as versions of a single story in the
conversational context. Comparison of two renditions of a story in separate
contexts revealed the range of permutations and paraphrases a teller may produce
to match the story with diverse topics and audience responses. Despite the
contextual differences between separate versions of the stories analyzed, the
similarity of the parallel clauses identified was quite substantial. Although one
can extract a primary sequence of narrative clauses in separate tellings of a story,
the closest similarities in phrasing often appear among the non-narrative clauses
of evaluation and background information, as well as in dialogue. The virtual
identity of certain phrases from one telling to the next suggests significant nearly
verbatim recall of whole chunks or a consistent use of specific narrative techniques at crucial points in a story. Clearly, frequent retelling leads some tellers

to crystalize and recycle stories as fairly complete units, sometimes with moveable sub-sections, tailoring them just as much as necessary to fit the current context.

My interest in remembering and verbalization in narrative performance led me to consider stories already familiar to the teller and listeners. These twice-told tales offer a further window on conversational storytelling. I argued that familiar stories are tellable under different circumstances than original stories. The tellability of familiar stories depends not on their newsworthy content, but on the dynamics of the narrative event itself, since familiar story content offers the opportunity for co-narration. Co-narration throws into relief the negotiated character of conversational storytelling, and it illustrates how narration balances memory and context to generate a coherent, understandable performance. Retelling serves an informing function even when the story is known to the participants, it helps coalesce group perspectives and values, and it augments rapport in multiple ways.

My investigation of storytelling contexts showed how conversationalists can manipulate topical talk and stories in progress to segue into stories of their own. Tellers employ prefaces and abstracts for their stories in order to gain the floor and to signal what sort of response is expected. Prefaces need not establish tellability qua originality or even topical relevance, if they only announce a story of current interest or a familiar story offering the possibility of co-narration. Thus, examination of storytelling in real conversational contexts revealed conditions on tellability different from those postulated in research based on elicited stories. Consideration of response stories provided another approach to conversational storytelling practices. I showed how they can be painstakingly fitted to the foregoing story, and how they co-determine how the foregoing story is interpreted.

In order to expand the corpus of conversational storytelling types, as well as to test and delimit my description of teller and listener strategies, I analyzed a wide range of narrative passages from naturally occurring conversation, particularly types which have received little or no attention in the study of narrative so far. The focus on temporal sequencing and narrative clauses in much narrative research have tended to narrow the data base by excluding collaborative stories as well as unsuccessful or incomplete stories, and marginal, narrative-like exchanges. The materials I analyzed exemplify many different interpersonal functions of storytelling in conversation such as conveying interpersonal information and values, aligning and re-aligning group members, demonstrating parallel experiences, enhancing rapport, and entertaining listeners. Conversationalists may employ storytelling for argumentation or to illustrate a point, and they tell third-person stories to inform one another of events and to express their feelings about them. Narrative-like accounts of recurrent experiences share personal experiences in similar ways. Narrative-like collaborative fantasies illustrate the negotiation of story line and perspective particularly clearly, since they do not depend on remembered events; and diffuse stories substantiate the idea that listeners can reconstruct a coherent narrative from bits and pieces of conversation.

Stories and narrative-like sequences emerge from and recede back into turn-by-turn talk, making it hard to determine the boundaries. Participants may collaborate in producing a story, making it hard to identify the teller or even the primary teller. Nevertheless, participants distill a coherent story from the talk, and this accounts for their appropriate responses — sometimes with parallel stories of their own. Conversely, listeners can recognize and comment on incompleteness and incoherence in stories as well. Problematic and marginal narrative passages provide a testing ground for the analytic methods proposed, but they also show listeners responding in ways which elucidate the data.

Finally, I extended the categories and methods developed to the telling of narrative jokes in conversation and to humorous stories in drama. Jokes observe special conditions on tellability, and they require special prefaces because of the high premium placed on newness and the competitive character of joking. Joke structure interacts with narrative structure to yield a story with a final humorous twist. I examined both successful and unsuccessful narrative joke performances in order to illustrate particular narrative processes. I then applied analyses developed for conversational storytelling to humorous stories from plays: the Nurse's story from Shakespeare's "Romeo & Juliet" and the story of the tailor from Beckett's "Endgame." Comparison of the Nurse's story with a parallel example from my own corpus showed the two tellers utilizing parallel strategies of verbalization, including nearly verbatim repetition of dialogue at the center of the story with variable evaluation, background and narrative elements. My preceding investigations of put-down stories and joke-telling practices provided a background and methods for the description of the story of the tailor from Beckett's "Endgame." Findings and methods from my foregoing investigations of conversational storytelling produced cogent analyses of the literary texts.

These conclusions suggest several directions for future research on conversational storytelling. For instance, I have said little about the frequency of past retellings and the proximity of the most recent retelling. Certainly, rehearsing a story helps stabilize its linguistic form, as Bartlett showed for written narratives, and recent practice must facilitate verbatim repetition, parallel structuring and close paraphrase. What is the effect of frequent retelling on personal stories versus canned narrative jokes and other third person narratives? What is the significance of the time between the experience and the telling? Do certain telling strategies loom larger in telling stories from the distant past? Or does the salience of the events reported count more? Would we, for example, find more consistency in retellings of a recent event than in an event of central importance to the teller from the distant past? These questions could be answered through appropriate empirical experiments in controlled situations. One could imagine a quantitative analysis measuring proportion scores for shared content across retellings. One could distinguish categories of content such as background, complicating action, dialogue and evaluation, then compare stability of common content for pairs of tellings. Samples could reflect different periods of time between tellings. And the sampling might contrast personal narratives with third-person stories as well. Such a quantitative analysis on a large corpus of tellings and retellings could prove extremely valuable. It could open new avenues of research, for instance on individual differences in telling strategies.

Other topics could be investigated based on conversational data already recorded and transcribed. I argued that storytelling goes beyond the recapitulation of past experience, allowing tellers to revisit and re-evaluate past experience. Indeed, narration may even put the teller back in touch with specific names or details assumed forgotten. I have not systematically investigated data relevant to this claim, but such a study would be well worth undertaking. One might collect passages from stories where tellers search for names and details or suddenly remember them. Thus, in the passage below, a teller explicitly declares his inability to remember a first name, but then supplies the missing name once he recalls it without any further comment.

> a very interesting thing in my experience.
> Sander was her name.
> I can't even remember her first name.
> and and she was out with us.
> there were three or four guys and her
> Julie Sander.
> we can't have been much older than thirteen, fourteen.

Again in the next excerpt, a second teller laments forgetting one name, but explains his remembering another because of the significance of the person in his memory. Of course, the name of the person can bear no particular importance to the audience except as a convenient label.

> and I don't even remember
> what the third person's name was,

> but the second person-
> I remember her name was Kate,
> because I sat all through freshman bio right behind her,
> and, y'know tried to catch her attention,

One might also investigate sequences where tellers experience difficulties in recovering details from memory. Passages like the following are instructive in this regard, since the teller himself reports the shakiness of his memory with "I think it was third base."

> and uh, I was playing soft ball.
> I used to play sixteen inch softball.
> and I had my uh finger run over sliding-
> which I think it was third base,
> and I broke the finger.

Again, the particular base the teller was sliding into plays no special informational role in the story. In fact, just where and how the teller broke his finger is irrelevant to the audience of this story as well. Nevertheless, the teller seems to feel the need to anchor his story with concrete remembrances from the past, and details create a feeling of immediacy in the storytelling performance.

Investigating data of these sorts could lead to a more complete account of memory in verbalization. The significance of names and details in remembering and verbalizing stories represents just one further direction for future research in conversational narrative.

Appendix

Appendix 1

Popsicle from Chafe (1998), discussed in chapter one.
Setting
1	(A)	and then another day,
2	(A)	… it was really hot it was in the summer and,
3	(A)	… my room was small.
4	(A)	It was like
5	(A)	… nine by twelve or something
6	(A)	it seemed spacious at the time.
7	(A)	… I came home,
8	(A)	I was really exhausted.
9	(A)	I was eating a popsicle [laugh].
10	(B)	[laugh]
11	(A)	… I was sitting there in my chair,
12	(A)	… just eating my popsicle and
13	(B)	[laugh]
14	(A)	… just looked.
15	(A)	… I mean my whole back door-.. wall was gla=ss. Complication
16	(A)	… [high] I noticed there was a gu-y-
17	(A)	… Who walked by.
18	(A)	… And no one ever walked by back there,
19	(A)	it was only a bamboo grove youknow
20	(A)	… And so I thought
21	(A)	… hm that's.. strange [laugh] you know,
22	(A)	someone must be lo=st.
23	(A)	… And so like-
24	(A)	when I got [laugh] done with my popsicle
25	(B)	[laugh]

26 (A)   ... [low] which was like five minutes later,
27 (A)   I went over to throw the stick away [laugh].
28 (A)   And the wastebasket was over by the back.. windows.
29 (B)   [laugh]
Climax 1
30 (A)   ... [high] And outside my window 1 [laugh],
31 (B)   (laugh]
32 (A)   and.. and crou=ched,
33 (A)   ... on the si=de,
34 (A)   was the same guy,
35 (A)   doing something weird with his pants [laugh].
36 (B)   [laugh]
37 (A)   Oh=,
38 (B)   [laugh]
39 (A)   oh=,
40 (A)   ... gosh,
41 (B)   [laugh]

Appendix 2

Two versions of the fairy tale "The three little pigs" related by two separate tellers, as discussed in chapter one.

Three Little Pigs 1

I am going to tell the story
of the three little pigs now.
okay.
once upon a time there lived a mother
with her three little pigs.
one day she said to them,
you are all big boys now
and you need to go out and live your lives
and build homes of your own
and take care of yourselves.
so they all three go out
and the first one decides to build his house of straw
and so he buys some straw from this farmer
an- and starts building

and he is done really soon
and he starts dancing and hopping around.
the second one decides to build his house out of sticks.
so he buys some sticks,
he starts gathering sticks
and then he builds his house,
and then, since it didn't take very long
since it was only sticks,
he starts playing his fiddle
or something like that.
And then the third one though was like pretty smart
as far as pigs go,
and he decided to build his house of bricks,
so he bought some bricks
and he worked really hard
and while he was working
his two brothers said,
hey why are you working so hard
I mean it's just a house.
and he said, well,
I got to work hard,
this is what I want to do.
so he kept working
and finally he was done.
and that night
the big bad wolf came to call
on the little pig in the straw house
and said
"little pig, little pig let me come in."
and the little pig in the straw house said,
"not by the hairs of my chinny chin chin."
And the wolf said,
"then I'll huff and I'll puff and I'll blow your house down."
And so he does that
and since it's made of straw
he is able to do that
and he eats the pig.
He goes to the next one,
the next night.

"little pig, little pig let me come in."
"not by the hair on my chinny chin chin."
so the second pig in the straw h-
eh in the stick house-
sorry- uhm says
is is sitting there
and he says,
"then I'll huff and I'll puff and I'll blow your house down."
and so he huffs and he puffs
and he blows his house down.
and basically that pig gets eaten too.
then then the third pig
the next night
the wolf decides he is hungry again
and so he goes to the third pig's house,
and he says,
"little pig, little pig let me come in."
and the little pig
in the third house
who is smart says,
"not by the hair on my chinny chin chin."
and the wolf says,
"then I'll huff and I'll puff and I'll blow your house down."
so he huffs and he puffs
and he tries to blow the house down,
but he can't,
so he tries again.
"Then I'll huff and I'll puff and I'll blow your house down."
but he can't do it
because the house is made of brick
instead of straw or sticks.
and he is determined
and so he tries to come in the chimney,
but the pig in the brick house hears him
and he sets a boiling pot of water-
a water pot-
a pot with boiling water on the stove,
and when the wolf decides to come through the chimney
he falls down through the chimney

and into the boiling pot of water.
and the little pig eats wolf stew for supper.
and so that's a happy end too,
the end.

Three Little Pigs 2
one day the ma pig
said to the three little pigs
that they should go out and build homes of their own.
the first little pig found a pile of straw
and he built his house out of straw.
the second little pig found some sticks
and he built his house out of sticks.
the third little pig got some bricks from a mason
and built his out of bricks.
the very next day the wolf came
and knocked on the pig-who-built-his-house-with-stick's door.
"little pig, little pig let me come in," he said.
the little pig said,
"not by the hair of my chinny chin chin."
then the wolf said,
"so I'll huff and I'll puff and I'll blow your house down."
and he huffed and he puffed
and he smashed the house
and he ate the pig.
the next day he went to the second pig's house.
the second pig
he built his house out of sticks.
the wolf said,
"Little pig, little pig let me in."
and the pig said,
"not by the hair of my chinny chin chin."
the wolf said,
"so I'll huff and I'll puff and I'll blow your house down."
so he blew
and he smashed it down
and he ate that pig.
now the pig who built his house out of bricks was smarter
the wolf said,

"little pig, little pig let me come in."
and the pig said,
"not by the hair on my chinny chin chin."
so the wolf tried to blow it down
but he couldn't because it was ouf out of bricks
so the wolf said "I have an idea.
I know this great place where you can get turnips."
there is a great garden where you can get turnips,
I'll meet you there at nine o'clock.
the wolf wanted to meet the pig at the turnip place-
at the turnip patch at nine o'clock
but the pig in the brick house
who was smarter
said ahm said okay.
but the next- but the next day
he went there at eight o'clock,
picked all the turnips
and came home
and when the wolf came to call,
the pig told him,
"I've already been to the turnip patch
and gotten all the turnips I need."
so the wolf said there's a great apple tree that he knew
and he told the pig where it was
and he said to meet him there at eight.
and the pig was smarter,
the next day he went to the apple tree,
got all the apples at seven o'clock
and then came back.
and when the wolf said come on,
let's go to the apple tree,
the pig was already inside the house
and said,
"I already got the apples at seven o'clock."
and the next day
the wolf said there's a fair
and we need to go to the fair
and the wolf said,
"I'll go to the fair at six o'clock."

and the pig was smarter and went at five o'clock
but the wolf knew the pig was going to come earlier
so the wolf came earlier too.
so the pig hid in a butter-churn.
and the pig got inside the butter-churn
and suddenly started rolling all the way down a big hill
an- all the way down,
it kept rolling and rolling
till he hit his front door
and he went in his brick house very fast
and the wolf came
and the wolf said,
now I have a better plan.
and he wanted to go down the chimney
but the pig heard him
and he put a fire under the chimney
in the fire-place,
and when the wolf came down the chimney
he got burned and then he was dead.
the end.

Appendix 3

Bakery

A series of connected stories told by two young women about a bakery where they have both worked part-time in the past. The formulaic story openers are cited in chapter three, and the final story **Change**, beginning at line 253, is analyzed in chapter four.

Bakery

Brianne:	does Sheila still work there?
Addie:	yeah,
	this is the latest thing.
	this just happened today.
Brianne:	uh-huh.
Addie:	um, Sheila was sick,
	um, last night.
Brianne:	uh-huh.

Addie: she was really *sick*.
             she didn't even have Thanksgiving dinner.
Brianne: {compassionate sigh}
Addie: she was *that* sick.
             she's- like, I don't know,
             some kind of stomach flu thing.
Brianne: oh, dear.
Addie: and, um, {tsk}
             so anyway, she had to work today.
             and obviously she wasn't feeling too hot
             [this morning].
Brianne: [no.]
             I don't suppose.
Addie: so, y'know?
             so, um, she didn't go,
             and I don't know,
             if she called in
             or had my mom call in or something.
             I think my mom called in and said she was sick.
Brianne: uh-huh.
Addie: so anyway.
             you know my mom and I went to Monroe today.
Brianne: uh-huh.
Addie: and anyway, so-
             Keith swore that it was Sheila in the car.
             now Sheila heard all this through Alison.
             because Alison, I guess, worked today.
             and, um, sh-
             he swore that it was her riding in the car. {laughs}
Brianne: {laughing} no way.
Addie: and I guess he said to Alison,
             cause Alison, um,
             he asked her, Alison,
             if she could stay a little later
             and she said "No,
             because I have to go to Monroe to get some things,
             y'know I have to run some errands."
             and he thought that it was a scam
             that Sheila was going with them.

Brianne:	oh, no.
Addie:	and that's why Sheila didn't come in to work.
Brianne:	oh, no.
Addie:	and so he said, y'know,
	"I- If I find out that-
	that you and Sheila were in Monroe
	you *both* are going to be fired" {laughs}
Brianne:	"yeah, sure,
	go ahead and fire them, y'know,
	then you could just work that much more, Keith,
	y'know, you want to work forty hours a day,
	don't you?"
Addie:	{laughing} and so I guess, Sheila,
	[Sheila was so mad]
Brianne:	[oh, man.]
	not to trust your employees at all.
Addie:	yeah.
	Shiela said that one time when Alison was sick,
	um, they called her house
	like six times during the course of the day
	check- to try to check up on her and see.
	and finally her s- older sister was so frustrated
	she just yelled down
	"*look*, she's *sick*
	and she's in *bed*,
	what do you want?"
Brianne:	oh my *God*.
Addie:	Sheila was laughing.
	she was like,
	she was so *mad*,
	she was like
	"I just want to go down there,
	like, sure Keith, I'll work." {both women laughing}
	and I just want to be handing a customer a plate
	with a doughnut,
Brianne:	*yes*. {laughing}
Addie:	and *throw up*.
	and then say
	"oh, excuse me, sir,

| | let me get you another one. {laughing} |
| Brianne: | {laughing} that would be great. |

{Addie leaves to let the dog in, then returns}

Brianne:	oh, jeez.
Addie:	and she's like
	"if he does that to me one more time
	I'm going to *dump* a pan of *dough*nuts on his head." {laughing}
Brianne:	{laugh} isn't that awful?
Addie:	yeah.
Brianne:	not to even trust her,
	I mean, how often does Sheila call [in sick?]
Addie:	[oh, like] never.
Brianne:	this is probably like [the first *time*.]
Addie:	[the second time] maybe.
	yeah.
Brianne:	second time.
	oh, jeez.
Addie:	so then they called her tonight.
	and uh asked her to work tomorrow.
	and she said yes
	but she still doesn't feel so well.
	she was *so* upset.
	she was so *mad*.
Brianne:	I mean-
Addie:	but y'know she wasn't scheduled.
	they just called her up
	and asked her to work tomorrow morning.
Brianne:	how often does she work now?
Addie:	oh, I don't really know for sure.
	I guess she works weekends pretty much.
	and she has gone in a few times before school
	at five thirty [in the morning.]
Brianne:	[no way.]
Addie:	yeah.
Brianne:	she *has*n't.
Addie:	yeah.
Brianne:	oh, God.
Addie:	yep.
Brianne:	oh man.

	first of all,
	if I were running a *store*
	that sold *food*
	and my em[ployee called in]
Addie:	[yeah.]
Brianne:	and said she was *sick*,
	I would have to trust her.
	and I would not want her [to come back.]
Addie:	[right.]
Brianne:	especially not before her next scheduled time.
	I'd want *her* to decide, y'know?
	I mean I don't want her hanging around my *food*
	if she's *sick*.
	what kind of a health [standard is that?]
Addie:	[they're so] goofy.
Brianne:	oh, man.
Addie:	she- okay.
	there was this lady,
Brianne:	isn't that awful?
Addie:	yeah.
Brianne:	oh, my God.
Addie:	{laughing} there is this other story too.
	this is a good one.
Brianne:	oh.
Addie:	um, some lady named Judy or something like that,
Brianne:	Mom told me there was a Judy that worked there.
Addie:	yeah.
	that *worked*.
	{laughing} I like it.
Brianne:	for a while. {laughing}
Addie:	yeah.
	but um she-
	okay, apparently.
	what was it,
	something like she had a hair appointment?
Brianne:	uh-huh.
Addie:	I don't know the whole story.
	but, I don't know,
	she- she was late for work or something like this

or she had told them in advance
that she had this appointment
and that she wasn't going to be in on time.
or I don't know.
but anyway,
the deal was
that Astrid did not let her forget it for two weeks.
she- she went around the store bitching about it.
"yeah she had a hair appointment,
I bet"
or something like
"oh-" y'know, "maybe I should get *my* hair done today"
or some snotty [thing like that.]

Brianne: [oh, my God.]
          oh, jeeze.
Addie: and Shiela's like,
          y'know, she's like
          "I don't even *want* to be sick,
          because I don't want to hear them *bitch* about it
          for two weeks afterwards" y'know? {laughing}
Brianne: oh, no.
          oh, isn't that [awful?]
Addie: [oh, well.]
Brianne: so, y'know,
          some things never change. {laughing}
Addie: no, apparently not.
          they're never going to [change.]
Brianne: [never.]
          she's crazy.
Addie: everybody's going to keep quitting.
          that Lauri girl quit a *long* time ago
          Shiela said.
Brianne: and Judy's quit too by now.
Addie: Judy, yeah.
Brianne: and Cindy tried it there
Addie: yeah.
Brianne: *two* different times.
          and left the second time too.
Addie: um-hm.

Brianne: {lauging} oh god, it's crazy.
Addie: it'll never get any better.
           it's always going to be like that. {laughs}
Brianne: man.
Addie: she's just a case and a half.
Brianne: oh, god. {laughing}
Addie: now someone heard that her and Keith-
           they were on the rocks with their marriage. {laughing}
Brianne: oh man, I bet they are.
Addie: well they were before
           but I mean I've never seen them really getting along.
           they were never um-hm.
Brianne: yeah, well.
Addie: and after this- this bakery bit here.
           I mean, they have not gotten any better.
           and now they have to spend more time together.
Brianne: um-hm.
Addie: I mean Keith has to work out in the *front* now.
Brianne: Keith? {lauging}
Addie: Keith. {lauging}
           he has to work out in the *front*.
Brianne: really?
Addie: yes because.
           I was-
           oh god, Mom and Grandma,
           we went shopping the other day
           and they're like "come on"
Brianne: Grandma Kerry?
Addie: {laughing} no, no.
           Grandma Helen. {laughing}
Brianne: {laughs} yeah.
Addie: Grandma Helen and Mom and I went shopping.
           and then we had *snacks* there {giggling}.
           it was the first time I'd been back.
Brianne: was *she* there?
Addie: she was there
           and he was there.
Brianne: did she say hi to you
           [or anything like that?]

Addie: [no, I kind of] avoided her
              and she didn't see me.
              but *he* was there, serv-
              Keith was serving.
Brianne: did they ask you for change? {laughing}
Addie: I don't know.
              Mom paid.
              I'm sure they did.
              they still do it.
              they do it.
Brianne: it- it was *so* funny in your letter.
              I was cracking up *so* hard.
              Manuela was like "what's so funny?"
              I'm like, "I can't even tell you
              because you won't even think it's funny but,"
Addie: wh- which one was it?
              when I told you about Mom and the *change*?
Brianne: yeah {laughs}.
Addie: she gave her a five dollar bill.
              [and-]
Brianne: [and she] promptly freaked.
Addie: and she freaked out
              because she didn't have enough change to give her.
              Mom gave her the five,
              "and the *change*?
              to go *with* this?
              [that's an awful lot of change to give *back*.]
Brianne: [she didn't have enough *ones* or whatever.]
              oh my God.
Addie: oh they're terrible.
Brianne: I know.
Addie: oh aren't they *aw*ful?
Brianne: of all the things she freaks out about,
Addie: I know.
Brianne: and she doesn't freak out about that.
Addie: oh, {laughs}.
Brianne: that's just the worst.

Notes

Chapter 1

1. The relevant section from the first story is reproduced in *Appendix 1*.

2. Two transcribed versions of "The three little pigs" are included in *Appendix 2* for purposes of comparison.

3. A set of transcriptions, including all the stories and jokes cited in the text, along with a growing number of related examples can be found at my website: http://www.uni-saarland.de/fak4/norrick

Chapter 2

1. Relevant sources on the alternation between the past tense and the (historical) present tense in conversational narrative in English are Wolfson (1982), Schiffrin (1981), Johnstone (1987), Fleischmann (1990) and Chafe (1994). A general consensus exists that the tenses themselves have no specific meaning; it is rather the switch between them that partitions one narrated event from the other. This switch may also be bound up with evaluation according to Schiffrin. And in particular, the alternation between *said* and *say* in reconstructed dialogue can reflect the relative status of the teller and the figure whose speech is recreated according to Johnstone.

Chapter 4

1. Tannen (1978) also discusses an unsatisfactory narrative performance "Fainting on the subway." She cites the example by way of showing how frames for narrative forms may differ among conversational participants. Expectations about what constitutes a tellable story prompt auditors to question the teller about the point of the story. In parallel fashion, Polanyi (1979) uses Tannen's "Fainting on the subway" to illustrate reactions to a perception that conditions on tellability have been violated. The passage below represents another unsuccessful narrative performance, but here the problem stems from an unwarranted presupposition that the story is familiar to the listeners. The unsuccessful joke performance **Singing Telegram** in chapter six similarly suffers from an unfulfilled presupposition of familiarity.

Chapter 7

1. In particular, the inference follows from Grice's so-called *Maxim of Quantity* (Grice 1975). According to this maxim, one should say as much as is necessary for the present purpose of talk, so that use of the indefinite article *a* and the indefinite *another* invites the generalized conversational implicature that the speaker can give no more precise information about the two Irishmen.

2. Other versions of "Endgame" contain an editorial change from *will* to *shall* in this line. Compare in particular the edition available at the Beckett site: WWW.geocities.com/HotSprings /5518/endgame3.html.
   The version with "Shall I tell" is certainly more like a normal conversational offer to tell a familiar story, and hence more appropriate in the context of the play. By the same token, the "Shall I tell" formulation renders even more startling Nell's negative rejoinder: "No. What for?"

References

Acheson, James. 1986. "Chess with the audience: Samuel Beckett's Endgame". *Critical essays on Samuel Beckett*, ed. by Patrick A. McCarthy. Boston: G. K. Hall.

Bamberg, Michael. 1994. "Actions, events, scenes, plots and the drama: Language and the constitution of part-whole relationships". *Language Sciences* 16. 39–79.

Bartlett, Frederic C. 1932. *Remembering: A study in experimental and social psychology*. Cambridge: Cambridge University Press.

Bateson, Gregory. 1953. "The position of humor in human communication". *Cybernetics, ninth conference*, ed. by H. von Foerster, 1–47. New York: Josiah Macy, Jr. Foundation.

———. 1954 (1972). "A theory of play and fantasy". *Steps to an ecology of mind*, ed. by G. Bateson, 177–93. San Francisco: Chandler.

Bauman, Richard. 1986. *Story, performance, and event*. Cambridge: Cambridge University Press.

Beckett, Samuel. 1986. *The Complete Dramatic Works*. London: Faber and Faber.

Bergson, Henri. 1900 (1911). *Laughter: An essay on the meaning of the comic*. New York: Macmillan

Blum-Kulka, Shoshana. 1993. "'You gotta know how to tell a story': Telling, tales, and tellers in American and Israeli narrative events at dinner". *Language in Society* 22. 361–402.

——— & Catherine E. Snow. 1993. "Developing autonomy for tellers, tales, and telling in family narrative events". *Journal of Narrative and Life History* 2. 187–217.

Boggs, Stephen T. 1985. *Speaking, Relating, and Learning: A study of Hawaiian children at home and at school*. Norwood: Ablex.

Brooke, Nicholas. 1968. *Shakespeare's early tragedies*. London: Methuen.

Burton, Deidre. 1980. *Dialogue and discourse*. London: Routledge & Kegan Paul.

Cederborg, Ann-Christin & Karin Aronson. 1994. "Conarration and voice in family therapy: Voicing, devoicing and orchestration". *Text* 14. 345–70.

Chafe, Wallace, ed. 1980a. *The pear stories*. Norwood: Ablex.

———. 1980b. "The development of consciousness in the production of a narrative". *The Pear Stories*, ed. by Wallace Chafe, 9–50. Norwood: Ablex.

———. 1982. "Integration and involvement in speaking, writing, and oral literature". *Spoken and written lnaguage: Advances in discourse processes, vol. 9*, ed. by Deborah Tannen, 35–54. Norwood: Ablex.

———. 1985. "Linguistic differences produced by differences between speaking and writing". *Literacy, language, and learning*, ed. by D. R. Olson, N. Torrance & A. Hildyard, 105–123. London: Cambridge University Press.

———. 1986. "Beyond Bartlett: Narratives and Remembering". *Poetics* 15. 139–151.

———. 1991. "Repeated verbalizations as evidence for the organization of knowledge". *Proceedings of the fourteenth international congress of linguists*, ed. by W. Bahner, J. Schildt & D. Viehweger, 57–68. Berlin: Academie-Verlag.

———. 1994. *Discourse, consciousness and time*. Chicago: University of Chicago Press.

———. 1997. "Polyphonic topic development". *Conversation: Cognitive, communicative and social perspectives*, ed. by T. Givón, 41–53. Amsterdam & Philadelphia: Benjamins.

———. 1998. "Things we can learn from repeated tellings of the same experience". *Narrative Inquiry* 8. 269–285.

——— & Jane Danielewicz. 1987. "Properties of spoken and written language". *Comprehending oral and written language*, ed. by R. Horowitz & S. Jay Samuels, 55–82. London: Academic Press.

Clark, Herbert. 1997. "Dogmas of understanding". *Discourse Processes* 23:3. 567–98.

Cohn, Ruby. 1969. "Endgame". *20th Century interpretations of Endgame*, ed. by Bell G. Chevigny, 40–52. Englewood Cliffs: Prentice Hall.

———. 1970. "The laughter of sad Sam Beckett". *Samuel Beckett now*, ed. by Melvin J. Friedman, 185–97. Chicago: University of Chicago Press.

Culler, Jonathan. 1975. "Defining narrative units". *Style and structure in literature*, ed. by R. Fowler, 123–42. Ithaca: Cornell University Press.

Duranti, Alessandro. *1986. "The audience as co-author: An introduction"*. *Text* 6:3.239–47.

Erickson, Frederick. 1982. "Money tree, lasagna bush, salt and pepper: Social construction of topical cohesion in a conversation amongItalian-Americans".

Analyzing discourse: Text and talk, ed. by D. Tannen, 43–71. Washington, D.C.: Georgetown University Press.

Ervin-Tripp, Susan & A. Küntay. 1997. "The occasioning and structure of conversational stories". *Conversation: Cognitive, communicative and social perspectives*, ed. by T. Givón, 133–166. Amsterdam & Philadelphia: Benjamins.

Everett, Barbara. 1972. "Romeo and Juliet: The nurse's story". *Critical Quarterly* 14. 129–139.

Falk, Jane. 1980. "The conversational duet". *Berkeley Linguistics Society: Proceedings of the Sixth Annual Meeting*, 1980, 507–514.

Fillmore, Charles J. 1976. "The need for a frame semantics within linguistics". *Statistical Methods in Linguistics*. 5–29.

————. 1985. "Frames and the semantics of understanding". *Quaderni di Semantica: Rivista Internazionale di Semantica Teorica e Applicata* 6. 222–54.

Ferguson, Liane & Paul Yachnin. 1981. "The name of Juliet's nurse". *Shakespeare Quarterly* 32. 95–97.

Ferrara, Kathleen. 1994. *Therapeutic ways with words*. New York: Oxford University Press.

Fleischman, Suzanne. 1990. *Tense and narrativity: From medieval performance to modern fiction*. Austin: University of Texas Press.

Fletcher, B. S. 1978. *A student's guide to plays of Samuel Beckett*. London: Faber.

Fludernik, Monika. 1996. *Towards a 'natural' narratology*. London: Routledge.

Freud, Sigmund. 1905 (1989). *Jokes and their relation to the unconscious*. New York: Norton.

————. 1950. *The interpretation of dreams*. New York: Modern Library.

Fry, William F. 1963. *Sweet madness: A study of humor*. Palo Alto: Pacific Books.

Goffman, Erving. 1967. *Interaction ritual*. Chicago: Aldine.

————. 1974. *Frame analysis*. Cambridge, Mass.: Harvard University Press.

Goodwin, Charles. 1986. "Audience diversity, participation and interpretation". *Text* 6:3.283–316.

————. 1987. "Forgetfulness as an interactive resource". *Social Psychology Quarterly* 50. 115–31.

Goodwin, Marjonie H. 1997a. "Towards families of stories in context". *Journal of Narrative and Life History* 7. 107–112.

————. 1997b. "By-play: Negotiating evaluation in story-telling". *Towards a social science of language: Papers in honour of William Labov: 2. Social interaction and dicourse structures*, ed. by G. R. Guy, C. Feagin, D. Schiffrin & J. Baugh, 77–102. Amsterdam & Philadelphia: Benjamins.

Grice, H. P. 1975. "Logic and conversation". *Syntax and semantics, vol. 3: Speech acts*, ed. by P. Cole, 113–127. New York: Academic.

Gumperz, John J. 1982a. *Discourse strategies*. Cambridge: Cambridge University Press.

———. 1982b. "The linguistic bases of communicative competence". *Analyzing discourse: Text and talk (Georgetown University Roundtable on Languages and Linguistics 1981)*, ed. by Deborah Tannen, 323–34. Washington, D.C.: Georgetown University Press.

Halliday, M. A. K. 1967. "Notes on transitivity and theme in English, Part 2". *Journal of Linguistics* 3. 199–244.

———. 1985. *Introduction to functional grammar*. London: Arnold.

———. 1987. "Spoken and written modes of meaning". *Comprehending oral and written language*, ed. by R. Horowitz & S. Jay Samuels, 55–82. London: Academic Press.

Heath, Shirley Brice. 1982. "Protean Shapes in literacy events: Ever-shifting oral and literate traditions". *Spoken and written lnaguage: Advances in discourse processes, vol. 9*, ed. by Deborah Tannen, 91–118. Norwood: Ablex.

Hockett, Charles F. 1960 (1977). "Jokes". *The View From Language*, ed. by Charles F. Hockett, 257–289. Athens, Ga.: University of Georgia Press.

Hopper, Paul. 1988. "Emergent grammar and the a priori grammar postulate". *Linguistics in context*, ed. by Deborah Tannen, 117–34. Norwood, N.J.: Ablex.

———. 1997. "Dualisms in the study of narrative: A note on Labov and Waletzky". *Journal of Narrative and Life History* 7. 75–82.

Hymes, Dell. 1962. "The ethnography of speaking". *Anthropology and human behavior*, ed. by T. Gladwin & W. C. Sturtevant, 13–53. Washington, D.C.: The Anthropology Society of Washington.

———. 1972. "Models of the interaction of language and social life". *Directions in sociolinguistics*, ed. by J. J. Gumperz & D. Hymes, 35–71. New York: Holt.

———. 1974. *Foundations in sociolinguistics: An ethnographic approach*. Philadelphia: University of Pennsylvania Press.

———. 1981. *"In vain I tried to tell you": Essays in Native American Ethnopoetics*. Philadelphia: University of Pennsylvania Press.

———. 1985. "Language, memory and selective performance: Cultee's 'Salmon Myth' as twice told to Boas". *Journal of American Folklore* 98. 391–434.

Ingarden, Roman. 1973. *The cognition of the literary work of art*, trans. by Ruth Ann Crowly & Kenneth R. Olsen. Evanston: Northwestern University Press.

Iser, Wolfgang. 1978. *The act of reading: A theory of aesthetic response*. Baltimore: John Hopkins University Press.

———. 1981. "The art of failure: The stifled laugh in Beckett's theater". *The Bucknell Review* 26:1. 139–89.

Jakobson, Roman. 1960. "Closing statement: Linguistics and poetics". *Style in language*, ed. by Thomas Sebeok, 350–377. Cambridge, Mass.: MIT Press.

Jefferson, Gail. 1978. "Sequential aspects of storytelling in conversation". *Studies in the organization of conversational interaction*, ed. by Jim Schenkein, 219–48. New York: Academic Press.

———. 1979. "A technique for inviting laughter and its subsequent acceptance/declination". *Everyday language: Studies in ethnomethodology*, ed. by G. Psathas, 79–96. New York: Irvington.

———. 1984. "On the organization of laughter in talk about troubles". *Structures of social action*, ed. by J. M. Atkinson & J. Heritage, 346–69. Cambridge: Cambridge University Press.

———. 1985. "An exercise in the transcription and analysis of laughter". *Handbook of Discourse Analysis, vol. 3: Discourse and Dialogue*, ed. by Teun A. van Dijk, 25–34. London: Academic Press.

Johnstone, Barbara. 1987. "'He says … so I said': Verb tense alternation and narrative depictions of authority in American English". *Linguistics* 25. 33–52.

———. 1990. *Stories, community and place: Narratives from middle America*. Bloomington: Indiana.

———. 1993. "Community and contest: midwestern men and women creating their worlds in conversational stortytelling". *Gender and conversational interaction*, ed. by Deborah Tannen, 62–80. Oxford: Oxford University Press.

———. 1996. *The linguistic individual*. Oxford: Oxford University Press.

Jung, Carl G. 1985. *Dreams*. London: Ark.

Kawin, Bruce F. 1972. *Telling It Again and Again: Repetition in Literature and Film*. Ithaca: Cornell University Press.

Kenner, Hugh. 1969. "Life in a Box". *20th Century interpretations of Endgame*, ed. by Bell G. Chevigny, 53–60. Englewood Cliffs: Prentice Hall.

Koestler, Arthur. 1964. *The Act of creation*. New York: Macmillan.

Kreider, Paul V. 1975. *Repetition in Shakespeare's plays*. New York: Octagon Books.

Labov, William. 1972. *Language in the inner city*. Philadelphia: University of Pennsylvania Press.

———. 1997. "Some further steps in narrative analysis". *Journal of Narrative and Life History* 7. 395–415.

——— & Joshua Waletzky. 1967. "Narrative analysis: Oral versions of personal experience". *Essays on the verbal and visual arts*, ed. by June Helm, 12–44. Seattle: University of Washington Press.

——— & David Fanshel. 1977. *Therapeutic discourse*. New York: Academic Press.

Lewis, Paul. 1989. *Comic effects: Interdisciplinary approaches to humor in literature*. Albany: SUNY.

Linde, Charlotte. 1993. *Life stories*. New York: Oxford University Press.

Mayes, Patricia. 1990. "Quotation in spoken English". *Studies in Language* 14. 323–363.

Michaels, Sarah & Cook-Gumperz, Jenny. 1979. "A study of sharing time with first grade students: Discourse narratives in the classroom". *Berkeley Linguistics Society: Proceedings of the Fifth Annual Meeting*, 647–60.

Middleton, D. & D. Edwards. 1990. "Introduction". *Collective remembering*, ed. by D: Middleton & D. Edwards, 1–22. London: Sage.

Miller, George. 1956. "The magical number seven, plus or minus two". *Psychological Review* 63. 81–97.

Nash, Walter. 1985. *The language of humor: Style and technique in comic discourse*. London: Longman.

Norrick, Neal R. 1984. "Stock conversational witticisms". *Journal of Pragmatics* 8. 195–209.

———. 1986. "A frame-theoretical analysis of verbal humor: Bisociation as schema conflict". *Semiotica* 60. 225–45.

———. 1987. "Functions of repetition in conversation". *Text* 7. 245–64.

———. 1988. "Binomial meaning in texts". *Journal of English Linguistics* 21:1.72–87.

———. 1993a. *Conversational Joking*. Bloomington: Indiana University Press.

———. 1993b. "Repetition in canned jokes and spontaneous conversational joking". *Humor* 6. 385–402.

———. 1997. "Twice-told tales: Collaborative narration of familiar stories". *Language in Society* 26. 199–220.

———. 1998a. "Retelling stories in spontaneous conversation". *Discourse Processes* 25. 75–97.

———. 1998b. "Retelling again". *Narrative Inquiry* 8. 373–378.

Ochs, Elinor, Ruth Smith & Carolyn Taylor. 1989. Dectective stories at dinner-time: Problem solving through co-narration. Cultural Dynamics 2. 238–57.

———, Carolyn Taylor, Dina Rudolph & Ruth Smith. 1992. "Storytelling as a theory-building activity". *Discourse Processes* 15. 37–72.

——— & Lisa Capps. 1997. "Narrative authenticity". *Journal of Narrative and Life History* 7. 83–89.

Ong, Walter. 1982. *Orality and literacy: The technologizing of the world*. London: Methuen.

Polanyi, Livia. 1979. "So what's the point?". *Semiotica* 25. 207–41.

———. 1981. "Telling the same story twice". *Text* 1. 315–36.

———. 1985. *Telling the American story*. Norwood: Ablex.

Pratt, Mary Louise. 1977. *Toward a speech act theory of literary discourse*. Bloomington: Indiana University Press.

Prince, Gerald. 1973. *A grammar of stories*. The Hague: Mouton.

Propp, Vladimir. 1968. *Morphology of the folktale*. Austin: University of Texas Press.

Quasthoff. Uta M. 1980. *Erzählen in Gesprächen: Linguistische Untersuchungen zu Strukturen und Funktionen am Beispiel einer Kommunikationsform des Alltags*. Tübingen: Narr.

Raskin, Victor. 1985. *Semantic mechanisms of humor*. Dordrecht: Reidel.

Rees, Joan. 1983. "Juliet's nurse: Some branches of a family tree". *Review of English Studies* 34. 43–47.

Reik, Theodor. 1962. *Jewish wit*. New York: Gamut Press.

Ricks, Christopher. 1993. *Beckett's dying words*. Oxford: Clarendon.

Romaine, Suzanne. 1984. *The Language of Children and Adolescents*. Oxford: Blackwell.

Rummelhart, David E. 1975. "Notes on a schema for stories". *Representation and understanding*, ed. by D. B. Bobrow & A. Collins, 211–36. New York: Academic Press.

Ryave, Alan L. 1978. "On the achievement of a series of stories". *Studies in the organization of conversational interaction*, ed. by J. Schenkein, 113–32. New York: Academic Press.

Sacks, Harvey. 1972. "On the analyzability of stories by children". *Directions in sociolinguistics*, ed. by J. J. Gumperz & D. Hymes, 325–45. New York: Holt, Rinehart and Winston.

———. 1974. "An analysis of the course of a joke's telling". *Explorations in the ethnography of speaking*, ed. by R. Bauman & J. Sherzer, 337–353. Cambridge: Cambridge University Press.

———. 1992. *Lectures on conversation,* 2 vols., ed. by G. Jefferson. Oxford: Blackwell.

———, Emanuel Schegloff & Gail Jefferson. 1974. "A simplest systematics for the organization of turn-taking for conversation". *Language* 50. 696–735.

Schegloff, Emanuel A. 1992. "In another context". *Rethinking Context,* ed. by A. Duranti & C.Goodwin, 191–227. Cambridge: Cambridge University Press.

———. 1997. "Narrative analysis: Thirty years later". *Journal of Narrative and Life History* 7. 97–106.

Schiffrin, Deborah. 1981. "Tense variation in narrative". *Language* 57. 45–62.

———. 1984. "How a story says what it means and does". *Text* 4. 313–46.

Scollon, Ron & Suzanne B. K. Scollon. 1984. "Cooking it up and boiling it down: Abstracts in Athabaskan children's story retellings". *Coherence in Spoken and Written Discourse,* ed. by Deborah Tannen, 173–97. Norwood: Ablex.

Sherzer, Joel. 1981. "Tellings, retellings and tellings within tellings: The structuring and organization of narrative in Kuna Indian discourse". *Case Studies in the Ethnography of Speaking,* ed. by R. Bauman & J. Sherzer, 249–73. Austin: Southwest Educational Development Laboratory.

Shuman, Amy 1986. *Storytelling rights.* New York: Cambridge University Press.

Simon Keller, Richard. 1982. "Dialectical laughter". *Modern Drama* 25. 505–513.

Smith, B. H. 1981. "Narrative versions, narrative theories". *On narrative,* ed. W. J. T. Mitchell, 209–232. Chicago: University of Chicago Press.

Spielman, Roger W. 1987. "Collateral information in narrative discourse". *Journal of Literary Semantics* 16:3.200–226.

Stubbs, Michael. 1983. Discourse analysis. Chicago: University of Chicago Press.

Tannen, Deborah. 1978. "The effect of expectations on conversation". *Discourse Processes* 1. 203–209.

———. 1979. "What's in a frame? Surface evidence for underlying expectations". *New directions in discourse processing,* ed. by Roy O. Freedle, 137–181. Norwood, N.J.: Ablex.

———. 1980. "A comparative analysis of oral narrative strategies: Athenian Greek and American English". *The Pear Stories,* ed. by Wallace Chafe, 51–87. Norwood: Ablex.

———. 1982. "The oral/literate continuum in discourse". *Spoken and written language: Advances in discourse processes, vol. 9,* ed. by Deborah Tannen, 1–16. Norwood: Ablex.

———. 1984. *Conversational style.* Norwood: Ablex.

————. 1987a. "Repetition in conversation: Toward a poetics of talk". *Language* 63. 574–605.

————. 1987b. "Repetition in conversation as spontaneous formulaicity". *Text* 7. 215–44.

————. 1989. *Talking voices: Repetition, dialogue, and imagery in conversational discourse*. Cambridge: Cambridge University Press.

————. ed. 1993. *Framing in Discourse*. Oxford: Oxford University Press.

van Dijk, Teun A. 1972. *Some aspects of text grammar*. The Hague: Mouton.

Watson, Karen Ann. 1975. "Transferable communicative routines: strategies and group identity in two speech events". *Language in Society* 4. 53–72.

Wolfson, Nessa. 1982. "The conversational historical present in American English narrative". *Topics in Socio-Linguistics* 1. Dordrecht: Foris.

Name Index

Subject Index

CURRENT ISSUES IN LINGUISTIC THEORY

E. F. K. Koerner, Editor

Zentrum für Allgemeine Sprachwissenschaft, Typologie
und Universalienforschung, Berlin
efk.koerner@rz.hu-berlin.de

Current Issues in Linguistic Theory (CILT) is a theory-oriented series which welcomes contributions from scholars who have significant proposals to make towards the advancement of our understanding of language, its structure, functioning and development. CILT has been established in order to provide a forum for the presentation and discussion of linguistic opinions of scholars who do not necessarily accept the prevailing mode of thought in linguistic science. It offers an outlet for meaningful contributions to the current linguistic debate, and furnishes the diversity of opinion which a healthy discipline must have. A complete list of titles in this series can be found on the publishers' website, *www.benjamins.com*

292 NICOLOV, Nicolas, Kalina BONTCHEVA, Galia ANGELOVA and Ruslan MITKOV (eds.): Recent Advances in Natural Language Processing IV. Selected papers from RANLP 2005. 2007. xii, 307 pp.

291 BAAUW, Sergio, Frank DRIJKONINGEN and Manuela PINTO (eds.): Romance Languages and Linguistic Theory 2005. Selected papers from 'Going Romance', Utrecht, 8–10 December 2005. 2007. viii, 338 pp.

290 MUGHAZY, Mustafa A. (ed.): Perspectives on Arabic Linguistics. Papers from the annual symposium on Arabic linguistics. Volume XX: Kalamazoo, Michigan, March 2006. 2007. xii, 247 pp.

289 BENMAMOUN, Elabbas (ed.): Perspectives on Arabic Linguistics. Papers from the annual symposium on Arabic Linguistics. Volume XIX: Urbana, Illinois, April 2005. 2007. xiv, 304 pp.

288 TOIVONEN, Ida and Diane NELSON (eds.): Saami Linguistics. 2007. viii, 321 pp.

287 CAMACHO, José, Nydia FLORES-FERRÁN, Liliana SÁNCHEZ, Viviane DÉPREZ and María José CABRERA (eds.): Romance Linguistics 2006. Selected papers from the 36th Linguistic Symposium on Romance Languages (LSRL), New Brunswick, March-April 2006. 2007. viii, 340 pp.

286 WEIJER, Jeroen van de and Erik Jan van der TORRE (eds.): Voicing in Dutch. (De)voicing – phonology, phonetics, and psycholinguistics. 2007. x, 186 pp.

285 SACKMANN, Robin (ed.): Explorations in Integrational Linguistics. Four essays on German, French, and Guaraní. 2008. ix, 239 pp.

284 SALMONS, Joseph C. and Shannon DUBENION-SMITH (eds.): Historical Linguistics 2005. Selected papers from the 17th International Conference on Historical Linguistics, Madison, Wisconsin, 31 July - 5 August 2005. 2007. viii, 413 pp.

283 LENKER, Ursula and Anneli MEURMAN-SOLIN (eds.): Connectives in the History of English. 2007. viii, 318 pp.

282 PRIETO, Pilar, Joan MASCARÓ and Maria-Josep SOLÉ (eds.): Segmental and prosodic issues in Romance phonology. 2007. xvi, 262 pp.

281 VERMEERBERGEN, Myriam, Lorraine LEESON and O.A. CRASBORN (eds.): Simultaneity in Signed Languages. Form and function. 2007. viii, 360 pp. (incl. CD-Rom).

280 HEWSON, John and Vit BUBENIK: From Case to Adposition. The development of configurational syntax in Indo-European languages. 2006. xxx, 420 pp.

279 NEDERGAARD THOMSEN, Ole (ed.): Competing Models of Linguistic Change. Evolution and beyond. 2006. vi, 344 pp.

278 DOETJES, Jenny and Paz GONZÁLEZ (eds.): Romance Languages and Linguistic Theory 2004. Selected papers from 'Going Romance', Leiden, 9–11 December 2004. 2006. viii, 320 pp.

277 HELASVUO, Marja-Liisa and Lyle CAMPBELL (eds.): Grammar from the Human Perspective. Case, space and person in Finnish. 2006. x, 280 pp.

276 MONTREUIL, Jean-Pierre Y. (ed.): New Perspectives on Romance Linguistics. Vol. II: Phonetics, Phonology and Dialectology. Selected papers from the 35th Linguistic Symposium on Romance Languages (LSRL), Austin, Texas, February 2005. 2006. x, 213 pp.

275 NISHIDA, Chiyo and Jean-Pierre Y. MONTREUIL (eds.): New Perspectives on Romance Linguistics. Vol. I: Morphology, Syntax, Semantics, and Pragmatics. Selected papers from the 35th Linguistic Symposium on Romance Languages (LSRL), Austin, Texas, February 2005. 2006. xiv, 288 pp.

274 GESS, Randall S. and Deborah ARTEAGA (eds.): Historical Romance Linguistics. Retrospective and perspectives. 2006. viii, 393 pp.

273 FILPPULA, Markku, Juhani KLEMOLA, Marjatta PALANDER and Esa PENTTILÄ (eds.): Dialects Across Borders. Selected papers from the 11th International Conference on Methods in Dialectology (Methods XI), Joensuu, August 2002. 2005. xii, 291 pp.

272 GESS, Randall S. and Edward J. RUBIN (eds.): Theoretical and Experimental Approaches to Romance Linguistics. Selected papers from the 34th Linguistic Symposium on Romance Languages (LSRL), Salt Lake City, March 2004. 2005. viii, 367 pp.

271 BRANNER, David Prager (ed.): The Chinese Rime Tables. Linguistic philosophy and historical-comparative phonology. 2006. viii, 358 pp.

270 GEERTS, Twan, Ivo van GINNEKEN and Haike JACOBS (eds.): Romance Languages and Linguistic Theory 2003. Selected papers from 'Going Romance' 2003, Nijmegen, 20–22 November. 2005. viii, 369 pp.

269 HARGUS, Sharon and Keren RICE (eds.): Athabaskan Prosody. 2005. xii, 432 pp.

268 CRAVENS, Thomas D. (ed.): Variation and Reconstruction. 2006. viii, 223 pp.

267 ALHAWARY, Mohammad T. and Elabbas BENMAMOUN (eds.): Perspectives on Arabic Linguistics. Papers from the annual symposium on Arabic linguistics. Volume XVII–XVIII: Alexandria, 2003 and Norman, Oklahoma 2004. 2005. xvi, 315 pp.

266 BOUDELAA, Sami (ed.): Perspectives on Arabic Linguistics. Papers from the annual symposium on Arabic linguistics. Volume XVI: , Cambridge, March 2002. 2006. xii, 181 pp.

265 CORNIPS, Leonie and Karen P. CORRIGAN (eds.): Syntax and Variation. Reconciling the Biological and the Social. 2005. vi, 312 pp.

264 DRESSLER, Wolfgang U., Dieter KASTOVSKY, Oskar E. PFEIFFER and Franz RAINER (eds.): Morphology and its demarcations. Selected papers from the 11th Morphology meeting, Vienna, February 2004. With the assistance of Francesco Gardani and Markus A. Pöchtrager. 2005. xiv, 320 pp.

263 BRANCO, António, Tony McENERY and Ruslan MITKOV (eds.): Anaphora Processing. Linguistic, cognitive and computational modelling. 2005. x, 449 pp.

262 VAJDA, Edward J. (ed.): Languages and Prehistory of Central Siberia. 2004. x, 275 pp.

261 KAY, Christian J. and Jeremy J. SMITH (eds.): Categorization in the History of English. 2004. viii, 268 pp.

260 NICOLOV, Nicolas, Kalina BONTCHEVA, Galia ANGELOVA and Ruslan MITKOV (eds.): Recent Advances in Natural Language Processing III. Selected papers from RANLP 2003. 2004. xii, 402 pp.

259 CARR, Philip, Jacques DURAND and Colin J. EWEN (eds.): Headhood, Elements, Specification and Contrastivity. Phonological papers in honour of John Anderson. 2005. xxviii, 405 pp.

258 AUGER, Julie, J. Clancy CLEMENTS and Barbara VANCE (eds.): Contemporary Approaches to Romance Linguistics. Selected Papers from the 33rd Linguistic Symposium on Romance Languages (LSRL), Bloomington, Indiana, April 2003. With the assistance of Rachel T. Anderson. 2004. viii, 404 pp.

257 FORTESCUE, Michael, Eva Skafte JENSEN, Jens Erik MOGENSEN and Lene SCHØSLER (eds.): Historical Linguistics 2003. Selected papers from the 16th International Conference on Historical Linguistics, Copenhagen, 11–15 August 2003. 2005. x, 312 pp.

256 BOK-BENNEMA, Reineke, Bart HOLLEBRANDSE, Brigitte KAMPERS-MANHE and Petra SLEEMAN (eds.): Romance Languages and Linguistic Theory 2002. Selected papers from 'Going Romance', Groningen, 28–30 November 2002. 2004. viii, 273 pp.

255 MEULEN, Alice ter and Werner ABRAHAM (eds.): The Composition of Meaning. From lexeme to discourse. 2004. vi, 232 pp.

254 BALDI, Philip and Pietro U. DINI (eds.): Studies in Baltic and Indo-European Linguistics. In honor of William R. Schmalstieg. 2004. xlvi, 302 pp.

253 CAFFAREL, Alice, J.R. MARTIN and Christian M.I.M. MATTHIESSEN (eds.): Language Typology. A functional perspective. 2004. xiv, 702 pp.

252 KAY, Christian J., Carole HOUGH and Irené WOTHERSPOON (eds.): New Perspectives on English Historical Linguistics. Selected papers from 12 ICEHL, Glasgow, 21–26 August 2002. Volume II: Lexis and Transmission. 2004. xii, 273 pp.

251 KAY, Christian J., Simon HOROBIN and Jeremy J. SMITH (eds.): New Perspectives on English Historical Linguistics. Selected papers from 12 ICEHL, Glasgow, 21–26 August 2002. Volume I: Syntax and Morphology. 2004. x, 264 pp.

250 JENSEN, John T.: Principles of Generative Phonology. An introduction. 2004. xii, 324 pp.

249 BOWERN, Claire and Harold KOCH (eds.): Australian Languages. Classification and the comparative method. 2004. xii, 377 pp. (incl. CD-Rom).

248 WEIGAND, Edda (ed.): Emotion in Dialogic Interaction. Advances in the complex. 2004. xii, 284 pp.

247 PARKINSON, Dilworth B. and Samira FARWANEH (eds.): Perspectives on Arabic Linguistics. Papers from the Annual Symposium on Arabic Linguistics. Volume XV: Salt Lake City 2001. 2003. x, 214 pp.

246 HOLISKY, Dee Ann and Kevin TUITE (eds.): Current Trends in Caucasian, East European and Inner Asian Linguistics. Papers in honor of Howard I. Aronson. 2003. xxviii, 426 pp.

245 QUER, Josep, Jan SCHROTEN, Mauro SCORRETTI, Petra SLEEMAN and Els VERHEUGD (eds.): Romance Languages and Linguistic Theory 2001. Selected papers from 'Going Romance', Amsterdam, 6–8 December 2001. 2003. viii, 355 pp.

244 PÉREZ-LEROUX, Ana Teresa and Yves ROBERGE (eds.): Romance Linguistics. Theory and Acquisition. Selected papers from the 32nd Linguistic Symposium on Romance Languages (LSRL), Toronto, April 2002. 2003. viii, 388 pp.

243 CUYCKENS, Hubert, Thomas BERG, René DIRVEN and Klaus-Uwe PANTHER (eds.): Motivation in Language. Studies in honor of Günter Radden. 2003. xxvi, 403 pp.

242 SEUREN, Pieter A.M. and Gerard KEMPEN (eds.): Verb Constructions in German and Dutch. 2003. vi, 316 pp.

241 LECARME, Jacqueline (ed.): Research in Afroasiatic Grammar II. Selected papers from the Fifth Conference on Afroasiatic Languages, Paris, 2000. 2003. viii, 550 pp.

240 JANSE, Mark and Sijmen TOL (eds.): Language Death and Language Maintenance. Theoretical, practical and descriptive approaches. With the assistance of Vincent Hendriks. 2003. xviii, 244 pp.

239 ANDERSEN, Henning (ed.): Language Contacts in Prehistory. Studies in Stratigraphy. Papers from the Workshop on Linguistic Stratigraphy and Prehistory at the Fifteenth International Conference on Historical Linguistics, Melbourne, 17 August 2001. 2003. viii, 292 pp.

238 NÚÑEZ-CEDEÑO, Rafael, Luis LÓPEZ and Richard CAMERON (eds.): A Romance Perspective on Language Knowledge and Use. Selected papers from the 31st Linguistic Symposium on Romance Languages (LSRL), Chicago, 19–22 April 2001. 2003. xvi, 386 pp.

237 BLAKE, Barry J. and Kate BURRIDGE (eds.): Historical Linguistics 2001. Selected papers from the 15th International Conference on Historical Linguistics, Melbourne, 13–17 August 2001. Editorial assistance Jo Taylor. 2003. x, 444 pp.

236 SIMON-VANDENBERGEN, Anne-Marie, Miriam TAVERNIERS and Louise J. RAVELLI (eds.): Grammatical Metaphor. Views from systemic functional linguistics. 2003. vi, 453 pp.

235 LINN, Andrew R. and Nicola McLELLAND (eds.): Standardization. Studies from the Germanic languages. 2002. xii, 258 pp.

234 WEIJER, Jeroen van de, Vincent J. van HEUVEN and Harry van der HULST (eds.): The Phonological Spectrum. Volume II: Suprasegmental structure. 2003. x, 264 pp.

233 WEIJER, Jeroen van de, Vincent J. van HEUVEN and Harry van der HULST (eds.): The Phonological Spectrum. Volume I: Segmental structure. 2003. x, 308 pp.

232 BEYSSADE, Claire, Reineke BOK-BENNEMA, Frank DRIJKONINGEN and Paola MONACHESI (eds.): Romance Languages and Linguistic Theory 2000. Selected papers from 'Going Romance' 2000, Utrecht, 30 November–2 December. 2002. viii, 354 pp.

231 CRAVENS, Thomas D.: Comparative Historical Dialectology. Italo-Romance clues to Ibero-Romance sound change. 2002. xii, 163 pp.

230 PARKINSON, Dilworth B. and Elabbas BENMAMOUN (eds.): Perspectives on Arabic Linguistics. Papers from the Annual Symposium on Arabic Linguistics. Volume XIII-XIV: Stanford, 1999 and Berkeley, California 2000. 2002. xiv, 250 pp.

229 NEVIN, Bruce E. and Stephen B. JOHNSON (eds.): The Legacy of Zellig Harris. Language and information into the 21st century. Volume 2: Mathematics and computability of language. 2002. xx, 312 pp.

228 NEVIN, Bruce E. (ed.): The Legacy of Zellig Harris. Language and information into the 21st century. Volume 1: Philosophy of science, syntax and semantics. 2002. xxxvi, 323 pp.

227 FAVA, Elisabetta (ed.): Clinical Linguistics. Theory and applications in speech pathology and therapy. 2002. xxiv, 353 pp.

226 LEVIN, Saul: Semitic and Indo-European. Volume II: Comparative morphology, syntax and phonetics. 2002. xviii, 592 pp.

225 SHAHIN, Kimary N.: Postvelar Harmony. 2003. viii, 344 pp.

224 FANEGO, Teresa, Belén MÉNDEZ-NAYA and Elena SEOANE (eds.): Sounds, Words, Texts and Change. Selected papers from 11 ICEHL, Santiago de Compostela, 7–11 September 2000. Volume 2. 2002. x, 310 pp.

223 FANEGO, Teresa, Javier PÉREZ-GUERRA and María José LÓPEZ-COUSO (eds.): English Historical Syntax and Morphology. Selected papers from 11 ICEHL, Santiago de Compostela, 7–11 September 2000. Volume 1. 2002. x, 306 pp.

222 HERSCHENSOHN, Julia, Enrique MALLÉN and Karen ZAGONA (eds.): Features and Interfaces in Romance. Essays in honor of Heles Contreras. 2001. xiv, 302 pp.

221 D'HULST, Yves, Johan ROORYCK and Jan SCHROTEN (eds.): Romance Languages and Linguistic Theory 1999. Selected papers from 'Going Romance' 1999, Leiden, 9–11 December 1999. 2001. viii, 406 pp.

220 SATTERFIELD, Teresa, Christina TORTORA and Diana CRESTI (eds.): Current Issues in Romance Languages. Selected papers from the 29th Linguistic Symposium on Romance Languages (LSRL), Ann Arbor, 8–11 April 1999. 2002. viii, 412 pp.

219 ANDERSEN, Henning (ed.): Actualization. Linguistic Change in Progress. Papers from a workshop held at the 14th International Conference on Historical Linguistics, Vancouver, B.C., 14 August 1999. 2001. vii, 250 pp.

218 BENDJABALLAH, Sabrina, Wolfgang U. DRESSLER, Oskar E. PFEIFFER and Maria D. VOEIKOVA (eds.): Morphology 2000. Selected papers from the 9th Morphology Meeting, Vienna, 24–28 February 2000. 2002. viii, 317 pp.

217 WILTSHIRE, Caroline R. and Joaquim CAMPS (eds.): Romance Phonology and Variation. Selected papers from the 30th Linguistic Symposium on Romance Languages, Gainesville, Florida, February 2000. 2002. xii, 238 pp.

216 CAMPS, Joaquim and Caroline R. WILTSHIRE (eds.): Romance Syntax, Semantics and L2 Acquisition. Selected papers from the 30th Linguistic Symposium on Romance Languages, Gainesville, Florida, February 2000. 2001. xii, 246 pp.

215 BRINTON, Laurel J. (ed.): Historical Linguistics 1999. Selected papers from the 14th International Conference on Historical Linguistics, Vancouver, 9–13 August 1999. 2001. xii, 398 pp.

214 WEIGAND, Edda and Marcelo DASCAL (eds.): Negotiation and Power in Dialogic Interaction. 2001. viii, 303 pp.

213 SORNICOLA, Rosanna, Erich POPPE and Ariel SHISHA-HALEVY (eds.): Stability, Variation and Change of Word-Order Patterns over Time. With the assistance of Paola Como. 2000. xxxii, 323 pp.

212 REPETTI, Lori (ed.): Phonological Theory and the Dialects of Italy. 2000. x, 301 pp.

211 ELŠÍK, Viktor and Yaron MATRAS (eds.): Grammatical Relations in Romani. The Noun Phrase. with a Foreword by Frans Plank (Universität Konstanz). 2000. x, 244 pp.

210 DWORKIN, Steven N. and Dieter WANNER (eds.): New Approaches to Old Problems. Issues in Romance historical linguistics. 2000. xiv, 235 pp.

209 KING, Ruth: The Lexical Basis of Grammatical Borrowing. A Prince Edward Island French case study. 2000. xvi, 241 pp.

208 ROBINSON, Orrin W.: Whose German? The *ach/ich* alternation and related phenomena in 'standard' and 'colloquial'. 2001. xii, 178 pp.

207 SANZ, Montserrat: Events and Predication. A new approach to syntactic processing in English and Spanish. 2000. xiv, 219 pp.

206 FAWCETT, Robin P.: A Theory of Syntax for Systemic Functional Linguistics. 2000. xxiv, 360 pp.

205 DIRVEN, René, Roslyn M. FRANK and Cornelia ILIE (eds.): Language and Ideology. Volume 2: descriptive cognitive approaches. 2001. vi, 264 pp.

204 DIRVEN, René, Bruce HAWKINS and Esra SANDIKCIOGLU (eds.): Language and Ideology. Volume 1: theoretical cognitive approaches. 2001. vi, 301 pp.

203 NORRICK, Neal R.: Conversational Narrative. Storytelling in everyday talk. 2000. xiv, 233 pp.

202 LECARME, Jacqueline, Jean LOWENSTAMM and Ur SHLONSKY (eds.): Research in Afroasiatic Grammar. Papers from the Third conference on Afroasiatic Languages, Sophia Antipolis, 1996. 2000. vi, 386 pp.

201 DRESSLER, Wolfgang U., Oskar E. PFEIFFER, Markus A. PÖCHTRAGER and John R. RENNISON (eds.): Morphological Analysis in Comparison. 2000. x, 261 pp.

200 ANTTILA, Raimo: Greek and Indo-European Etymology in Action. Proto-Indo-European *agⵊ-. 2000. xii, 314 pp.

199 PÜTZ, Martin and Marjolijn H. VERSPOOR (eds.): Explorations in Linguistic Relativity. 2000. xvi, 369 pp.

198 NIEMEIER, Susanne and René DIRVEN (eds.): Evidence for Linguistic Relativity. 2000. xxii, 240 pp.

197 COOPMANS, Peter, Martin EVERAERT and Jane GRIMSHAW (eds.): Lexical Specification and Insertion. 2000. xviii, 476 pp.

196 HANNAHS, S.J. and Mike DAVENPORT (eds.): Issues in Phonological Structure. Papers from an International Workshop. 1999. xii, 268 pp.

195 HERRING, Susan C., Pieter van REENEN and Lene SCHØSLER (eds.): Textual Parameters in Older Languages. 2001. x, 448 pp.

194 COLEMAN, Julie and Christian J. KAY (eds.): Lexicology, Semantics and Lexicography. Selected papers from the Fourth G. L. Brook Symposium, Manchester, August 1998. 2000. xiv, 257 pp.

193 KLAUSENBURGER, Jurgen: Grammaticalization. Studies in Latin and Romance morphosyntax. 2000. xiv, 184 pp.

192 ALEXANDROVA, Galina M. and Olga ARNAUDOVA (eds.): The Minimalist Parameter. Selected papers from the Open Linguistics Forum, Ottawa, 21–23 March 1997. 2001. x, 360 pp.

191 SIHLER, Andrew L.: Language History. An introduction. 2000. xvi, 298 pp.

190 BENMAMOUN, Elabbas (ed.): Perspectives on Arabic Linguistics. Papers from the Annual Symposium on Arabic Linguistics. Volume XII: Urbana-Champaign, Illinois, 1998. 1999. viii, 204 pp.

189 NICOLOV, Nicolas and Ruslan MITKOV (eds.): Recent Advances in Natural Language Processing II. Selected papers from RANLP '97. 2000. xi, 422 pp.

188 SIMMONS, Richard VanNess: Chinese Dialect Classification. A comparative approach to Harngjou, Old Jintarn, and Common Northern Wu. 1999. xviii, 317 pp.

187 FRANCO, Jon A., Alazne LANDA and Juan MARTÍN (eds.): Grammatical Analyses in Basque and Romance Linguistics. Papers in honor of Mario Saltarelli. 1999. viii, 306 pp.

186 MIŠESKA TOMIĆ, Olga and Milorad RADOVANOVIĆ (eds.): History and Perspectives of Language Study. Papers in honor of Ranko Bugarski. 2000. xxii, 314 pp.

185 AUTHIER, Jean-Marc, Barbara E. BULLOCK and Lisa A. REED (eds.): Formal Perspectives on Romance Linguistics. Selected papers from the 28th Linguistic Symposium on Romance Languages (LSRL XXVIII), University Park, 16–19 April 1998. 1999. xii, 334 pp.

184 SAGART, Laurent: The Roots of Old Chinese. 1999. xii, 272 pp.

183 CONTINI-MORAVA, Ellen and Yishai TOBIN (eds.): Between Grammar and Lexicon. 2000. xxxii, 365 pp.

182 KENESEI, István (ed.): Crossing Boundaries. Advances in the theory of Central and Eastern European languages. 1999. viii, 302 pp.

181 MOHAMMAD, Mohammad A.: Word Order, Agreement and Pronominalization in Standard and Palestinian Arabic. 2000. xvi, 197 pp.

180 MEREU, Lunella (ed.): Boundaries of Morphology and Syntax. 1999. viii, 314 pp.

179 RINI, Joel: Exploring the Role of Morphology in the Evolution of Spanish. 1999. xvi, 187 pp.

178 FOOLEN, Ad and Frederike van der LEEK (eds.): Constructions in Cognitive Linguistics. Selected papers from the Fifth International Cognitive Linguistics Conference, Amsterdam, 1997. 2000. xvi, 338 pp.

177 CUYCKENS, Hubert and Britta E. ZAWADA (eds.): Polysemy in Cognitive Linguistics. Selected papers from the International Cognitive Linguistics Conference, Amsterdam, 1997. 2001. xxviii, 296 pp.

176 VAN HOEK, Karen, Andrej A. KIBRIK and Leo NOORDMAN (eds.): Discourse Studies in Cognitive Linguistics. Selected papers from the 5th International Cognitive Linguistics Conference, Amsterdam, July 1997. 1999. vi, 187 pp.

175 GIBBS, JR., Raymond W. and Gerard J. STEEN (eds.): Metaphor in Cognitive Linguistics. Selected papers from the 5th International Cognitive Linguistics Conference, Amsterdam, 1997. 1999. viii, 226 pp.

174 HALL, T. Alan and Ursula KLEINHENZ (eds.): Studies on the Phonological Word. 1999. viii, 298 pp.

173 TREVIÑO, Esthela and José LEMA (eds.): Semantic Issues in Romance Syntax. 1999. viii, 309 pp.

172 DIMITROVA-VULCHANOVA, Mila and Lars HELLAN (eds.): Topics in South Slavic Syntax and Semantics. 1999. xxviii, 263 pp.

171 WEIGAND, Edda (ed.): Contrastive Lexical Semantics. 1998. x, 270 pp.

170 LAMB, Sydney M.: Pathways of the Brain. The neurocognitive basis of language. 1999. xii, 418 pp.

169 GHADESSY, Mohsen (ed.): Text and Context in Functional Linguistics. 1999. xviii, 340 pp.

168 RATCLIFFE, Robert R.: The "Broken" Plural Problem in Arabic and Comparative Semitic. Allomorphy and analogy in non-concatenative morphology. 1998. xii, 261 pp.

167 BENMAMOUN, Elabbas, Mushira EID and Niloofar HAERI (eds.): Perspectives on Arabic Linguistics. Papers from the Annual Symposium on Arabic Linguistics. Volume XI: Atlanta, Georgia, 1997. 1998. viii, 231 pp.

166 LEMMENS, Maarten: Lexical Perspectives on Transitivity and Ergativity. Causative constructions in English. 1998. xii, 268 pp.

165 BUBENIK, Vit: A Historical Syntax of Late Middle Indo-Aryan (Apabhramśa). 1998. xxiv, 265 pp.

164 SCHMID, Monika S., Jennifer R. AUSTIN and Dieter STEIN (eds.): Historical Linguistics 1997. Selected papers from the 13th International Conference on Historical Linguistics, Düsseldorf, 10–17 August 1997. 1998. x, 409 pp.

163 LOCKWOOD, David G., Peter H. FRIES and James E. COPELAND (eds.): Functional Approaches to Language, Culture and Cognition. Papers in honor of Sydney M. Lamb. 2000. xxxiv, 656 pp.

162 HOGG, Richard M. and Linda van BERGEN (eds.): Historical Linguistics 1995. Volume 2: Germanic linguistics.. Selected papers from the 12th International Conference on Historical Linguistics, Manchester, August 1995. 1998. x, 365 pp.

161 SMITH, John Charles and Delia BENTLEY (eds.): Historical Linguistics 1995. Volume 1: General issues and non-Germanic Languages.. Selected papers from the 12th International Conference on Historical Linguistics, Manchester, August 1995. 2000. xii, 438 pp.

160 SCHWEGLER, Armin, Bernard TRANEL and Myriam URIBE-ETXEBARRIA (eds.): Romance Linguistics: Theoretical Perspectives. Selected papers from the 27th Linguistic Symposium on Romance Languages (LSRL XXVII), Irvine, 20–22 February, 1997. 1998. vi, 349 pp. + index.

159 JOSEPH, Brian D., Geoffrey C. HORROCKS and Irene PHILIPPAKI-WARBURTON (eds.): Themes in Greek Linguistics II. 1998. x, 335 pp.

158 SÁNCHEZ-MACARRO, Antonia and Ronald CARTER (eds.): Linguistic Choice across Genres. Variation in spoken and written English. 1998. viii, 338 pp.

157 LEMA, José and Esthela TREVIÑO (eds.): Theoretical Analyses on Romance Languages. Selected papers from the 26th Linguistic Symposium on Romance Languages (LSRL XXVI), Mexico City, 28–30 March, 1996. 1998. viii, 380 pp.

156 MATRAS, Yaron, Peter BAKKER and Hristo KYUCHUKOV (eds.): The Typology and Dialectology of Romani. 1997. xxxii, 223 pp.

155 FORGET, Danielle, Paul HIRSCHBÜHLER, France MARTINEAU and María Luisa RIVERO (eds.): Negation and Polarity. Syntax and semantics. Selected papers from the colloquium Negation: Syntax and Semantics. Ottawa, 11–13 May 1995. 1997. viii, 367 pp.

154 SIMON-VANDENBERGEN, Anne-Marie, Kristin DAVIDSE and Dirk NOËL (eds.): Reconnecting Language. Morphology and Syntax in Functional Perspectives. 1997. xiii, 339 pp.

153 EID, Mushira and Robert R. RATCLIFFE (eds.): Perspectives on Arabic Linguistics. Papers from the Annual Symposium on Arabic Linguistics. Volume X: Salt Lake City, 1996. 1997. vii, 296 pp.

152 HIRAGA, Masako K., Chris SINHA and Sherman WILCOX (eds.): Cultural, Psychological and Typological Issues in Cognitive Linguistics. Selected papers of the bi-annual ICLA meeting in Albuquerque, July 1995. 1999. viii, 338 pp.

151 LIEBERT, Wolf-Andreas, Gisela REDEKER and Linda R. WAUGH (eds.): Discourse and Perspective in Cognitive Linguistics. 1997. xiv, 270 pp.

150 VERSPOOR, Marjolijn H., Kee Dong LEE and Eve SWEETSER (eds.): Lexical and Syntactical Constructions and the Construction of Meaning. Proceedings of the bi-annual ICLA meeting in Albuquerque, July 1995. 1997. xii, 454 pp.

149 HALL, T. Alan: The Phonology of Coronals. 1997. x, 176 pp.

148 WOLF, George and Nigel LOVE (eds.): Linguistics Inside Out. Roy Harris and his critics. 1997. xxviii, 344 pp.

147 HEWSON, John: The Cognitive System of the French Verb. 1997. xii, 187 pp.

146 HINSKENS, Frans, Roeland van HOUT and W. Leo WETZELS (eds.): Variation, Change, and Phonological Theory. 1997. x, 314 pp.

145 HEWSON, John and Vit BUBENIK: Tense and Aspect in Indo-European Languages. Theory, typology, diachrony. 1997. xii, 403 pp.

144 SINGH, Rajendra (ed.): Trubetzkoy's Orphan. Proceedings of the Montréal Roundtable on "Morphonology: contemporary responses" (Montréal, October 1994). In collaboration with Richard Desrochers. 1996. xiv, 363 pp.

143 ATHANASIADOU, Angeliki and René DIRVEN (eds.): On Conditionals Again. 1997. viii, 418 pp.

142 SALMONS, Joseph C. and Brian D. JOSEPH (eds.): Nostratic. Sifting the Evidence. 1998. vi, 293 pp.

141 EID, Mushira and Dilworth B. PARKINSON (eds.): Perspectives on Arabic Linguistics. Papers from the Annual Symposium on Arabic Linguistics. Volume IX: Washington D.C., 1995. 1996. xiii, 249 pp.

140 BLACK, James R. and Virginia MOTAPANYANE (eds.): Clitics, Pronouns and Movement. 1997. 375 pp.

139 BLACK, James R. and Virginia MOTAPANYANE (eds.): Microparametric Syntax and Dialect Variation. 1996. xviii, 269 pp.

138 SACKMANN, Robin and Monika BUDDE (eds.): Theoretical Linguistics and Grammatical Description. Papers in honour of Hans-Heinrich Lieb. 1996. x, 375 pp.

137 LIPPI-GREEN, Rosina L. and Joseph C. SALMONS (eds.): Germanic Linguistics. Syntactic and diachronic. 1996. viii, 192 pp.

136 MITKOV, Ruslan and Nicolas NICOLOV (eds.): Recent Advances in Natural Language Processing. Selected Papers from RANLP '95. 1997. xii, 472 pp.

135 BRITTON, Derek (ed.): English Historical Linguistics 1994. Papers from the 8th International Conference on English Historical Linguistics (8 ICEHL, Edinburgh, 19–23 September 1994). 1996. viii, 403 pp.

134 EID, Mushira (ed.): Perspectives on Arabic Linguistics. Papers from the Annual Symposium on Arabic Linguistics. Volume VIII: Amherst, Massachusetts 1994. 1996. vii, 261 pp.

133 ZAGONA, Karen (ed.): Grammatical Theory and Romance Languages. Selected papers from the 25th Linguistic Symposium on Romance Languages (LSRL XXV) Seattle, 2–4 March 1995. 1996. vi, 330 pp.

132 HERSCHENSOHN, Julia: Case Suspension and Binary Complement Structure in French. 1996. xi, 200 pp.

131 HUALDE, José Ignacio, Joseba A. LAKARRA and R.L. TRASK (eds.): Towards a History of the Basque Language. 1996. 365 pp.

130 EID, Mushira (ed.): Perspectives on Arabic Linguistics. Papers from the Annual Symposium on Arabic Linguistics. Volume VII: Austin, Texas 1993. 1995. vii, 192 pp.

129 LEVIN, Saul: Semitic and Indo-European. Volume I: The Principal Etymologies. With observations on Afro-Asiatic. 1995. xxii, 514 pp.

128 GUY, Gregory R., Crawford FEAGIN, Deborah SCHIFFRIN and John BAUGH (eds.): Towards a Social Science of Language. Papers in honor of William Labov. Volume 2: Social interaction and discourse structures. 1997. xviii, 358 pp.

127 GUY, Gregory R., Crawford FEAGIN, Deborah SCHIFFRIN and John BAUGH (eds.): Towards a Social Science of Language. Papers in honor of William Labov. Volume 1: Variation and change in language and society. 1996. xviii, 436 pp.

126 MATRAS, Yaron (ed.): Romani in Contact. The history, structure and sociology of a language. 1995. xvii, 208 pp.

125 SINGH, Rajendra (ed.): Towards a Critical Sociolinguistics. 1996. xiii, 342 pp.

124 ANDERSEN, Henning (ed.): Historical Linguistics 1993. Selected papers from the 11th International Conference on Historical Linguistics, Los Angeles, 16–20 August 1993. 1995. x, 460 pp.

123 AMASTAE, Jon, Grant GOODALL, M. MONTALBETTI and M. PHINNEY (eds.): Contemporary Research in Romance Linguistics. Papers from the XXII Linguistic Symposium on Romance Languages, El Paso/Juárez, February 22–24, 1992. 1995. viii, 381 pp.

122 SMITH, John Charles and Martin MAIDEN (eds.): Linguistic Theory and the Romance Languages. 1995. xiii, 240 pp.

121 HASAN, Ruqaiya, Carmel CLORAN and David G. BUTT (eds.): Functional Descriptions. Theory in practice. 1996. xxxvi, 381 pp.

120 STONHAM, John T.: Combinatorial Morphology. 1994. xii, 206 pp.

119 LIPPI-GREEN, Rosina L.: Language Ideology and Language Change in Early Modern German. A sociolinguistic study of the consonantal system of Nuremberg. 1994. xiv, 150 pp.

118 HASAN, Ruqaiya and Peter H. FRIES (eds.): On Subject and Theme. A discourse functional perspective. 1995. xii, 414 pp.

117 PHILIPPAKI-WARBURTON, Irene, Katerina NICOLAIDIS and Maria SIFIANOU (eds.): Themes in Greek Linguistics. Papers from the First International Conference on Greek Linguistics, Reading, September 1993. 1994. xviii, 534 pp.

116 MILLER, D. Gary: Ancient Scripts and Phonological Knowledge. 1994. xvi, 139 pp.

115 EID, Mushira, Vicente CANTARINO and Keith WALTERS (eds.): Perspectives on Arabic Linguistics. Papers from the Annual Symposium on Arabic Linguistics. Volume VI: Columbus, Ohio 1992. 1994. viii, 238 pp.

114 EGLI, Urs, Peter E. PAUSE, Christoph SCHWARZE, Arnim von STECHOW and Götz WIENOLD (eds.): Lexical Knowledge in the Organization of Language. 1995. xiv, 367 pp.

113 MORENO FERNÁNDEZ, Francisco, Miguel FUSTER and Juan Jose CALVO (eds.): English Historical Linguistics 1992. Papers from the 7th International Conference on English Historical Linguistics, Valencia, 22–26 September 1992. 1994. viii, 388 pp.

112 CULIOLI, Antoine: Cognition and Representation in Linguistic Theory. Texts selected, edited and introduced by Michel Liddle. Translated with the assistance of John T. Stonham. 1995. x, 161 pp.

111 TOBIN, Yishai: Invariance, Markedness and Distinctive Feature Analysis. A contrastive study of sign systems in English and Hebrew. 1994. xxii, 406 pp.

110 SIMONE, Raffaele (ed.): Iconicity in Language. 1995. xii, 315 pp.

109 PAGLIUCA, William (ed.): Perspectives on Grammaticalization. 1994. xx, 306 pp.

108 LIEB, Hans-Heinrich: Linguistic Variables. Towards a unified theory of linguistic variation. 1993. xiv, 261 pp.

107 MARLE, Jaap van (ed.): Historical Linguistics 1991. Papers from the 10th International Conference on Historical Linguistics, Amsterdam, August 12–16, 1991. 1993. xviii, 395 pp.

106 AERTSEN, Henk and Robert J. JEFFERS (eds.): Historical Linguistics 1989. Papers from the 9th International Conference on Historical Linguistics, New Brunswick, 14–18 August 1989. 1993. xviii, 538 pp.

105 HUALDE, José Ignacio and Jon Ortiz de URBINA (eds.): Generative Studies in Basque Linguistics. 1993. vi, 334 pp.

104 KURZOVÁ, Helena: From Indo-European to Latin. The evolution of a morphosyntactic type. 1993. xiv, 259 pp.

103 ASHBY, William J., Marianne MITHUN and Giorgio PERISSINOTTO (eds.): Linguistic Perspectives on Romance Languages. Selected Papers from the XXI Linguistic Symposium on Romance Languages, Santa Barbara, February 21–24, 1991. 1993. xxii, 404 pp.

102 DAVIS, Philip W. (ed.): Alternative Linguistics. Descriptive and theoretical modes. 1996. vii, 325 pp.

101 EID, Mushira and Clive HOLES (eds.): Perspectives on Arabic Linguistics. Papers from the Annual Symposium on Arabic Linguistics. Volume V: Ann Arbor, Michigan 1991. 1993. viii, 347 pp.

100 MUFWENE, Salikoko S. and Lioba MOSHI (eds.): Topics in African Linguistics. Papers from the XXI Annual Conference on African Linguistics, University of Georgia, April 1990. 1993. x, 304 pp.

99 JENSEN, John T.: English Phonology. 1993. x, 251 pp.

98 EID, Mushira and Gregory K. IVERSON (eds.): Principles and Prediction. The analysis of natural language. Papers in honor of Gerald Sanders. 1993. xix, 382 pp.

97 BROGYANYI, Bela and Reiner LIPP (eds.): Comparative-Historical Linguistics: Indo-European and Finno-Ugric. Papers in honor of Oswald Szemerényi III. 1993. xii, 566 pp.

96 LIEB, Hans-Heinrich (ed.): Prospects for a New Structuralism. 1992. vii, 275 pp.

95 MILLER, D. Gary: Complex Verb Formation. 1993. xx, 381 pp.

94 HAGÈGE, Claude: The Language Builder. An essay on the human signature in linguistic morphogenesis. 1993. xii, 283 pp.

93 LIPPI-GREEN, Rosina L. (ed.): Recent Developments in Germanic Linguistics. 1992. xii, 163 pp.

92 **POYATOS, Fernando:** Paralanguage: A linguistic and interdisciplinary approach to interactive speech and sounds. 1993. xii, 478 pp.

91 **HIRSCHBÜHLER, Paul and E.F.K. KOERNER (eds.):** Romance Languages and Modern Linguistic Theory. Selected papers from the XX Linguistic Symposium on Romance Languages, University of Ottawa, April 10–14, 1990. 1992. viii, 416 pp.

90 **KING, Larry D.:** The Semantic Structure of Spanish. Meaning and grammatical form. 1992. xii, 287 pp.

89 **BURRIDGE, Kate:** Syntactic Change in Germanic. Aspects of language change in Germanic with particular reference to Middle Dutch. 1993. xii, 287 pp.

88 **SHIELDS, JR., Kenneth:** A History of Indo-European Verb Morphology. 1992. viii, 160 pp.

87 **BROGYANYI, Bela and Reiner LIPP (eds.):** Historical Philology: Greek, Latin, and Romance. Papers in honor of Oswald Szemerényi II. 1992. xii, 386 pp.

86 **KESS, Joseph F.:** Psycholinguistics. Psychology, linguistics, and the study of natural language. 1992. xiv, 360 pp.

85 **BROSELOW, Ellen, Mushira EID and John McCARTHY (eds.):** Perspectives on Arabic Linguistics. Papers from the Annual Symposium on Arabic Linguistics. Volume IV: Detroit, Michigan 1990. 1992. viii, 282 pp.

84 **DAVIS, Garry W. and Gregory K. IVERSON (eds.):** Explanation in Historical Linguistics. 1992. xiv, 238 pp.

83 **FIFE, James and Erich POPPE (eds.):** Studies in Brythonic Word Order. 1991. x, 360 pp.

82 **VAN VALIN, JR., Robert D. (ed.):** Advances in Role and Reference Grammar. 1992. xii, 569 pp.

81 **LEHMANN, Winfred P. and Helen-Jo Jakusz HEWITT (eds.):** Language Typology 1988. Typological Models in the Service of Reconstruction. 1991. vi, 182 pp.

80 **COMRIE, Bernard and Mushira EID (eds.):** Perspectives on Arabic Linguistics. Papers from the Annual Symposium on Arabic Linguistics. Volume III: Salt Lake City 1989. 1991. xii, 274 pp.

79 **ANTONSEN, Elmer H. and Hans Henrich HOCK (eds.):** STAEFCRAEFT: Studies in Germanic Linguistics. Selected papers from the 1st and 2nd Symposium on Germanic Linguistics, University of Chicago, 4 April 1985, and University of Illinois at Urbana-Champaign, 3–4 Oct. 1986. 1991. viii, 217 pp.

78 **KAC, Michael B.:** Grammars and Grammaticality. 1992. x, 259 pp.

77 **BOLTZ, William G. and Michael C. SHAPIRO (eds.):** Studies in the Historical Phonology of Asian Languages. 1991. viii, 249 pp.

76 **WICKENS, Mark A.:** Grammatical Number in English Nouns. An empirical and theoretical account. 1992. xvi, 321 pp.

75 **DROSTE, Flip G. and John E. JOSEPH (eds.):** Linguistic Theory and Grammatical Description. Nine Current Approaches. 1991. viii, 354 pp.

74 **LAEUFER, Christiane and Terrell A. MORGAN (eds.):** Theoretical Analyses in Romance Linguistics. Selected papers from the Linguistic Symposium on Romance Languages XIX, Ohio State University, April 21–23, 1989. 1991. viii, 515 pp.

73 **STAMENOV, Maxim I. (ed.):** Current Advances in Semantic Theory. 1991. xi, 565 pp.

72 **EID, Mushira and John McCARTHY (eds.):** Perspectives on Arabic Linguistics. Papers from the Annual Symposium on Arabic Linguistics. Volume II: Salt Lake City, Utah 1988. 1990. xiv, 332 pp.

71 **O'GRADY, William:** Categories and Case. The sentence structure of Korean. 1991. vii, 294 pp.

70 **JENSEN, John T.:** Morphology. Word structure in generative grammar. 1990. x, 210 pp.

69 **WANNER, Dieter and Douglas A. KIBBEE (eds.):** New Analyses in Romance Linguistics. Selected papers from the Linguistic Symposium on Romance Languages XVIII, Urbana-Champaign, April 7–9, 1988. 1991. xviii, 385 pp.

68 **BALL, Martin J., James FIFE, Erich POPPE and Jenny ROWLAND (eds.):** Celtic Linguistics/ Ieithyddiaeth Geltaidd. Readings in the Brythonic Languages. Festschrift for T. Arwyn Watkins. 1990. xxiv, 470 pp.

67 **LEHMANN, Winfred P. (ed.):** Language Typology 1987. Systematic Balance in Language. Papers from the Linguistic Typology Symposium, Berkeley, 1–3 Dec 1987. 1990. x, 212 pp.

66 **ANDERSEN, Henning and E.F.K. KOERNER (eds.):** Historical Linguistics 1987. Papers from the 8th International Conference on Historical Linguistics, Lille, August 30-September 4, 1987. 1990. xii, 577 pp.

65 **ADAMSON, Sylvia M., Vivien A. LAW, Nigel VINCENT and Susan WRIGHT (eds.):** Papers from the 5th International Conference on English Historical Linguistics. 1990. xxi, 583 pp.

64 **BROGYANYI, Bela (ed.):** Prehistory, History and Historiography of Language, Speech, and Linguistic Theory. Papers in honor of Oswald Szemerényi I. 1992. x, 414 pp.

63 **EID, Mushira (ed.):** Perspectives on Arabic Linguistics. Papers from the Annual Symposium on Arabic Linguistics. Volume I: Salt Lake City, Utah 1987. 1990. xiii, 290 pp.